THE MAVEN MARKETER

HOW TO STOP WASTING MONEY ON ADVERTISING AND BUILD A LEGENDARY BUSINESS

BRANDON WELCH

MAVEN PUBLISHING
A DIVISION OF FRANK & MAVEN

MAVEN PUBLISHING
A DIVISION OF FRANK & MAVEN
book@frankandmaven.com

MAVEN

Published by Maven Publishing, a division of Frank & Maven.

ISBN 978-1-7358467-0-5

Library of Congress Control Number: 2020925210

First Edition

Editing and Book Production by Ashley Mansour, LA Writing Coach
Interior Book Design by Carla Green, Clarity Designworks

mavenmethodtraining.com

To the dreamers who get up and
do something about it.

CONTENTS

"The master in the art of living makes little distinction between his work and his play, his labor and his leisure, his mind and his body, his information and his recreation, his love and his religion. He hardly knows which is which. He simply pursues his vision of excellence at whatever he does, leaving others to decide whether he is working or playing. To him he's always doing both."

—*James A. Michener*

AN INTRODUCTION FOR THE WISE

It's time to declare war on wasted advertising.

American businesses spend $1.2 trillion buying ads every year. But 8 out of 10 business owners are not confident that their advertising is working for them.

That's $1.2 *trillion*! *Trillion*—with a *t*!

You would think that by now, with all that money, someone somewhere would've discovered how to make advertising a more rewarding purchase. Businesses should start demanding a safer return on their investments. I can't think of any other product that would be so continually purchased and return such poor results.

Yet millions of ads are sold daily, and very few businesspeople can tell you exactly *how* or *why* these ads work.

As business owners, we're constantly bombarded with numerous options in marketing. Salespeople from TV, radio, print, digital, social media, email, networking, billboards, vehicle graphics, and sponsorships all beg us to spend a little bit of our budget with them.

We are overwhelmed by new shiny objects. Digital targeting, text message marketing, reputation management, and search engines leave us wondering: How do we make these things work when we know nothing about them?

We are forever haunted by the fear of making the wrong decisions and wasting our hard-earned money.

Yet we risk it all because we want our dreams to come to life. We want to build ourselves the freedom of our dream lifestyle, take our family on vacations, and leave a legacy.

However, for too many of us, the advertising doesn't deliver.

I've watched hundreds of business owners waste, literally, millions of dollars trying to achieve ad results, *trying to grow their dream,* but they may as well be tossing coins into a wishing well.

The most devastating reality is that incredible businesses never grow to their fullest potential.

I'm not talking about publicly traded companies that have no heart. I'm talking about *real-life* family businesses, businesses owned by people like you and me—hard workers who want to provide jobs for their communities and support good causes.

I see so many of them struggle, be taken advantage of, and fail, all because of one stupid thing: advertising.

It infuriates me, and that's why I'm declaring war!

In the last 15 years, I've been face-to-face with the problem. After countless experiments implementing nearly every type of advertising, I finally refined a process that cuts through the confusion:

The Maven Method.

Today, the Maven Method is the exact set of principles my team uses to grow family-owned companies all across the United States.

Using this method, our clients have scaled their companies beyond what they could have ever imagined, making many of them millionaires in the process.

The Maven Method is a reverse-engineered recipe of the success I found after working with over 500 different businesses. We use this method to achieve wildly profitable returns on marketing for companies in a multitude of categories, including professional services, medical practices, home improvement, automotive service, retail, e-commerce, and even nonprofits.

Unlike much of the marketing teaching in the world today that is based on a single marketing category or platform, the Maven Method is universally applicable because it's based on human connection.

This method doesn't require any special technology or sophisticated tools. It takes the guesswork out of creating a marketing plan and eliminates wasted dollars in your budget.

If you're already achieving success in marketing, this book will help you understand why as well as how to double down on your efforts.

If you're uncertain, like so many, this book can serve as your go-to reference for what to do when you're unsure how to move forward.

As Otto von Bismarck famously said, "Only a fool learns from his own mistakes. The wise man learns from the mistakes of others."

This book is for you: *the wise.*

Borrow what I have learned the hard way so that you can skip ahead to your success.

You don't have to exhaust yourself trying to find the right way to market your company. You don't have to endure the financial and emotional stress of coming up short. Save all that energy for the things you really *want* to do.

My family, friends, and clients have paid the price for me to earn this wisdom firsthand. You don't have to pay another penny for it—you're holding the lessons in your hand. I give you permission to skip over the marketing school of hard knocks and jump into a confident, repeatable process for growth.

You are already capable of growing your company beyond your wildest dreams. But the Maven Method—these essential lessons—will help you do it faster.

My first lesson was by far the most expensive, most traumatic, and most life-changing event I've ever lived through. It's deeply personal. And until recently, I wasn't really comfortable sharing it.

But I've decided to trade that fear to serve a greater purpose. If one person can avoid the pain that my family had to endure, I will consider this book a great success.

It began with the most painful type of learning that any of us can imagine—losing everything.

CHAPTER 1

THE MISGUIDED MARKETER

"It's over. We're putting the key in the door," Dad said in a defeated voice that I'd never heard before.

The sun was radiating my whole body, but I stood there cold with my hands shaking.

It was supposed to be the most amazing week of my life—my honeymoon in Hawaii. Waves rolled onto the beach in front of me. Palm trees were dancing against the blue sky. Seagulls soared above and cawed into the ocean breeze.

One minute before, I felt as if I were on top of the world. Yet seconds into this call, I'd never felt more defeated.

Dad had received the news that our bank wasn't going to come through with the loan we needed for operating cash. Other debts from building our new facility had reached a tipping point, the economy was tanking, our cash flow wasn't where it needed to be, and we were completely out of options.

The company that we never thought could fail was dead in the water, along with my career and everything that I'd worked for.

"Are we really out of options?" I said in denial. "Isn't there something we can do to keep it going?"

Dad was even more crushed than I was. "There's nowhere to get the money. It's just not going to happen."

It was his company and his dream. And it was my dream to take it over one day. He had worked his whole life perfecting the craft of restoring and selling cars. No matter how banged up, busted, or broken they were, he was the master at making them new again. He could fix *anything.*

Two years before, we had taken his life experience and started a new business with it: The Works Auto Center. It was a body shop, mechanic repair shop, tire shop, and automotive detail all under one roof. We'd invested heavily in equipment and a new building and had over 30 employees.

Up until that fateful moment on the balcony of my honeymoon suite, my life was in seemingly perfect order. I'd been continuously helping my dad build his business. It was the only job I thought I'd ever need, and I had visions that one day I'd turn the concept into a franchise and take over the world.

I had left for my honeymoon believing things were going to be just fine. I knew money was tight, but I just thought we'd get through it somehow.

Suddenly it was clear that things were never going to turn around.

I was especially devastated for my dad. He had spent his life savings and leveraged everything he had to bring this new business to life. We employed great people and had a great reputation, great facilities, and *great marketing* that should've brought us all the customers we'd ever need.

Or so I thought.

That part was on me—marketing, sales, and advertising. That was my role in the family business. I worked with all the media companies, wrote our commercials, built our website, and managed the company's social media. More importantly, I controlled our advertising budget.

I had worked hard for the last two years to bring new customers to our door. I had spent tens of thousands of dollars on TV, radio, print, and digital ads to tell the world about our great new business.

I had failed. I had failed big time.

I had spent big money that didn't deliver the results we needed.

I believed the ad salespeople when they told me how many new customers they could bring me. I believed them when they preached, "You have to spend money to make money!" I believed that their commercial schedules, endorsements, billboard placements, calls to action, and graphics were all a recipe for instant success.

But none of it had worked, and I had let my entire family down. I was devastated, scared, and angry.

How would I pay my mortgage?

Would the first chapter of our marriage be spent fighting about money?

What would my friends think?

How would I recover professionally?

I couldn't help but feel that I had been misguided with bad marketing advice.

The advertising salespeople had a lot of enthusiasm—they promised their marketing would work. They made me feel smart and capable.

Our commercials were packed with all the great things that I thought the public should know about our company. The salespeople told me my ads sounded "professional," and I thought I was doing the right thing.

It was clear that I never had a real method to guide me. I was acting on my own assumptions, and all the salespeople were happy to agree with me and encourage me as long as we would give them our money.

In the end, I realized that it was no different from risking it all on a high-stakes poker game. I was a misguided marketer. Sound familiar?

And now, the lesson was clear: *I should have never risked what I wasn't willing to lose.*

CHAPTER 2
INSIDE THE BUSINESS OF ADVERTISING SALES

After all I'd been through, I completely rejected the idea of being in advertising sales. *I hated those people.*

But there I was—sitting in front of Kent, the guy who would give me my first job in the advertising business.

My dad had no choice but to liquidate everything. Our family business was finished; there was nothing I could do to hold on to that dream.

So I went out looking for a job, not sure what I even wanted to do with my life.

As I drove past the businesses in my town, I tried to imagine what it would be like to work for them. What would it be like to have a regular eight-to-five job?

I was used to putting in 60-hour weeks. I had been happy to work weekends and do whatever it took to make our customers happy. But the thought of giving up my autonomy, my sense of creativity, and my identity made me sick to my stomach.

I imagined trying to show my value to a potential employer. What would I say: "Uh, yeah, I was the sales and marketing manager of a company that went bankrupt"?

The aimless drive through town led me to a place I was familiar with—one of the stations where I had bought advertising.

I'm not sure why, but I decided to pull into the parking lot and sit there for a minute. My wounds were still fresh. Even seeing the station logo reminded me of all the money I had wasted. I sat there contemplating all the things I should've done differently.

Suddenly I saw Kent's car pull in. Kent was one of the salesmen I'd bought ads from, but he was *different* from the rest. Kent was the only one who never tried to sell me something I didn't need. I decided to flag him down, thinking that maybe he would know of a job opening somewhere.

He was genuine as always. "Hey, stranger. What brings you here?"

"Honestly? I'm looking for a job."

"Oh man! What happened? Is everything okay?"

"I'm not really sure how to answer that, Kent."

He invited me into his office. He listened to my story and shared his surprise that things hadn't turned out well.

"I thought you were on your way to the top!"

"Yeah, that makes two of us who were wrong."

Kent could tell I felt defeated.

"How can I help?"

"What do you think I should do?" I sighed, still in disbelief that I was this helpless.

"Well, you would kill it in the advertising business. We're about to hire in the sales department. You interested?"

Absolutely not, I thought. Secretly, I was surprised that he even thought I'd be qualified for the job. I didn't want to be rude, so I told him I'd think about it and that I'd keep in touch.

At dinner that night, I told my wife, Valerie, what Kent had suggested. "Wouldn't that be ridiculous?" I chuckled. "Me, an ad salesman?" *She knew my infuriation with the advertising sales world.*

"Go do it better," she said, as if the answer were written on the wall.

Was she crazy? Had she forgotten how badly I'd failed? Did she not witness what my family just went through?

"You know what it's like to be a business owner better than anyone, right? Sounds like a pretty good opportunity."

Maybe she was right. *Maybe I could make a difference. Maybe I could change the outcome for other family businesses.*

Kent called me the next week. Before I knew it, he offered me a job, and I accepted. I was officially an ad salesman for a TV station and I was about to find out exactly how this business worked.

INSIDE THE AD SALES WORLD

My first week on the job was awesome. The people were amazing; the newsroom was incredible. *I was in the big leagues.* It was exciting!

I showed up dressed in slacks with a pressed shirt and a new tie. Not exactly my normal dress code, but I was ready to play the part. It didn't take long for me to meet my first challenge.

My bosses put me through two weeks of corporate sales training videos. During my training, I heard things like:

» "It's a numbers game. Knock on 40 doors, get 10 appointments, sell 2 deals. Rinse. Repeat."

» "Overcome objections!"

» "Position your product!"

» "Prospect! Prospect! Prospect!"

» "Close the deal!"

It felt like they were asking me to be the ruthless salesperson I had been misguided by when I was on the other side of the table.

Those same tactics had been used on me from other salespeople to get money from my dad's business. Obviously, those tactics had worked on me, but it made me sick to think about using them on someone else.

What about the results? Was anyone going to discuss how to make the ads work? What if a marketing campaign failed? Would I be able to give the business a refund?

The answer was clearly *no*. This was a sales job—*a competitive one*. Everyone I worked with definitely cared about their customers, but the system of advertising sales didn't have any recourse for businesses that got bad results.

Ad reps from all over town, and even my own colleagues, were trying to call on as many businesses as possible. We were all dressed alike and trained to say the same things. That's exactly the problem with advertising sales: Ad salespeople are primarily trained and paid to "get the sale" from business owners, not how to grow their companies.

My very first week in the ad business I came face-to-face with the exact reason so many business owners fail to get a return on their ads: *No one is focused on how to actually make advertising work!*

Because salespeople have only one way of earning a paycheck—by selling ads—they naturally focus on growing *their* sales revenue, not necessarily their *clients'*. But I wanted to know how my clients were going to grow instead of failing like I had before.

I quickly realized that if I was going to be successful in the ad business and feel good about myself, I had to dig deeper on my own. I became obsessed with studying everything I possibly could about successful ads.

I took courses, read books, and attended webinars. I relentlessly searched for case studies of ad campaigns that had actually grown small businesses. And I asked every business owner I could get in front of "What has worked for you in advertising and what has failed?"

I knew my job was to sell advertising, but I couldn't do it without knowing how to get good results. *I was not willing to be a careless spender, and risk being thought of as a crook.* My life experience in small business was directly at odds with my job description.

My colleagues were awesome people with good intentions, but none of them had gone through what I had. None of them knew what it was *really* like to be a part of a struggling business. None of them knew what it was like to risk everything on your company's advertising.

So, I completely ignored their corporate sales training and tried to do my job the only way it felt right, given what I had experienced: *to talk to business owners like they were business owners, not sales prospects.* This attitude would eventually lead me to my first big breakthrough, but I still had a lot to learn.

In hindsight, the opportunity to experiment with hundreds of small business owners' ad budgets was the education of a lifetime. However, at the time it was a journey laden with failures, and I struggled to believe that I could actually make a difference.

But through those failures I finally put my finger on exactly why so many businesses go broke on advertising: It's a broken system.

CHAPTER 3

THE BROKEN SYSTEM OF ADVERTISING IN AMERICA

I quickly learned that the world of the advertising sales professional is far different from the world of the small business owner. I also came to see that this was really no fault of the salespeople or their sales managers, or even the TV station owners. They were all really amazing people, some of whom became my best friends.

However, I did find that there was a problem that had developed over generations of misaligned training in the industry: *My bosses' bosses hadn't ever taught them how to make their ads work, so how were my bosses going to teach me?*

Moreover, the industry hasn't demanded that this change because there's always a new business to chase. When one client fails, there's always another business that you can pitch to in order to make your sales quota. And, while no one wants these businesses to fail, no one is exclusively focused on learning how to make them succeed.

Like my family, most business owners don't know what they don't know, yet they're always looking for the "next best thing." When they get poor results from one advertising station after a few months, they cancel their contract with them and assume it was the station's fault. Then they'll either go advertise with another station, quit altogether, or even worse—they never recover from their bad investment.

Now I was part of this broken system of advertising sales. **An ad salesperson's job goes something like this:**

1. "Cold call" five new businesses daily to try to get an appointment.

2. Business owners rarely have the time or desire to talk to me, but eventually one of the five business owners agrees to a meeting.

3. Attend the meeting and tell the potential client all the great things about my station and our great advertising packages.

4. Give a proposal packed with a bunch of different programs, emphasizing all the free stuff they'll get as clients. Promise them that they can cancel any time after three months if their advertising campaign with us isn't working.

5. The potential client signs the contract and hopes for the best.

6. After the ads are sold, send a production crew to record the new client's ad.

7. The business owner feels excited. A few of their friends comment on the ad, and they're happy until they're writing a check for the third month in a row without gaining much new business in return.

8. The business owner determines the ad isn't working, so they cancel the contract and chalk it up to "I tried that, and it didn't work." Boom. Money wasted.

I watched that same song and dance happen dozens of times. I began to see that this cycle was at the core of wasted money and failed advertising.

No salesperson ever *wants* their contracts to be canceled. But they also don't know how to explain bad results. More importantly, they don't have a method for how to attain *good* results in the first place.

The problem here isn't that advertising salespeople lie. It's that they are seldom trained on much more than how to position their product, overcome objections, and distract the client with shiny new objects. They are *paid* to get the sale. So, the sale itself is the *focus*.

But to get the sale, they must provide some sort of explanation to the business owner about how all of it works. And their explanation is everything that is *wrong* with the way advertising is being bought and sold.

Their explanation usually revolves around one of three myths.

I call them myths, because they are misleading and are used to justify some really bad decisions. And, while these myths are partially true, they don't fully provide a method for advertising success.

THREE MYTHS PLAGUING ADVERTISING:

1. **The Branding Myth**—You just have to get your name out there!

2. **The Targeting Myth**—The secret for success is to reach your perfect target customer!

3. **The Educate the Public Myth**—The world just needs to be educated about your product!

These same myths are the ones I believed in our family business, and they let me down big time. I thought I just needed to get our business's name out there. I thought that targeting the perfect person would bring us all the customers we would ever need. And I believed our company's ads should be jam-packed with educating the public about our services. Yet after spending tens of thousands of dollars on advertising with these beliefs, our company still failed. I knew there had to be more to the story.

Now I was responsible for other people's money, and I had to find a better explanation, *a better method* for getting results.

I realized that these three myths weren't created or committed to by any single vindictive person. They were a culmination of bad habits and bad excuses that were developed over time in the advertising sales world. And because there's plenty of money to go around, most salespeople can meet their sales goals and keep their jobs, and life is good for them. They never have to deal with the realities of these misleading myths.

There is no rhyme or reason, no proven system, and no ultimate accountability for bad results in ad sales. Sure, an advertiser can cancel a contract and the salesperson won't earn more commission, but for the business owners like my family who had tried and failed, there's no recourse. We could not "un-bankrupt" ourselves, and there was no refund.

Decades of ad sales culture have taught ad sales reps the bad excuses to cite when clients have bad results.

» "Just gotta keep getting your name out there. Ya gotta do some branding!"

» "We'll change the targeting and try to find more of your perfect customer!"

» "Cram everything you can into that ad! Mention your name and phone number three times! They'll listen!"

The problem, however, isn't just the fault of the advertising salesperson. *Small businesses have believed and acted on the same false beliefs for decades.* This broken system isn't due only to how the ads are being sold; it's also with the way the ads are being bought and agreed to in the first place by the business owner or marketing manager.

If business owners were more aware of *how to make ads work,* they wouldn't buy bad plans and seek out bad advice.

Due to my experience from both sides of the table, as a buyer and seller of failed advertising, I was more anxious than ever to figure out how to change the outcomes. I was determined to make advertising work. But first I had to fully unlearn the three myths of advertising.

CHAPTER 4
THE BRANDING MYTH

As a salesperson, I became keenly aware that a really good way to get advertising sales was to promote the idea of *branding*. Branding is a fancy term that I assume someone somewhere used with good intentions to describe the result of a *brand* becoming well-known. For decades, however, it has been misused and misunderstood by advertising salespeople and businesses all over the world.

Because I had failed my family's business by using the word *branding* to justify all my advertising expenses, I was suspicious of the term when it became my job to get results for the money other people were spending with me. I saw the branding term used virtually in every sales presentation where I was present.

You might be thinking, "The biggest companies in the world invest millions into branding. It couldn't possibly be a myth!" The problem, however, isn't that branding isn't a thing; it is that very few truly understand how branding is accomplished. Branding is a term that gets tossed around anytime someone can't explain what's happening with an ad budget. All too often, it's a small business owner or a salesperson who's trying to justify money being spent on advertising. The salesperson in the room says, "Ah, well, we just have to brand ourselves!" Or the business owner exclaims, "We gotta get our name out there!"

Suddenly, the conversation is finished as if that's all there is to the story. Nobody ever talks about what branding means or where "out there" is. Yet, the business owner then commits to TV and radio contracts, Facebook ads, search engine optimization (SEO) services, print, billboards, and countless other marketing expenses based on this extremely shallow assumption that it is "branding" their business.

This is the Branding Myth at work.

The Branding Myth assumes that simply by *paying money* to have your name and your product advertised, you will receive more business. You assume that by "having your name out there," people will suddenly care, remember, and automatically want to buy from you. You assume that the consistency of the colors in your logo, slogans, and fonts used are somehow the secret to business growth. And you refer to it all as *branding*. By placing your hope in branding by these stereotypical assumptions, you completely lose sight of how human beings *actually* behave, and you even forget about how you behave in your own life.

I became very uncomfortable using the word *branding* because it has so many different and ambiguous meanings for everyone. I began to think:

» When is the last time you bought anything just because "the name was out there"?

» When is the last time you bought anything just because an ad played on a TV channel that you happened to watch?

» When is the last time you bought anything due to the logo's shape or color?

You know the truth as well as I do: If an ad doesn't speak to you or about you, you ignore it like the other 5,000 ads you previously saw that day. This number isn't an exaggeration, either.

According to a study performed in 2007 by the market research firm Yankelovich, the average American is exposed to over 5,000 selling messages every 24 hours. Yes, there are 5,000 messages out there daily just in your own little world.

How silly is it to believe that we can change human behavior by simply randomly shouting at them with our brand name? Yet, ad professionals and business owners act on this bad conventional wisdom every single day. This is true even at the highest levels.

THE SUPER BOWL EXAMPLE:

I use the Super Bowl as an example because it's a universally known spectacle for advertising. The Super Bowl broadcast typically commands an audience of about a hundred million people.

Yet, everyone who watches forgets many of the ads by the next morning.

With an audience this big—one of the biggest audiences in the world—it's easy to see that just getting a brand name out there doesn't make a whole lot of difference, right? But during advertising sales pitches everyone spends hours talking about the number of commercials, impressions, rating points, targeting, Facebook likes and shares—how to get their names "out there" to supposedly "brand" themselves—but where *very little* time is spent talking about the customer they're trying to win over.

Both business owners and salespeople forget to talk about customers' needs and their desires in life. **This is the fundamental problem.** It's where the Branding Myth fails us.

In my family's company, I was guilty of using branding to justify every one of our random marketing expenses. In the heat of the ad sales world, at times I was also guilty of using branding to sell ads. Every one of my clients and friends in this industry have been guilty of it as well. But it's complete and total baloney. The term *branding* is far too often what we say just to make ourselves feel good and that we're making a sophisticated marketing investment in our business.

The Branding Myth comes disguised in numerous other catchy ad phrases that promote false hope:

» *Top-of-Mind Awareness*

» *Brand Awareness*

» *Brand Recall*

All these concepts—the goal of which is to become a well-known and well-liked company—are *good*. But most of the time, these buzzwords are utilized to justify spending money without further understanding how it will actually lead people to do business with you.

Before I continue, I'd like to clarify one thing. Putting your message "out there" is a part of the advertising success formula. That said, you are completely fooling yourself if you think the secret to growth is just being out there. You're missing the mark if you think people just need to know your brand name.

I've seen countless businesses fail at marketing because they thought making noise about their name was all they needed to do.

Now, I know what you might be thinking:

» But people say they hear my business's ads all the time!

» But I've been branding for years!

» But I'm reaching thousands of people!

I hear you. **All these things are likely true.** But I have news for you: That's *not* what is actually driving your success.

Knowing that people are seeing and hearing your company's brand name feels good. But no one really cares at all about a brand or a name unless it's tied to something that helps them meet a need, overcome a pain, achieve a better future, or defeat a fear. Your *name* means nothing by itself without intrinsic value being tied to it.

True Branding Is More Than Name Awareness

True branding is the emotional connection we have with a company's personality, values, and commitments over time as they offer to make our lives better. The *brand name* simply helps us recall those feelings we have about a company.

True branding is a connection with a company that's very similar to a connection you'd have with a friend. This type of connection happens in the same part of the mind. True branding is achieved by much more than name repetition. In fact, name awareness is really not persuasive at all.

I'll use a few really well-known examples for some proof of this:

When someone says "Coca-Cola," what feelings do you get? Many I've asked this question to remember a childhood memory, nostalgia, or easier times. For me, it was my grandma's kitchen. I smell her cooking, feel her house's warmth, and remember the innocence of sitting down at her kitchen table with our "have a Coke" ritual.

Do you have your own story like this about Coke? Or is yours with Pepsi? How about Dr Pepper, Mr. Pibb, Sprite, or 7UP? If you responded differently to any of these brand names, then you can clearly see how the *name* of each of them has nothing to do with how you feel.

Each brand name of Coke, Pepsi, Dr Pepper, Mr. Pibb, Sprite, and 7UP has received *billions* of dollars in advertising over the years. You could not find an American unaware of any of these brand *names*. Yet, most of us have an overwhelming preference to one of these, right? *Don't you dare bring me Pepsi when I order Coke.*

Why?

Because we've connected complex feelings to that brand name—memories, sensory experiences, and emotions that make us feel good.

True branding happens when we have feelings for a company.

Feelings can be created in a number of ways—*sounds, sights, smells, tastes,* and *relationships* that we experience over time with a company. These feelings can be developed in person, such as when we experience a product/service firsthand, or visit a location and interact with the employees of a company. But they can also be developed in the imagination by the words, sounds, and images you choose to put in your advertising.

Regardless of where we develop the feelings for a company, though, the name of the brand only has *meaning* when it becomes *attached* to these feelings. *Name awareness means nothing without feelings attached to the name.*

Don't believe me?

Think of the first and last name of your favorite childhood teacher. Did his or her name have any significance before they had an impact on your life? Have you met others by that person's first name? And does that name have as much meaning on its own? You can do this exercise by thinking about other names of people you feel strongly about, such as your mom, dad, wife, husband, kids, best friend, or a childhood bully.

Truly branded companies have the exact same kind of connection. They invoke the same kind of feelings with their audience. Take any automotive brand for example: Ford, Chevy, Dodge, Toyota, Lexus, Audi, Porsche, BMW, Tesla, Harley-Davidson, etc.

How about fashion? Do the names Patagonia or North Face do anything for you? How about Nike or Adidas? Coach or Chanel?

All of these company names are *out there* in a huge way. But that's not what makes them well-branded. Each one of these brand names commands millions of dollars in advertising annually. But you only feel strongly about certain ones because they've spoken to you over and over about things that matter to you, which creates that emotional, feeling experience. And you *don't* have a strong feeling about certain names because they haven't spoken to you about things that matter to you; therefore, you have no emotional connection to them and no feeling about them.

Names don't matter; feelings do. The name merely *recalls* the feeling.

You absolutely must remember this before you step forward into the activities of branding or getting your name out there. You absolutely *must* go deeper to understand the feelings, experiences, and stories that you connect to your brand name that make it *worth remembering*.

ACHIEVING TRUE BRANDING

Achieving *true branding* based on feelings can be accomplished in the exact same way every human relationship is built:

1. Talk to people about what matters to them (not to your company).

2. Speak to them in an entertaining or emotional way.

3. Spend consistent time together (advertise to them every day).

Talk to people about what matters to them: When you make your ads about more than your name and about more than your products, you greatly increase your chances of listeners paying attention to you. You can talk about four basic things to accomplish this: a need, a pain, a hope, or a fear your audience has.

Speak to them in an entertaining or emotional way: Humans are suckers for entertainment. This is the true art of advertising, but it doesn't mean you have to be a creative genius. Entertainment simply means that you're being interesting in your delivery of whatever you're saying. You can accomplish this using humor, sadness, rhythm, music, personality quirks, photography, videography, or the style of how you talk. The biggest thing to avoid is sounding like an ad. Avoid letting the customer know it's an ad by using words, phrases, colors, and a delivery style that are unique, not predictable.

Spend consistent time together: Repetition is required for even the best ads in the world. If you're trying to be remembered often, then you must speak often by committing to a consistent media schedule with a consistent audience. Don't frequently change where your ads are placed. Display them in a place where a consistent group of people will see them often.

In the following chapters, I introduce the Maven Method, the process I developed after repeatedly coming into contact with the same failures with the Branding Myth. I show you exactly what to do to create meaningful ads *instead* of ambiguous branding. I share the specific process I now successfully use to create authentic connection, entertainment, and consistency that works in advertising for our clients.

But no matter what you do in marketing, it's crucial to remember that you must avoid making bad excuses for bad results, and be immediately skeptical of using "branding" or "getting your name out there" as an excuse to buy advertising.

Just like the Branding Myth, another myth plagues the advertising industry and is causing huge waste and disappointing results for the money that companies spend. It's called the Targeting Myth.

CHAPTER 5
THE TARGETING MYTH

I want to ask you a question. If I tell you "I'm going to target you," how does that make you feel? Like a human? An animal? Valued? Used?

Because you are a real human being, you're probably already seeing the fundamental problem with the Targeting Myth: It immediately takes the humanness out of advertising.

Business owners spend a great deal of energy wondering which advertising platform will be the *magic* ingredient in growing their sales opportunities. They test and try TV, radio, direct mail, magazines, billboards, internet ads, Facebook, or Instagram, hoping for really fast and obvious results. Because they are afraid to waste money, they dip their pinky toe into the waters of each of these different media platforms to try and feel out which one will work best. They obsess over tracking results, asking people:

- » Where did you hear about us?
- » Did you hear our radio ad?
- » Did you see our billboard?
- » Was it our Facebook post that brought you in?
- » Did you find us on Google?

Because marketing and advertising conversations are often led by advertising salespeople, any talk about strategy is quickly directed around the audience strength and targeting abilities of different advertising products and stations. Meaning, each advertising salesperson is focused on telling you why their particular product is the perfect one to reach your "perfect target customer."

On both sides of the buying and selling of advertising—with both the business owner and the salesperson—the conversation heavily revolves around one belief: *To be successful in advertising, you just have to target the right audience.*

This is the Targeting Myth.

And it's one of the biggest reasons so many companies go broke buying ads. This Targeting Myth was at the core of all false hope and bad results that devastated my family's company. In my job as an ad salesman, I began to see just how much faith business owners and ad salespeople put into targeting.

"What is targeting?" you might be wondering. Targeting happens anytime we make a conscious decision in our media to reach a certain type of person. Targeting uses rating points data, audience surveys, and digital ad technology in an effort to place an ad in front of a person a business owner believes will be most likely to buy from them.

Like the other myths outlined in this book, the Targeting Myth is not the fault of any one person. Ad salespeople *love* to talk about the strength of their audience, and most business owners *love* to imagine reaching their perfect target customer.

That's all fine and good. *This* can *help in the success of a campaign.*

But the Targeting Myth fails us when we assume that *reaching our perfect audience* is all that's *required* to make our ads work.

In my job of selling TV ads, I was trained to sell based on my station's strengths. And the easiest "strength" to talk about was the product audience—*who our TV station was reaching.*

Specifically, we would talk at length about demographics of the TV programs and internet ads that we would sell. The conversation went something like this:

Ad salesperson: "Research says your customer is most likely a 25- to 34-year-old female. Does that sound right?"

Business owner: "Yeah! That's exactly who my customer is!"

Ad salesperson: "Good news! We have a huge audience of that exact person! We can target your perfect customer if you just buy our station/program/website audience (versus another type of media)."

Business owner (thinking to themselves): "Wow! This sounds exactly like what I've been needing—a bunch of my target customers located all in one place."

The ad salesperson closes the sale, and the confidence is placed largely on the targeting working.

This exact sales process is repeated across just about every advertising sales organization. TV ads, radio, newspaper, magazine, direct mail, social media, and digital marketing people make the same promise every single day: *"All you need to do is target the right audience."*

When I first started buying advertising, this made perfect sense to me. When it was my job to start selling ads, I followed the same logic: Reach the perfect target audience, and the rest will take care of itself. But once again, I came face-to-face with the failures of the broken advertising system.

After several months in advertising sales, contract renewals started coming around with the clients who had trusted me with their money. I'd made great friends with them, but this was the point where business had to be business. Enthusiastically, I returned to my previous buyers with another new advertising plan; it was a way to keep our business relationship going and my sales revenue coming in. Their responses were devastating, however:

» We just can't justify spending this money.
» People aren't saying they've seen our ads!
» You told me I would be seeing results by now.

Most of the buyers I had sold advertising to believed that *they* had been *sold*, not helped.

I was disappointed in myself and in the product I had sold them. They had trusted me with their money, and I had trusted my perfect audience to deliver great results. It was the same chilling moment I'd had on that Hawaii balcony—I was failing at the exact thing that I'd spent so much time studying.

I thought, "How could this be? I'd made a perfect plan to reach all the right people!" I had all the fancy research tools. I was a *sophisticated* advertising pro.

It was because I had believed in the Targeting Myth.

I was especially concerned for my client Duane. He'd given me his last $8,000 to help grow his new window replacement company. Specifically, he needed that $8,000 to produce him "leads," people who would see his ad and call him so that he could schedule an in-home presentation to sell them windows.

I was honest with him that the results would take time, which is what I was trained to say. Duane believed that advertising on my station would bring in enough sales in the short term to pay for his ads and make him a little profit. I let him advertise with us based on these expectations, knowing that he needed to sell only a few jobs to make up for this expense.

My research told me that his *key demographic* is adults between the ages of 35 and 64 years old. (Key demographic is just a fancy term for the people most likely to buy from you.) I'd used sophisticated software to confirm that this group most likely owned homes and could spend the money on the window replacements Duane sold.

I, therefore, selected my best TV programs for his audience— the ones that would reach the most 35- to 64-year-olds for the least amount of money. For example, a total of 30,000 people of this exact target demographic watched the noon news on my station every day.

I sold the media and promised him results based on one thing: We will reach your target audience!

Instead, we aired three months' worth of his commercials with virtually no results. Duane asked to meet.

Duane carried a smog of fear into the conference room with him. His hair was rustled, and his face was rough. He sighed and sank down into the chair across from me and said defeatedly, "I have no leads, Brandon. I'm out of money."

I stared across the table, witnessing his agony. Stress was strangling the life out of him. Duane looked exactly like another failed business owner I'd known too well—my dad.

I had no answers for him, but I was willing to do anything to help turn this around.

"Give me 24 hours," I said.

That night, I read tirelessly, seeking for some sort of magic answer to give Duane. I looked through my targeting software and programs list, hoping to find Duane an audience that might react better and more efficiently.

None of the options I found looked better than what we were already doing.

So I decided to focus on the only other thing I could think of—the commercial itself. Was the commercial to blame?

I replayed it repeatedly on my computer screen.

"Homeowners, if you're looking to replace your windows, now is the time! We have high-quality, high-efficiency windows starting at $187! Call 883-2000 to schedule a free estimate!"

The ad's call to action was clear; its production quality was high.

I showed it to my wife and asked her opinion.

"Yeah, it's fine. If I were thinking about buying windows, I might call," Valerie said, as she went back to reading her book.

Suddenly it hit me. The stupid ad was only talking about the product—it wasn't giving anyone a real reason to consider buying it!

Valerie had said the magic words—*If I were thinking about windows . . .*

That's a pretty big *if.* I wondered how many people were thinking about purchasing windows during the afternoon news on a given day. My research showed me, statistically, that only about 50 out of 30,000 people at any given time were thinking of purchasing windows. So, what about the other 29,950 people? Were they simply ignoring the ad?

Yep. They were. My commercial wasn't giving anyone else reasons to consider purchasing the product. The price, the offer, the brand name, the phone number, and the entire category didn't matter to *anyone* else because I wasn't talking to them about anything that mattered to them. I was putting Duane's name out there and targeting the *exact* people he needed to reach. Yet, the Targeting Myth and the "getting your name out there" myth, the Branding Myth, led me to believe that's all I needed to do.

The problem wasn't that I had the wrong audience; it was that the commercial wasn't giving them reasons to care. If they weren't already thinking about buying windows, they'd quickly ignore it.

I had included all the information Duane thought was important: his name, phone number, website, and the word "homeowners." (*Business owners always want to cram all their information into their ads as if the people watching are just waiting to write down their phone number and call them.*)

For three months, I had aired Duane's commercial without thinking twice about the feelings we were creating. The commercial looked good. It looked professional. Duane loved it because it contained all the buzzwords, and he looked good on camera.

But professionally produced ads with all the buzzwords don't make people pay attention, even if they're targeted to the exact perfect audience.

I started to remember all the great things I'd learned studying legendary ad writers:

» "Talk to the customer in the language of the customer about what matters to the customer," advised Roy Williams.

» "A *good advertisement* is one that sells the product without drawing attention to itself," shouted David Ogilvy.

» "Don't tell me how good you make it [product]; tell me how good it makes me when I use it," echoed Leo Burnett.

I had clearly failed to listen to these guys the first time around. But now it couldn't have been clearer that to save Duane's marketing, I needed to apply their wisdom. I went back to the drawing board and asked myself:

» **What am I really selling here?**
Warm living rooms and low utility bills, not windows.

» **What needs does this customer have? What pains do they currently face?**
They are cold in their homes. They have high energy bills. Their old windows are ugly.

» **What are the customer's hopes and dreams?**
Having more money to go on vacation, getting compliments on their beautiful home, and being able to open their windows and enjoy spring air.

My ad wasn't addressing a *single* thing that the target customer actually wanted. So no matter how much target research I had done, it was never going to work. The commercial was saying things that didn't matter!

With this realization, I rewrote the ad that night:

How did you feel the last time you paid your energy bill?

You know, energy costs aren't getting any cheaper.

By installing more-efficient windows, you could be investing that money into the value of your home instead of donating it to the utility company AND have more money to take your family on vacation!

I'm Duane, and I have energy-saving windows that will make your home more beautiful and efficient, starting at just $187. Call me today, and I'll take the pain out of high energy bills before the summer heat gets here.

© *Frank & Maven Partners in Communication 2020*

The next day, I rushed a production order to reshoot the ad and then called Duane.

"I need you here Thursday. Look sharp and bring your best smile," I said.

I convinced Duane to advertise with us for another month, although we both knew he wouldn't be able to pay for it if my new ad wasn't successful. We aired it on the station the following week.

"It will probably take a few weeks before we can judge anything," I told him. To be honest, I wasn't sure what to expect, or when to expect it.

The middle of the next week Duane called me. He inquired, "Did my commercial just play?"

"Sure did," I said.

"Brandon, I think you're on to something. Just got four leads. I got two yesterday, too."

"That's amazing," I said. Honestly, I was still a little surprised by what had just happened. "Please keep me posted."

I sat back in my chair and thought about every failure I'd had in marketing up until that moment in my career.

I wondered: "*Could it really be that easy? Could choosing the right words make that big of a difference?*"

By the week's end, the answer was clearly yes. Duane had enough appointments to fill his entire calendar for the following week.

Duane began selling his window installations like crazy. He paid his advertising bills and sold over $1 million in the next nine months. He quickly became the number-one seller in his Midwest franchise group and, not long after, a household name in his market.

It was undeniably clear: The audience targeting had very little to do with our marketing campaign's success. *It was how I changed the ad's message that made all the difference.*

Looking back, I realize that that one golden epiphany forever changed my ability to truly help businesses grow. *It's not about whom you target; it's what you say to them that makes the difference.*

I had placed all my faith in the targeting and efficiency of the media, which had nearly failed me and Duane, and it continues to fail countless other business owners.

I had followed the Targeting Myth that nearly every advertising salesperson leans on: "Reach the right people, and you'll win."

I learned the hard way that the best media plan in the world cannot save a bad message.

It took me five years and hundreds of thousands of dollars of other people's money to learn that media can do only one thing: *Place a message in front of a potential buyer.* No matter how much targeting, technology, or efficiency is behind your media plan, if your message doesn't sell, then the audience isn't buying.

Businesses tend to blame targeting and the media because that's what they're paying for in their mind.

However, in any failed advertising endeavor, I always ask, "Did you fire the ad writer, too?"

For some of us, that's a tough question. We are often our own ad writers. It's *our* creative ideas that we take to the production team and ask the team to put them together, right? As business owners and media people, we have a brainstorm, we develop a vision for the ad, and because we are paying for it, we expect the production team to follow our lead, right?

As I lay out the Maven Method, I'll teach you a process for writing with creativity that sells, but before you read further, I feel it is paramount to call out this monster of a myth:

Targeting and the media do not make your advertising work.

Targeting and the media platform can do only one thing: Place your message in front of a potential buyer. But if your message is fundamentally flawed, the best media and the best targeting in the world will not save you.

You might be asking, "If all of this is true, does the advertising platform even matter?"

Short answer: Not if your ad misses the mark.

Long answer: A well-tuned TV, radio, print, billboard, or digital campaign *can* make your message go *a lot* farther, and sometimes it can even speed up the results you want to achieve.

Knowing how to negotiate your media schedule can save you and your business tons of money. In fact, I have literally saved my clients hundreds of thousands of dollars on their advertising spending by understanding targeting and negotiating their advertising based on the targeting and audience.

That said, your ad could be shown during every Super Bowl commercial break and still not move the needle if it fails to connect with the audience about something that already matters to them. You can have a perfectly selected broadcast schedule, full of watchers who meet your perfect demographics, and still come up empty-handed. You can have the most sophisticated digital or social media targeting that pinpoints your perfect customer and still strike out.

The Targeting Myth leads you to believe that your advertising platform is the problem. You'll prematurely cancel your contract with whoever sold it to you and go on blaming the wrong reason for your failures, missing the opportunity to focus on what *actually* will make all the difference. Don't fall for the Targeting Myth and then make rapid changes to your advertising for fear of not reaching the right audience.

Instead, choose the media to the best of your ability and then spend the rest of your time *obsessing* over the customer you are writing your ad for.

Become serious about what their needs and pains are! Get obsessed with their hopes and fears!

Get realistic about how your product can actually make their life better!

In other words, uncover what you are *really* selling.

Learning that begins by *unlearning* the third common myth that fails us in advertising.

It's called the Educate the Public Myth.

CHAPTER 6
THE EDUCATE THE PUBLIC MYTH

Do you ever find yourself wondering how many years of combined experience your local plumber has?

Or how about the industrial certifications of a diesel mechanic?

And would you feel so enlightened to hear how many convenient locations a local credit union has?

These are all lines from real ads that you've probably heard before. These companies believed you simply needed *to be educated* before you would buy.

Is it working?

Writing ads about the customer's needs may seem like common sense, but it isn't common practice. When we start the task to sit down and write ads about our businesses, our minds naturally go to the products or services that our companies sell. We *assume* because we need to sell more of our products or services that we must use our ads to *educate the public* about them.

This is the Educate the Public Myth.

The Educate the Public Myth assumes that all that's required for success in advertising is for people to know more information about a product/service.

When attempting to sell you advertising, the average salesperson will usually ask the following:

» "What is your unique selling proposition?"

» "What do you want people to know about your company?"

» "What do you need to educate the public about your product or service?"

Business owners happily answer these questions with rambling bullet points:

» "We pride ourselves on service!"

» "We've been in business 26 years!"

» "We need to educate our customers about our difference in *quality*!"

» "We have 186 years of combined experience!"

Have you been guilty of putting out ads that sound like this?

This part of the advertising process often goes unnoticed. In traditional media sales, the salesperson is usually in charge at this point. To no fault of his own, he's just trying to get the ad on the air so he can begin billing the client. And the business owner happily goes along answering the questions that are assumed to be the *right* questions.

But it is from this seemingly intelligent starting point that the ad is doomed. This is the biggest point of failure in most small business marketing today.

If you need any proof, look no further than your own life and your own experience. When your local auto shop advertises "We pride ourselves on service!" do you believe them?

When was the last time that you, as a consumer, needed to be "educated" about a product you weren't already thinking of?

During 99.9 percent of your time, do you feel the need to be "educated" about the difference between vinyl windows and wooden windows? The different types of shingles? What "ASE" certified means? But these ads are all over the place, aren't they?

Somewhere in the history of advertising, we forgot that our job, as advertisers, is not to *educate* people. Our job is to *inspire* people.

Information is not inspirational. To inspire someone, you must first meet them at their current feelings—their interests, pains, fears, and their way of viewing the world. I ask you again to look at your own life. You pay attention to things that are in your best interest, right?

The reason we ignore most advertising is directly tied to our nature as human beings.

Yet most ads are plagued with empty phrases violating the rules of our psychological wiring. For example:

> » "For all your estate planning needs!"

> » "186 years of combined experience!"

> » "Your source for quality windows!"

> » "You've tried the rest, now try the best!"

The problem with these statements doesn't lie in the fact that they aren't *true*. The problem is simply that no one cares.

When you set out to *educate* the public on how awesome *your company* is, you're loading your gun with blanks. You should, instead, tell them how awesome *they* would be if they did the thing you want them to do. I experienced this firsthand with Bill, my friend and client, at his body shop when I visited.

Bill owned a successful body shop that had been passed down through three generations of owners. After nearly an hour of grilling him on why he thought people should do business with him, all I could get from him was the standard answer:

» "We treat people fairly."

» "We have great customer service."

» "We're a family business."

» "Do business with people you can trust!"

Bill was the most upstanding example of a hardworking business owner I'd ever met. I knew 100 percent that these statements were true.

However, I looked him straight in the eye and said, "Bill, every single one of your competitors is shouting that crap. Do you believe them?"

"Well, no," he quickly admitted.

"And neither does anyone else!" I shouted.

I wasn't going to take Bill's money and waste it by boring people to death with the same old drivel. So, I did the uncomfortable thing and kept digging.

"Tell me about the last customer that dropped their car off here."

"What do you mean?" he asked.

"Who was it? Literally, what was their name?"

He thought about it for a second. "Well, we had a lady this morning drop off a van. Lisa was her name, I think."

"Great! Tell me about Lisa," I said, as I leaned over the desk. "Tell me about her day. How do you think it started? What was she feeling this morning when she woke up?"

Bill pondered for another minute and said, "Well, she had two kids with her. She was probably in a hurry to get them to school."

"Tell me more," I said. "What do you think is more important to her than anything?"

"Her kids?" he said with uncertainty. I could tell he had no clue what any of our conversation had to do with his body shop.

"Yes! Now, stay with me," I pleaded, leaning in closer. "And why is she here?"

"She got in a fender bender on the way to drop them off at school," Bill stated.

"How did she feel in that moment when her car crashed into another one?" I asked.

"Scared. She was still a little frazzled when she arrived here."

"What did you tell her when she came here?"

"I told her not to worry and that we would have her van back to her by the weekend."

"Really? It's already Thursday."

"Yeah, I know. Dale will come in early and knock it out tomorrow."

"Who's Dale?" I dug deeper.

"He's our painter. Hardest-working guy you'll ever meet."

"Does he come in early often?"

"Oh sure. When he knows someone needs a favor, he does it all the time."

"How early?"

"Shoot, sometimes 3 or 4 a.m."

"You're kidding me," I said with genuine surprise.

"Nope. That's why the insurance companies like us so much."

"Because you get the car back to owners faster?"

"Yeah, and the insurance companies don't have to pay extra days for a rental car," he said, as he started rooting around on his desk for a report. "See right here, we're always winning on this report. It tells us how we're doing in comparison to other body shops in town. We get people's cars back to them two days faster than the average local body shop."

Bill had no idea, but that report he had dug up on his desk was pure gold.

"Dammit, Bill."

"What?" he said, a little alarmed.

"You're telling me you have a verifiable report that proves you're the fastest in town?"

"Well, yeah. I told you we take care of people!" Bill chuckled.

"Do you realize how many moms there are like Lisa?" I inquired.

"Sure. We see 'em every day."

"You were a hero for Lisa today, right?"

"Yeah. She mentioned they needed the van back before the kids' soccer tournament this weekend."

"I'll be back in 15 minutes," I said, and scurried out the door.

I went to my car and wrote the following ad:

It's 3 a.m. on Walnut Street. The rest of the world is sleeping, but Dale and the boys are wide awake. *tap tap tap*

Dale knows that you need your van to get everyone to soccer on Saturday; it just isn't going to happen any other way. So he's here so you can have your keys back before the kids get out of school.

That's the kind of promise we make at Bill Wilson's Auto Body: to get you back to your life. And the numbers prove it. Insurance companies tell us that we get cars back to folks two days faster than other shops in town.

When you've had a bad car day, bring it to Bill Wilson's Auto Body—the fastest way back to normal.

I ran back in and showed Bill the ad.

"I see what you mean now," he smiled.

We ran ads like that for the next two years, and Bill's company grew faster than it ever had in 50 years. By the following fall, he'd increased his company's gross sales by nearly $2 million and had to build another facility to handle the increased volume.

Had I not taken the time to find Bill's diamond of a story, his ad may have run and simply blended in with the ads for the other dozen shops in town. Bill would've been trying to "educate the public." But the public does not need to be educated; the public needs to be inspired. In fact, if you try to educate the public about body shops, they won't listen for more than a few seconds.

Bill had the courage to run an ad that spoke directly to the Lisas of the world about what matters most in their lives, *not his.*

That extra hour I spent digging into the life of the customer made a multimillion-dollar difference for Bill and his company. He had advertised for years, "educating the public" about his body shop, but he *never* had results like these. I had helped Bill see what he was *really selling*, and it made the million-dollar difference.

Uncovering what you are *really selling* will make the million-dollar difference for your company, too. But it requires that you give up a little bit of your ego and realize that, in fact, what you are *really* selling has very little to do with *you* at all.

CHAPTER 7

THE MAVEN METHOD WRITING PROCESS: WHAT YOU ARE REALLY SELLING

To tell people what you're selling seems pretty simple, doesn't it? You're an expert on your products and services. You could talk for hours about what you know. Yet usually that expertise is the very thing that blocks you from ever connecting with your audience.

Bill thought that his customer, Lisa, needed quality body shop repairs. But really, she just needed to get back to her life faster. She needed to get to the soccer tournament. She needed to know her vehicle was safe to carry her kids after the collision. She needed to overcome the hassle and embarrassment of not having a car.

Most business owners falsely assume that *product awareness* is their goal. But effective ads help people see much more than a product. They help them visualize a better life.

What you *think* you're selling is very rarely what you are *really* selling.

Here are some more examples:

> » Attorneys aren't selling estate planning; they're selling *happy families* who don't need to fight over money.

» Dentists aren't selling perfect smiles; they're selling *confidence* for dating, job interviews, and better selfie pics.

» Luxury restaurants aren't selling amazing food; they're selling romantic date nights.

» Eye doctors aren't selling perfect vision; they're selling being able to *experience* every detail of your daughter's wedding.

» Plastic surgeons aren't selling surgery; they're selling the ability to not be afraid of seeing yourself in a picture.

» Roofers aren't selling a roof; they're selling *no hassles in dealing with your insurance company.*

» Window replacement companies aren't selling windows; they're selling *lower utility bills, curb appeal,* and being able to sit on your couch *without a cold draft.*

As the old saying goes, "Nobody wants a half-inch drill bit. They want a half-inch hole." I'd argue even a step further that what they *really want* is for the shelf to be hung up. *That's what they're really buying.*

What's the *real thing* you are selling?

It's easy to see what someone else is selling when you consider products outside of your own business. But how do you uncover this for your products and your customers? Your curse of knowledge tries to prevent you from ever seeing it, but there *is* a method you can use for overcoming that. After I perfected this method, I was exponentially better at making ads work for people. I had finally overcome the other false beliefs, the *myths* that led me and so many others astray and that are at the root of businesspeople wasting money with advertising.

Over the next few years, I repeated the process I'd used with Bill on other clients: digging deep, begging them to not settle for just "getting their name out there," "targeting their perfect customer," and "educating the public." The results I started to see were everything I had imagined that advertising should be. Businesses that I helped were growing. In fact, their owners were *thriving*. They'd become more financially independent, paying off debt, hiring more employees, and taking more vacations with their family. Other business owners in my town heard about the results my campaigns were generating. I started receiving calls from other states.

That was when I left the ad sales job that had taught me so much, and I started an ad agency.

As I began to hire employees to help me, I realized I needed to quickly teach them what I had learned. I tracked my writing process on paper, putting it into a series of questions so that I could teach it and repeat the results that had made such an awesome impact for my previous clients. I took from all my experiences what I was able to do *intuitively* and formulated it into a series of guided questions—a repeatable method for writing good ads.

That writing process is now a critical part of my Maven Method. The rest of this book will be teaching the Maven Method—shifting from everything that's wrong in the broken system of advertising to what to do instead.

You may be asking, "What is a maven?" A *maven* is someone who gathers information for the sake of educating others. A maven has the heart of a teacher and seeks to share and give everything they can to the world so that others can achieve.

I didn't know it at the time, but all the tough lessons I had learned previously were shaping me into a maven so I could teach many others to avoid those mistakes. It's why the Maven Method exists.

The Maven Method of writing ads—discovering what you are really selling—follows four basic questions:

1. Who are you really talking to?

2. What are their needs, pains, hopes, and fears?

3. How can your product meet one of those needs, pains, hopes, or fears?

4. What is the most reasonable next step you can ask them to take?

While it may appear unsophisticated on the surface, this method has been behind every successful ad that I've written. I believe you can find the same success, and you don't even have to be a great writer.

By following this simple exercise, you can literally transform the profitability of your campaigns and immediately pull yourself out of irrelevance mode in your writing. Let's dig a little deeper into each of the four parts of this process.

STEP 1: WHO ARE YOU REALLY TALKING TO?

Take the time to vividly visualize *who* you are talking to.

Like the example with Bill's customer, Lisa, and his body shop, you must get very specific about this person. Pick a recent customer that exemplifies a customer you want to earn. Picture them in your mind. Call them by name. (This part of the process doesn't necessarily require scientific research.)

You *can* use customer research platforms to find who your most likely customers are demographically, but defining "who your customer really is" comes mostly from intuition and your experience. Use clues like their age, where they are from, the conversations you've had with them, bumper stickers they proudly display on their cars, and even their social media, to develop a general sense of *who* they really are. Contemplate the following:

» How do they spend their time?

» What do they value?

» Who do they most admire?

» Who do they need to impress?

» What's a day in their life like for them?

» What brands do they find attractive? Why?

This is a process also known as "defining your customer's avatar." A *customer avatar* is a picture and profile of your ideal customer. Ponder any and all characteristics about this person, so much so that you can see them in your mind and speak to them with empathy. Pretend you've just met this stranger on an airplane and you're trying to get to know them.

Literally defining "who" you are talking to enables you to stop writing boring, ineffective ads. Getting this clear picture naturally sets your brain up to speak *to* the person you are thinking about as if you were sitting across the table from them. Without having a specific person in mind, your ads are blank and your words are floating out in space. *And that's when it becomes too easy to write about things that don't matter.*

If your promises don't matter to **someone,** your ads won't matter to **anyone.**

It's important to note that you can have multiple avatars for your brand and your advertising, but it's very wise to speak to *only one avatar at a time.* When you focus on speaking directly to one type of customer, you'll find that most everyone will connect and recall your message better, even if it's not the exact person you were writing to. This physiological truth is known as the *eavesdropper effect.*

THE EAVESDROPPER EFFECT

Have you ever been in a room where someone else was talking on the phone? You can hear only one side of the conversation, but your brain can't help but listen, right? And you can't bring yourself to ignore the conversation until you figure out what the person is talking about.

The human brain is wired to listen to conversations, even when conversations don't pertain to us.

In the September 2010 issue of *Psychological Science,* Dr. Lauren Emberson shared her research on the undying tendency of our brains to tune into "halfalogues," a term she used to describe overhearing a one-sided conversation. A WebMD summary of her findings stated: "Overhearing half of a conversation 'has a really profound effect on the cognition of the people around you, and it's not because they're eavesdropping or they're bad people. Their cognitive mechanism basically means that they're forced to listen.'"

In other words, when dialogue is directed towards *someone*, everyone is more likely to pay attention.

Your ads can also be secretly written to start a one-way conversation with your person of interest, which causes the rest of the world to curiously listen in. By doing this, you force yourself to talk in *human* language, not *advertising* language.

To do this, you must be *real.* You must not cue your potential customer's brain that this is an ad, or they'll stop listening. You must have the courage to remove insider language about your product. Avoid jargon and just talk to people plainly.

You must make the conversation authentic.

» An estate planning attorney might say: *"You're going to leave it all to them someday, and they should get every penny."*

» A boat dealer might say: *"Time with your boys on the water— there's nothing like it."*

» A solar energy company might say: *"If you had an extra $150 a month in your pocket, what would you do with it?"*

The magic of talking this way is that far more people will listen to and be inspired by a conversation than they will to an information stream. They'll be far more capable of recalling that conversation as well—and the company tied to it.

You must find the courage to have an imaginary dialogue with the person you want to speak to as if you were sitting across the table from them. Strike up a conversation about things that matter to them. If you don't do this when you write your ads, you are very likely flapping your jaws to nobody. You might as well grab a megaphone and walk down the street shouting one-liners about your product and see who cares enough to stop and listen. We both know how that would probably turn out, right?

So, do the human thing and start your message process by visualizing the *someone* you're talking to so that you don't get ignored by *everyone*.

STEP 2: WHAT ARE THEIR NEEDS, PAINS, HOPES, AND FEARS?

This is where you must get very intentional about why anyone should care. Answer the following:

» What do they currently need that you can help them meet?

» What pains do they have in their life that you can help them relieve?

» What hopes or dreams do they have that you can help them realize?

» What fears for taking action can you help them overcome?

Following this simple exercise can literally transform the profitability of your advertising campaigns. In general, you want to speak to *one* of these needs, pains, hopes, or fears at a time. You might find that some needs, pains, hopes, and fears coincide with each other. But the central theme of each of these points should remain consistent.

Over the years, I have received some push back from my clients on limiting their ads to just one thing at a time. Due to the amount of money they're spending, eager business owners often want to cram all they can into 60-second or even 30-second ads. This comes from a place of anxiousness, usually. "Don't leave anything out" is what traditional wisdom tells us.

But traditional wisdom isn't really wise at all.

Lee Clow, an Apple ad executive, famously once demonstrated the concept of simplicity in a meeting with Steve Jobs. As the story goes, he crumpled up five pieces of paper. He threw one piece of paper at Jobs, which Jobs easily caught. Then Clow threw all five pieces of paper at Jobs, and Jobs didn't catch a single one.

Your mission is to make it impossible to not catch the **one thing** at a time you're selling. When you have something else to say, write an additional ad for that and run it as part of the campaign. But if you try to cram it all into one message, you're going to come up short.

When you have the courage to make your messages a sequential understanding over time, you fundamentally prepare the customer to build a full understanding of your brand in their mind. That's when magic happens. That's when you start to get big growth.

You might have multiple messages running in your campaign at once, or you might run one message for a while, then switch to another. But within that message, make it one *single* message. No afterthoughts, no throw-in details, and no speed reading to get through all of what you need to say. Let the ad breathe a little. Let your message be heard. Say something so valuable that it's the only thing you need to say!

SPEAKING TO NEEDS

Needs are simply that: What does a person need in their life right now? What does she need in her life? What do they need as a family? It could be more time to spend with the kids. It could be more money. It could be more respect from colleagues. It could be the feeling of accomplishment. It could be help losing weight. It could be a better relationship with their spouse.

Use this simple fill-in-the-blank technique to take yourself outside the box for a minute:

Their life would be better if they only had _____.

Even if it's unclear how the need directly relates to your product, write it down when it does come to mind. As you're visualizing the avatar you've created for your ideal client, model all the things you can imagine going on in their life.

SPEAKING TO PAINS

Defining the pain factors of your target can be very powerful in finding an emotional desire for your product. When the brain is in pain, it's wired to want to get out of it. Humans are naturally programmed to avoid pain when we can, so if your product or service can overcome your customer's pain, you have an immediate chance to be relevant. Here are a few of the questions you might ask when modeling your customer's pain:

» Where are they currently feeling frustration?

» What or who is annoying them?

» What is causing them sadness or grief?

» What is causing them financial stress?

» What do they find difficult in their lives?

» What do they wish they didn't have to do every day?

» How did they imagine their life would be different by now?

» What is keeping them from their desired situation?

SPEAKING TO FEARS

Fears are similar to pains, but fears more clearly model what may be causing your target to put off making a decision. You might ask:

» What is the worst thing that could happen if this person makes the wrong decision?

» What bad stories have they heard about this product category?

» Where have they failed in the past that might make them leery about buying this product again?

» What are they most afraid of losing?

Be thinking of how you might be able to position your product to overcome these fears.

SPEAKING TO HOPES

Speaking to the hopes, dreams, and other aspirations of a person is a very fast way to emotionally connect with them. When you can paint a better future for them, or even a better today for them, you earn the position to be a big part of their success. Ask them the following types of questions:

» What is a perfect world for them?

» What does this person dream of when they close their eyes?

» What is this person's idea of a fun day?

» Their life would be perfect if they only had _____.

» What would make them feel more important? What's their idea of accomplishment?

» What status do they wish to achieve?

» If money wasn't an object, how would they spend their time?

BANKING ON UNIVERSAL DESIRES

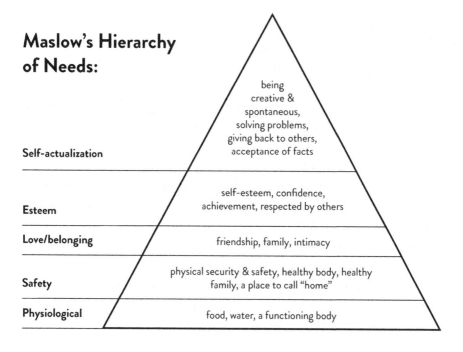

Maslow's Hierarchy of Needs:

- Self-actualization: being creative & spontaneous, solving problems, giving back to others, acceptance of facts
- Esteem: self-esteem, confidence, achievement, respected by others
- Love/belonging: friendship, family, intimacy
- Safety: physical security & safety, healthy body, healthy family, a place to call "home"
- Physiological: food, water, a functioning body

Abraham Maslow studied over 100,000 human beings in his career. If you've spent any time taking college psychology or studying human behavior, you've certainly heard of him.

Maslow's famous Hierarchy of Needs pyramid has been used to explain human behavior at its most basic level for decades. Maslow found that . . .

> » Most of us have our two most basic levels of needs met. Physiologically, most of us are nourished with plenty of food and water. Most of us have ample safety and shelter. If we don't have our most basic needs met, nothing else really matters.

> » Very few of us reach a peak point of sustained self-actualization—the peak at which we feel "okay," where we have the ability to focus on humanity at large and can

solve problems bigger than ourselves, taking our need to be right out of the equation.

» Most human beings spend their days searching for more love, a sense of belonging, and affirmation from others, or identity (Tiers 3 and 4 of the pyramid).

Knowing that the vast majority of the population needs more love, a sense of belonging, and a sense of identity, it's usually a good idea to write ads that help in these areas.

If you aren't in a particularly emotional type of business, you may be asking, "How can my product possibly give anyone more love and a sense of belonging?" The answer is in the angle of approach you take with your ads. There is almost always a deeper thing to connect on besides just your product.

Let's say you're an HVAC company.

Who you are talking to: Assume, for this example, that you are talking to a female homeowner. She's in her mid-30s and a stay-at-home mom. She has a job on the side, but it comes second to taking care of her family. Because she's more detail-oriented and organized than her husband, she's the one who typically makes the first call for home repairs. She's at home when her A/C goes out, and the problem is urgent for her. Let's give her a name: Jennifer.

What are Jennifer's needs?
» Being comfortable
» Having kids who aren't fussy
» Having enough time to get everything done
» Taking a break—a vacation
» Feeling like she's doing a good job
» Owning a nice home to entertain in
» Controlling her day and her life
» Being mindful of finances

What are Jennifer's pains?
- » Changing her day to work on this unexpected problem
- » Feeling the physical discomfort of a hot house
- » Experiencing her children's physical discomfort
- » Recognizing potential health dangers due to overheating
- » Knowing that she has to spend money
- » Taking the time and energy to go through the repair company selection process
- » Dealing with rude people (i.e., competition)

What are Jennifer's fears?
- » Making the wrong decision
- » Paying more than is necessary
- » Getting taken advantage of
- » Feeling dumb
- » Realizing a repair may affect her vacation or "fun" budget with the family

What are Jennifer's hopes?
- » Spending more time with family
- » Having happy and healthy kids
- » Traveling
- » Having a beautiful home
- » Making good money on the side
- » Having a happy spouse

Using this simple avatar as an example, do you see that just by using a little imagination and common sense how deeply we can begin to understand our customer? Do you see how much easier it is to speak to her when we call her "Jennifer," and we picture her as a young mom?

Sales and marketing guru Dean Graziosi once said, "People don't buy when they understand you. They buy when they feel understood." Going through the needs, pains, hopes, and fears exercise puts you in prime position to speak to potential clients as if they've been understood.

STEP 3: HOW CAN YOUR PRODUCT MEET ONE OF THOSE NEEDS, PAINS, HOPES, OR FEARS?

While this next part may seem like common sense, too, watch a commercial on TV and you'll see that common sense is not common practice. How often do people throw the details of their product at us and then fail to tell us what it even means to them?

A typical ad that violates the intelligence and attention of the public goes something like this:

Are you thinking about buying (product)?

(Company name) has (product) with (feature, feature, feature)!

So call (business name) for all your (product) needs.

Even if you've properly modeled your customer and understood their needs, pains, hopes, and fears, you still must *follow through* by connecting them to your product. You can do this by using a very small amount of words. For example:

Every mother on the planet wants the same thing: for her kids to be happy and healthy. That's why Smith Elder Law has advanced training in family counseling so we can help you navigate life's most difficult conversations with empathy and compassion.

Over the years, I've used the simple visual on the next page to ensure that I never lose focus in my ads. In the left column, I list all my potential client's needs, pains, hopes, and fears. On the right-hand side, I list all the benefits of my product or service. Then, just like a worksheet that my six-year-old brings home from school, I connect the needs, pains, hopes, and fears to the feature that overcomes or fulfills them.

Satisfying The Customer

Customer	Product Benefits
Needs	**Outcomes My Product Provides**
•	
•	•
•	
•	•
•	
	•
Pains	
	•
•	
•	•
•	
•	•
•	
	•
Hopes	
	•
•	
•	•
•	
•	•
•	
	•
Fears	
	•
•	
•	•
•	
•	
•	∿
•	

Your job as an ad writer is to so clearly see exactly what outcome you are trying to deliver that you naturally jump from the customer's life to your product feature and back to your customer's life through the ad.

THE "WHICH MEANS" TRICK

I first learned this trick from Roy Williams, author of *The Wizard of Ads,* and I've heard this wisdom echoed by many copywriting pros. Every time you catch yourself blabbing about a product or service's detail, make yourself finish the sentence with " . . . which means_____."

For example:

Our body shop technicians are I-CAR certified, which means they know how to restore your vehicle to its ultimate structural integrity so your family is safe.

Every one of our roofers is an employee, not a contractor, which means you'll never have an unverified stranger at your house.

The websites we build are stored on a redundant cloud server, which means we can restore them in a matter of minutes in the event of a hacker attack.

The GMC Terrain is equipped with Lane Assist Radar Technology, which means you'll never accidentally forget to check your blind spot again.

Our optometry clinic is equipped with the latest scanning technology, which means you don't have to get poked in the eye for your glaucoma test.

See the difference? This quick trick will make sure that you're always bringing the conversation back to your customer, instead of just talking about yourself.

STEP 4: WHAT'S THE MOST REASONABLE NEXT STEP YOU CAN ASK THEM TO TAKE?

Remember earlier when we discussed how few people are actually looking for your product today?

Remember the illustration about how 99.9 percent of people don't need to be educated in this very moment?

Well, even fewer are ready to take action! Often in advertising, we expect the holy grail of direct response. So we shout things at the end of our ads like "Call now, or visit our website!"

In high-demand commoditized products that we buy often, this information shouting can work. I particularly had good success with a restaurant one time when we ran a text message promotion for a discount. *Hundreds* responded within 30 seconds. Yet, what about the products where the buying cycle takes years? Is it reasonable to expect the phone to ring off the hook right after a 30-second sales pitch? Most of us would agree that, no, it would not be reasonable. But we hear the same clichéd calls to action every day.

Now, hear me clearly: I'm not saying you *shouldn't ask* for action, you absolutely *should*. What I am saying is your action should be *reasonable*. Ask yourself, "How long did it take for your last 10 customers to decide they were ready to buy what you sell?" Next, ask yourself, "How long did it take them to choose to buy it from you instead of someone else?"

What were the questions they had before taking action? Why didn't they act sooner? What finally made them comfortable enough to start looking?

We assume that most decisions are made from an impulsive logic, but this has been highly disputed by countless studies. The Google/Shopper Sciences study revealed that the average shopper uses more than 10 sources of information to make purchase decisions. It also concluded that as technology progresses, there is an increasing number of sources used.

Even when consumers do feel a direct response to your ad, it's not actually *that* ad that has done all the work. Friends and neighbors, social media, signs and graphics on vehicles that people drive by, and even your competitors' ads have long primed your ideal prospects for taking action until the lucky day when the stars align and your ad finally speaks to them enough to warrant action. Your best hope is to provide the most *reasonable* step to action, instead of blindly assuming that the customer is ready to purchase your product.

My favorite example of this is a small tweak we made to the call to action for one of my clients. He had been spending close to $1 million a year advertising his solar panel company. His call to action was "Call now to schedule an estimate." It's worth noting that before we came along, he was advertising this message across multiple TV stations, radio stations, and Facebook on weekends and during the nighttime when he wasn't even staffed with people to answer the phones.

Aside from that, we pointed out to him that the majority of search engine traffic for his product category revolved around terms related to "Are solar panels really worth the investment?" It was quite obvious that he was asking the majority of his service area to take an action that they weren't even close to being ready to take.

Solar was a very new product at the time, and people didn't quite understand what it could do for them. So, we shifted messaging to this question by building a "solar savings calculator" and adding it on his website. Then we changed the call to action on the ads to say:

Solar isn't for everyone. But you can find out if it's right for you. Go to ABCSolarCalculator.com to see how much money a system could save you.

Seems like a simple shift, right?

We literally quadrupled the amount of leads our client was receiving within a few days of making this change, *without* spending one extra penny or changing one single placement in his ad schedule. What was the difference? We made the call to action about the customer's desire, not ours. We made the next step *reasonable*.

The "call to schedule an in-home estimate" language was scaring people. Nobody was even close to ready to have a solar salesman in their home. But from the comfort of their own computer, they could get an idea of the cost and savings of a solar system. Naturally, this encouraged them to become willing prospects.

We estimated this one change made a seven-figure difference in his company the first year. Once again, a few words and the right method made a million-dollar difference. Never forget that words are the cheapest thing on the planet. But when chosen carefully, they can inspire life-changing action.

The Maven Method writing process will help you find these words and the right angle to help your ads convey them. It has *never* failed me. More importantly, every time I didn't use the Maven Method, I ended up with poor results. In hindsight I can see that every time I let a client run an ad about their product or service features without asking questions about a customer's life, the ads ended up falling short of our goals.

If you've had a disappointing result in your advertising, I'd be willing to bet nobody was asking these questions. Using the Maven Method writing process alone can single-handedly change your advertising outcomes because it forces you to get serious about the customer, not your product.

Bad ad writers ramble on about products, features, and useless information about the business. However, exceptional ad writers speak directly to the needs, pains, hopes, and fears of the customer. That's really the biggest difference! They don't rely on creativity and wordsmithing nearly as much as people think.

This Maven Method writing process helps you do the latter and make million-dollar ads, even if you don't consider yourself a creative or good writer. Once you know how to go deep, to find the desires of the customer and speak to them, you are prepared to win. I have proven this hundreds of times over since learning it.

After I understood this concept, I uncovered yet another lesson that greatly increased my chances of winning and scaling the results of our campaigns. This lesson was pivotal in my career and for the clients whom I served because it enabled me to finally predict *what* was going to happen with an ad campaign *before* I spent money on it. This also provided me with the final understanding of *why* some campaigns had worked while others had not.

The lesson was this: There are actually *three types of customers* at any given time for a business, and before you write an ad, you must decide which one you want to attract.

CHAPTER 8

UNDERSTANDING THE THREE TYPES OF CUSTOMERS

Over your lifetime, you'll buy thousands and thousands of different services and products for different reasons. But on any given day, you'll probably be in the market for only a couple dozen things at the most, right? And it would be really silly to ask you to spend thousands of dollars on stuff you don't want, right? *You are no different from anyone else you're advertising to.* Remembering that is key to setting expectations with your marketing.

As I perfected the Maven Method of writing, my clients went from just "making noise" and "getting their name out there" to truly connecting with their customers and inspiring them to buy. But there was still a problem: Even though my ads were making a much bigger impact, I didn't have a solid way to predict *when* they would start working. It drove me crazy that some clients would get instant results, while for others it would take months. I eventually learned that it had everything to do with understanding what I now call the three types of customers:

1. **Today customers:** People who already have a need for the product today.

2. **Tomorrow customers:** People who don't have a need for the product today but eventually will.

3. **Yesterday customers:** Those who've already purchased a product from you but will buy something from you again and/or send their friends and family to you.

Today, tomorrow, and yesterday customers refer to the different "modes" that a person can be in related to your product category. Most advertising is created without *any* strategic approach to which of these customers the business actually is trying to earn, and therefore the results are inconsistent. Advertisers fail when they simply create an ad that they assume will be relevant to everyone. In reality, human beings are more complex than that. (You are more complex than that, right?)

To fully understand how advertising will work for your business, you must first be able to differentiate among each of these three types of customers and understand that each requires a different type of strategy, a different message, and a different kind of media to win them over. The best marketing plans have a plan for all three customer types, but it's crucial that you understand which customer you are trying to earn at any given time.

In the following chapters, I outline the motivations for each customer type, followed by the specific type of messaging you must use to win them over and the media platforms that work best to reach them.

I first realized how important the three customer types were when I met Sam.

Sam and his dad, Gerald, owned a furniture store. They were, by all meanings of the phrase, a *family business.* Sam sold the furniture; his brother, Danny, put the furniture together; Sam's wife and mom collected the money; and Gerald delivered the furniture.

It was a Friday afternoon when I first met them in the middle of their empty store. They had called me because they wanted to buy ads to get some more store traffic, and they'd been to a seminar for furniture stores where everyone was talking about TV ads producing big results.

I asked Sam, "What do you think your customers want?"

"They want someone they can trust!" he piped up in a thick Arkansas drawl.

"Tell me more. Is trust a rare thing in your business?"

"You betcha! Too many badgers sellin' junk furniture. Stuff people don't really want. And then, they ain't nowhere to be found when it breaks."

"Can you give me an example?"

"Them big outfits in town that run big financin' sales. You walk in the door, and they start tellin' ya about all the interest-free payments while they sell ya things you never wanted."

"I see. So, how are you different?"

"We only sell people what they're lookin' for. And, we don't sell junk."

"Okay, I think I might be able to do something with that."

I knew Sam's expectations were going to be pretty high. The seminar he'd been to had been full of big-budget advertisers with sophisticated promotions and prime locations. He was a little guy on the outskirts of town and determined not to discount his furniture. I was confident, however, that I could write a message that would make a difference. I brought him this ad:

You count on your furniture to be there for you. After a long day, at your family dinners, your time relaxing together, and for a good night's rest.

These are the moments that make our work worth doing, and our lives worth living. You can't really put a price on that kind of comfort.

So, when you want a piece of furniture you can depend on, buy it from a family you can depend on.

No gimmicks, no pushy salespeople, and no junk. Come shop

with the Walter family at Walter Family Furniture, just off Highway 14, next to Sonic.

This ad spoke to the needs and pain factors that Sam believed in:

His customers needed quality and dependability.

They wanted to avoid the pain factors of pushy salespeople.

Sam loved the ad, so we ran it. After the first week, he called me.

"Are you sure our ads are runnin'?"

"Yes, sir. Your ads are running in the 6 and 9 p.m. news, just like we talked."

"Well, we can't tell! Nobody in the store this weekend."

"There are 50,000 people hearing your message every day, Sam. You'll soon be on their list of places to shop. Just be patient."

Sam wasn't buying it. Right then, I should've known it wasn't going to end well. It was a classic case of a need for instant gratification, but one week wasn't even close to a solid measurement period for *good* or *bad* results.

As Sam challenged the results, I wasn't even truly sure what to tell him. Some of my other furniture store clients *had* seen great results in a few weeks. *I knew there had to be a reason.*

That weekend I decided to do some research by mystery shopping some of Sam's competitors—the big-box furniture stores. It was no surprise that they were packed with people. I walked in the door of one, and Sara handed me a flier.

"Welcome to our sale! Everything in the store today qualifies for $0 down, 0 percent interest financing, and up to 30 percent off!"

Sara was an eager salesperson. She was like a robot, programmed to close the deal. She followed me around the store to remind me every three minutes, "This one qualifies for $0 down financing!" She was the exact pushy salesperson that Sam stood against in the ad we had written.

Finally I asked her, "You seem to have a lot of people in here today. Is that pretty common for a Saturday?"

"Oh yeah. When we have sales, you can count on a boatload of people, rain or shine."

"Why do you think that is?" The look on her face told me it was the dumbest question she'd ever heard.

"Because they need furniture!"

"Sure. But why do you think they're here and not somewhere else?"

"Well, they saw our ads and know we have the best deals."

"How often do you have those?"

"Pretty much every weekend."

"Can I ask you one more question?"

"Sure."

"How long has the average person worked here?"

"Hmm. I dunno. Maybe three months?"

"Thank you for your time. I'm just looking today, but I'll let you know when I'm ready to buy."

I had all the proof I needed. Nobody in that big-box store really cared about quality, relationships, or trust in whom they were buying from. They only cared about *price* and *convenience*.

Sara had been trained to constantly talk about financing because that's what *works* for the people who come into a big-box store. She was working in a high-pressure sales environment and, just like her peers, probably wouldn't last in that job for longer than a few months. Financing promotions, discount pricing, and high-pressure salespeople work for those who have an immediate need—*today*.

Having purchased furniture from this same store a couple of years before, I also knew firsthand that their quality wasn't great, and neither was their customer service. But at the time, I had a short-term need to buy furniture for a new house.

Years later, I would develop a relationship with my interior designer and buy furniture only from high-quality stores like Sam's. But at that point in my life, I didn't have the time or money to be a relationship-focused furniture customer.

When I had shopped with the big-box stores, I didn't care about trust, quality, or having a connection with whom I was buying from at that point in my life. I just needed furniture for the cheapest price possible for our starter house. In that moment, I was a *today* customer. The same was true for every person in that big-box store that day. Exactly zero people were there buying because they trusted a sales associate, or even the name on the furniture. Everyone was acting with a short-term mentality with the belief that they were getting it at the *right time* for the *right price*. Everyone in that store was a *today-focused* customer because that's what the store's advertising had attracted.

I saw exactly why Sam's ad wasn't bringing those people in: Sam's value proposition was a long-term promise. But the people in that big-box store didn't want a *tomorrow* promise, they needed a *today* promise of getting the cheapest, most convenient furniture.

Monday I called Sam with my discovery.

"Sam, you're going to have to make a choice."

"And what's that?" he asked.

"You're going to have to choose what kind of customer you're going to build your business off of: *today* customers or *tomorrow* customers."

"Well, we need money today, brother!" he replied.

"Then you're going to have to start playing the *today* game. Promotions and sales are what drive *today* results. Talking about values and comfort will build you future high-quality customers, but it will not make people rush into your store this weekend."

I explained to Sam what I had come to realize. There are two types of customers: today customers and tomorrow customers. Each customer cares about different things. At any given time, for any given product, the motivations of each customer are different.

Today customers are motivated by *price* and *convenience*. Today customers are fast and cheap to get, but they're not loyal to you and won't usually pay more for quality or for having a relationship with whom they're buying from.

Tomorrow customers are motivated by *value* and *relationships*. Tomorrow customers take more time to earn, but when they get around to buying, they'll shop with only you and be happy to pay more because in that moment quality and relationships will be more important than discounts.

I told Sam that today customers will show up *quickly* for whoever has the lowest perceived price or convenience. And they'll *leave* quickly for those exact same reasons.

But over time, far more tomorrow customers will show up and buy from you, and only you, if you have the courage to win them over before they need furniture.

When you show the public who you really are (easy-going and not pushy, like the ad I had written for Sam, for example), you build a relationship with them over time. By the time they decide to buy, they'll prefer doing business with someone they already trust. This is an example of earning a tomorrow customer.

Sam's ad was an awesome example of attracting a long-term customer. In his charming Southern voice, he was sitting on a couch in front of the camera, speaking about things of substance—time with family, relaxing, lifelong trust in a product, and no high-pressure buying. Any person can find value in these things, and I believe that ad would have worked very well over time. But those aspirations are not nearly as motivating to someone who needs furniture *now.*

This realization came to me in that big-box furniture store. Nobody was there because they held an immense amount of trust in this place. They obviously didn't have long-term relationships with the sales associates. (The average one had been there only three months, remember?) They weren't even necessarily looking for the quality of the kind of furniture Sam sold.

They simply had a *today* need for furniture, and they were taking the option of the least resistance. They quite clearly had a transactional mentality, so the transactional approach of financing, price discounting, and hype were motivating factors.

Sam's down-to-earth message of family business didn't stand a chance against this machine. Sam's ad, and more importantly his approach to business, placed him in the long-term relationship category. He was operating on a *tomorrow mentality* but expecting *today mentality* buyers.

Sam was also caught in the classic case of *being inside the bottle.* Meaning, he expected every person to know what he knows about his product and his industry, when, in fact, the average person thinks about buying furniture very few times in an entire year.

I told him that both approaches to today and tomorrow customers can be successful. And I reminded him about all the things he told me he wanted to stand for:

» Quality products

» No pushy sales gimmicks

» Being there for long-term support

If the people in "furniture today" buying mode had heard his ads years and months before, it's likely they would have attached themselves to the message of "When you buy a piece of furniture to depend on, buy it from a family you can depend on."

But they hadn't had enough time to consider a message like that. They had quite obviously chosen to care about something more important to them: money and convenience.

It was with Sam that I learned the lesson, *you cannot tell someone how to feel.* Advertising cannot change someone's preference or what they care about in a given moment. Advertising can only communicate what *you* are about. And if you are communicating something they care about, they will respond when they feel like responding.

In the case of Sam vs. the big-box stores, Sam's message was connecting with an audience; it just wasn't the one who was rushing out to buy furniture this weekend.

I knew Sam wasn't going to like my advice. I gave him the choice to change what he stood for or to wait for customers to come to him over time.

"So you're tellin' me people would rather do business with a pushy college kid than with our family?"

"No. I'm telling you they would rather feel like they are coming to the place where they're getting it the cheapest. Price wins over relationship when you *haven't had time* to build the relationship. Your ads have only been running a couple of weeks."

"Don't make any sense."

Sam grew frustrated, and within a week he discontinued his ads. I wished him well and never heard from him again. His store went out of business a few months later.

While I wasn't successful in getting him to buy into my plan, I felt very good about what I had learned. This was the first time I was truly able to explain what was happening and why; Sam's strategy was simply misaligned with his message.

I had stopped bad results before too much of his money was spent. While he didn't ultimately succeed, it wasn't due to bad marketing, at least not on my watch. It was because he was trying to earn *today* customers with a *tomorrow* business model and a *tomorrow* message.

TOMORROW CUSTOMERS

I knew I was on to something with today and tomorrow customers. But Mike and Gina helped me solidify this principle more than anyone.

After working their butts off for nearly a decade, their roofing company was holding its own in a very competitive market. They had built their business the old-fashioned way through hard work, patience, and doing the right thing for their customers. Outside of beginning their company's name with an A so they could get first alphabetical placement in the phone book, they hadn't marketed very much at all before I met them.

But despite his lack of marketing experience, Mike had the most spot-on intuition I'd ever seen about advertising when he said in our first meeting: "Nobody cares about a roofing company until they need one." He was keenly aware of the money his competitors were wasting by just getting their name out there and talking about discounts on roofs, because *very few* people need a roof at any given time.

I asked Mike, "How often do people need to buy a roof?"

"About every 20 years."

Some quick math told me that one roof every 20 years meant that only 5 percent of homes *per year* would need a roof ($1 \div 20 = 5\%$). And a little more math told me that a little less than half a percent of homes *per month* would need a roof ($5\% \div 12 = 0.41\%$). So, if the only message in our ad was "Get a discount on your roof," an ad about roofing would be irrelevant to 99.5 percent of the population at any given time!

For a product like Mike's, the question begged to be asked, "Why even advertise at all?"

So I dug further, asking Mike: "So when they do choose you, why is that?"

"Reputation," Mike said confidently. "You wouldn't believe how many horror stories there are about people getting screwed by out-of-town companies who leave a mess, tear up their house, and skip town."

"I see, and what about when you're up against another established local company?"

"I think they just like me better. I'm the first to tell them when they don't need a roof. Sometimes, I even fix stuff for no charge if it's easy."

"So, when people suddenly go looking for a roofer, who do you think they call?"

"I guess the one they like the most."

Mike didn't know it, but in that moment he defined the perfect recipe for success in advertising. He knew that most homeowners would not be buying a roof today. But *every homeowner* would buy a roof someday, even if it was 5, 10, or 20 years from now. Mike knew intuitively the value of a *tomorrow* customer, and his hard work up to that point had shown him that they were worth waiting for.

Unless a massive tornado or hailstorm event happens, there are very few today customers in the roofing business. All of Mike's competitors were speaking to the today customers by talking only about the product and their name. It was clear that if we were going to earn the *tomorrow* customer for Mike, we would have to build ads that were about more than just roofs. They had to have some extra feeling to them besides "roofing company," or statistically 99.5 percent of the audience would ignore them.

I asked myself the question "So if most people don't care about roofs right now, what do they care about? What can I say to make Mike the guy that they'll want to do business with one day?" My first step was to disrupt the typical form of local advertising. *We've all seen these typical ads, right?*

The owner is usually standing in front of his business, talking about his product or service, then says his name several times with some product jargon, then ends the ad by saying his phone number and website a couple of times.

Boooooorrrring!

Mike's intuition and my own experience told me that ads like that don't work. Within the first couple of seconds of a business owner talking about a product nobody needs, the ad is ignored. It's within the first couple of words even that a person mentally decides if they are in or out on listening further. In Mike's case, if he had started the ad with "When it's time to replace your roof . . . ", everyone who wasn't currently needing roofs would've opted out. Remember, 99.5 percent of the homeowner population is not in *today* mode for a roof in any given month.

However, if we start the ad about something else *universally interesting* or entertaining, we have a much greater chance of getting the attention of that 99.5 percent. This behavior has been scientifically explained. A summary from the website Science Daily explains that our very psychological and physiological nature is to conserve energy. Furthermore, researchers at Lund University found that "maintaining unnecessary association pathways requires energy for the brain," and they've been able to show how specific nerve endings learn and forget new information out of self-interest. Writer Thomas Oppong summarized this beautifully in a recent Medium.com article on a study from Florida State University:

> In the digital age, information comes at you like a tsunami. From the moment you wake up, notifications (news, social media, email, chat channels) fight for your attention. With all of the information vying for your attention, you make choices and use a lot of your mental energy before the day even starts. . . . Without your awareness, your brain creates shortcuts in the form of cognitive biases to help you process the influx of information as the day progresses.

Conclusion: It takes brain energy to listen and pay attention to information (i.e., ads). So, when the brain determines that an ad has no value or effect on its well-being, it ignores it to conserve energy.

So, how did we make people listen to Mike's roofing ad?

» *We could not let the public think that this was an ad about roofing.*

» *We had to talk to them about things that mattered to them.*

» *We had to do it in a disruptive, entertaining way.*

We decided to not put Mike on camera in a traditional way. Instead, we took hundreds of pictures of his face and turned him into an animated cartoon. We made a cartoon background of a neighborhood with houses, happy blue skies, birds chirping, and happy music to completely disrupt the clichéd look and feel of a local service company ad. We wanted it to be so immediately different that, during those first few seconds, the viewer wouldn't realize they were looking at an ad at all. We wanted to give them a *story*. We wanted them to watch the story and, as a by-product, make Mike "the guy they liked better."

As Mike had told me in the first meeting, people choose the guy they like better. So, if we could make Mike a guy they liked *before* they ever needed a roof, he would win their business. This is the way tomorrow customers are earned.

THE ADS

We recorded Mike saying friendly things like "Absolutely!"; "It was an easy fix, just a single shingle!"; and "No problem!"

Then we wrote a voiceover from the homeowner's point of view:

> "*I was taking the dog for a walk when a big storm rolled in. And then . . .*"
>
> *(Drip drip drip sound effects and visual of her leaking roof)*
>
> "*Oh no!*"
>
> "*I called Mike at Absolute Roofing and . . .*"
>
> *(Doorbell sound effects)*
>
> "*Wow, that was fast!*"
>
> *(Tap tap tap and visual of Mike on the ladder)*
>
> "*It was an easy fix! Just a single shingle!*"
>
> Homeowner: "*Wow! Thank you!*"

*"Aaaaaabsolutely!" (voiced with a happy delivery from a
group of Mike's staff)*

(End logo)

With fast-cut animations, a bright delivery, and colorful
graphics, our goal was for the commercial to entertain the viewer
before she even realized she'd watched an ad.

Mike and Gina were still unsure of what to expect, but with
their permission we ran this campaign of very short, frequent ads
that positioned a cartoon Mike as a happy-go-lucky helpful guy.

We approached the entire campaign with the goal to make
Mike a guy that people would already know in their minds. We
wanted people to feel as if they were seeing their happy-go-lucky
next-door neighbor on the screen. We were creating preference
in Mike's *tomorrow* customers, because they were hearing his
positive phrases and experiencing his light-hearted personality
long before they would ever need a roof.

Mike's phone didn't ring off the wall when his commercial
played. His website wasn't overrun with inquiries, at first. But
within about a year of starting the campaign, his business had
grown *over $1 million in sales* at a much faster rate than he'd ever
experienced in his last eight years in business. Mike and Gina's
business continued to grow, even in years where other roofing
companies struggled to find work. A few years later, their sales
volumes had nearly quadrupled. They were then able to hire a
sales team, build out management processes, and take their
company to an entirely new level.

Today, because of his commitment to earning tomorrow
customers, Mike's business enjoys an extremely low cost per
acquisition of customers and has grown much larger than the
competitors in town who have been around for decades.

Why? Because every year there is another 5 percent of his
market that needs roofs. And for the last five years, Mike has been
building favor with our town, so when they suddenly (finally)
need a roof, he's on top of their list.

While his competitors have been advertising to *today* customers with specials, discounts, and empty calls to action, we positioned Mike's ads to be short, sweet, and entertaining, expecting that very few people who will see them need his product *today*. We don't waste time talking about things that don't matter to the other 99.5 percent of the population. Instead, we show how happy and easy Mike is to work with in an entertaining ad.

We have proven that tomorrow customers are very much worth the effort to earn, and Mike has done very well because of that.

As I went further along in my career, I saw the theory of today and tomorrow customers continue to repeatedly prove itself. I deepened my understanding of this concept, which has single-handedly enabled me to avoid millions of wasted dollars in advertising for my clients.

The three customer types have become a key part of my Maven Method—how we get results repeatedly and expectedly for dozens of companies across the United States.

WHICH ONE SHOULD YOU ADVERTISE FOR?

By and large, the marketing world places a large amount of emphasis on the today customer. The need for instant gratification is alive and well. This is because we all have budgets to be accountable to, we all feel the pain of spending money, and it's our tendency to measure results in 30-day increments.

Certainly, some companies have no option but to realize a short-term payoff to advertising. Early on in my agency, I consulted dozens of start-ups that would give me the last dollars they had to their name in hopes of a result. They had no choice but to focus on *today* customers.

There is nothing fully wrong with a today customer. They give us seed money for all good things. And if you are starting a business, you might have no choice but to expect and look for today customers.

However, it's vital to understand that, if done properly, there's an exponentially greater return when you become the preferred company for *tomorrow* customers. Most product categories have an infinite amount of tomorrow customers, and if you commit to winning them over before they turn into *today* customers, you will grow your future business at a much faster rate than you can grow your current business.

PLANTING SEEDS

Age-old wisdom in the book of Ecclesiastes tells us that there is, "a time to plant, and a time to pluck up that which is planted."

Attracting tomorrow customers is a game of planting *today* so that you have an abundance of opportunities *tomorrow*. Your ads are your seeds. The consistency at which you run your ads is the water and fertilizer. And your patience is the time between the spring plant and the fall harvest. Only a fool would pull his crops up before they are done growing, right?

Similarly, if you have resources and enough patience to write ads for tomorrow customers, tomorrow customers will eventually grow into a field of customers you can harvest when the time is right. To rely only on *today* customers is like pulling up crops as soon as they pop out of the ground. The yield is not nearly as rich, and it's a lot more work.

In the following chapters, I lay out specifically how to set expectations for each customer type, but the major principles are as follows:

1. Ads that focus on competitive pricing, convenience, and limited-time offers attract more people who are buying *today*, but these messages are completely ignored and forgotten by people who aren't buying your product today (i.e., they have no long-term effect).

2. Ads that focus on broad needs, entertainment, and customer relationships will not be as persuasive to

today customers who are only concerned with price, but they earn you much better and much more committed customers *tomorrow* if you have the faith and patience to let the ads do their job. While the ad sales' start is slower, these ads produce more and more results the longer you commit to running them.

THE THIRD CUSTOMER TYPE— YESTERDAY CUSTOMER

Today and tomorrow customers dominate most of the conversation in marketing and advertising in America because that's where the large majority of media and advertising salespeople earn their money—through selling ads. However, a *very powerful* third type of customer exists that's almost always overlooked: the *yesterday customer.*

As a marketing guy, my days are filled with everyone asking different versions of the same question: "How do we get new customers?" When most companies jump into the assumption that all their business comes from *new customers*, they ignore their largest and most profitable asset—the people who have already done business with them, known as the yesterday customer.

THE PAIN OF A NEW CUSTOMER

Getting new customers is really tough to do when you think about it. It's expensive, and it requires patience, sales strategy, and a lot of hard work. Your chance of failure is really high when you try to earn new customers. New customers don't know how you operate. They don't have a relationship with you. They compare you to other options in the market. They're flighty and are more likely to complain. Their expectations aren't fully known.

Yesterday customers, by contrast, already know how to do business with you. And assuming you delivered as promised, they already trust you. Yesterday customers don't generally want to experience the pain of shopping for another option; it's easier for them to come straight back to you if they had a good experience.

Most importantly, yesterday customers are virtually free to market to! Most businesses spend hundreds of thousands of dollars annually trying to attract new customers with TV, radio, print, digital ads, billboards, and other forms of paid media. But with email marketing, social media, phone calls, and mailing addresses, you can influence yesterday customers for virtually no cost. *Yesterday customers* are the perfect sales equation: They like you, and they're easy and free to talk to.

EXTREME POTENTIAL

Of all the money and effort we spend on our clients, I estimate that the return on investment for yesterday customer marketing is 10:1 when compared to using paid advertising for today and tomorrow customers.

Every year, my company generates millions of dollars in sales with repeat customers for our clients. Kevin is one of my favorite examples.

Kevin owned a boat dealership in the smallest town you could possibly imagine. Through hard work, commitment, and an immense amount of care for his customers, Kevin had grown his business with a very small advertising budget.

It was the middle of winter—not exactly the best time to be selling boats. One of his competitors had been making a lot of noise by advertising on billboards and TV when Kevin came to me and asked, "What would it cost to compete with him?"

Familiar with exactly what his competitor was doing, I threw out an estimate: "Probably 30 grand a month."

"Wow. There's no possible way."

Kevin wasn't a whiner, but I could tell he was adding the numbers up in his head. If his competitor was spending that much on advertising, how many boats must they be selling?

My wheels were turning, too. *There had to be a way to beat this guy.*

"I've got another idea for you," I said.

"I'll try anything once as long as it doesn't cost me 30 grand," said Kevin.

"How many customers do you think your company has served in the last five years?"

"Gee, I dunno. Maybe 5,000?"

"All those people have boats, yes?"

"We don't sell anything else. If they did business with us, they have a boat."

"Do you have email addresses for any of them?"

He laughed. "Half of our customers don't even know how to spell email."

"Seriously, though, do you have email addresses for any of them?"

"Maybe a few in our system."

"Your job is to go find as many of them as you can. Let me know what you find."

Kevin is a sharp guy. After just a few days, he managed to pull a couple thousand emails from his system and put them into one document.

"I'm not sure what you're gonna do with them, but here they are," said Kevin as he turned over the document.

I smiled and asked him, "So all of these people have boats, right?"

"Presumably."

"Great," I said. "Here's the plan. We're going to load all of these into an email blast platform and send one giant call to action to them."

"And what's that going to be?"

"We're going to tell them that we want to buy their boat!"

"How do you know we want to buy their boat?"

"Because you're going to sell them their next one!" I exclaimed as I laid out the very simple ad copy for him:

Email Subject Line: We Want to Buy Your Boat

Our records indicate that you have a boat that matches a make and model that we are currently seeking for inventory.

If you would have any interest in selling it, we would like to make an offer to you.

Simply click here to provide a few details, and we will be in touch within 24 hours with an offer.

The "click here" button took the viewers to a page where they'd provide their boat's make, model, and condition information. We then instructed his salespeople to be ready to make trade-in offers.

We sent the email blast in the middle of the week on a day when it was literally snowing. We had no idea if the customer's email addresses were valid, or even if some of these customers were even alive. There were exactly *zero* people shopping for boats during this time, and his sales guys were sitting around with virtually nothing to do. What happened next frankly surprised even me a little.

Within hours of sending, Kevin had nearly 100 sales opportunities. Everyone sitting around on that snowy day seemed to be perfectly willing to talk about boats. Their inquiries came in through the website with paragraphs of text, which provided an immediate topic for the salespeople to start a conversation with. Kevin's salespeople had more leads than during their busiest time of year. After making offers to buy, they not only reconnected with old customers, but they'd made sales that they may never have had if Kevin's business hadn't taken advantage of this new advertising campaign.

Months ahead of their competitor, his business had opportunities that could *not have been earned* from new customers. This was a time of year when *new customers simply didn't exist—it was snowing!* We both realized in that moment the monumental power of the *yesterday customer.*

Since then, I have had countless six-figure results from placing even a small focus on yesterday customers. I will lay out specific tactics for advertising to yesterday customers throughout this book. But as we dig deeper into all the customers we have the potential to market to, it's important to remember that the yesterday customer is very often the most profitable.

THE REAL GOAL

The best marketing plans address all three customer types: today, tomorrow, and yesterday. As you strive to grow your companies, the most important thing to know is that you can't grow from just one type of customer. *Sustainable, profitable,* and *efficient* growth requires that you have an understanding of each of these types of customers and how they can affect your business.

As I discuss the advanced methods for marketing to each of these customer types, keep in the back of your mind that there's a time and place for every type of customer.

By now, I hope that you've seen through these successes and failures that advertising isn't simply a matter of what media you choose to buy, or even what you choose to say. Mastering advertising requires that you have complete clarity on *which type of customer* you're talking to and setting reasonable expectations for each of them.

No matter what you are doing to grow your business, always remember the following:

- » **Today customers** come quick, but they aren't the most profitable.

- » **Tomorrow customers** take longer to earn business from, but they're more profitable in the long run.

- » **Yesterday customers** are often the easiest to sell to *and* the most profitable.

Next I will dig into the Maven Method and the specific tactics for earning today, tomorrow, and yesterday customers. At the end of the next section, you should have a full understanding of when to choose each of these customers, what to say that makes a difference, and which media to use for each.

CHAPTER 9

THE TODAY CUSTOMER

You wake up, turn on your shower, and the water is cold. You're now a today customer for a plumber.

Your child woke up with a splitting toothache. You're now a today customer for a dentist.

You turn the key to your ignition, and your car won't start. You're now a today customer for a mechanic.

You will make a purchase decision today for these things because it is no longer an option to wait.

The today customer is the person who's actively trying to buy in your product category *today*. A customer enters *today mode* when they have decided that their need, pain, hope, or fear cannot wait any longer to be satisfied. *This customer type must find a solution quickly.*

Once today customers have committed to finding a provider, they make their purchase decision in a very short amount of time based on the information that's available to them. And if they don't have a previously determined preference for a certain company or product, they'll usually choose the one that is the cheapest, fastest, or most convenient for them.

It's important to clarify that today customers are customers who *do not* have a previous relationship or preference to do business with you or another company.

Today simply means that they are searching for businesses like yours today, and they're not *warm* to buying from you or any of your competitors yet. Simply put, no one has won them over yet, no one has made a *tomorrow* customer out of them yet with marketing. Therefore, the today customer needs to be won over in a very short time period.

Today customers seem to be what most business owners want from advertising. After all, why would anyone want to waste their time talking to someone who isn't a today buyer?

This is the question, and the reality, that dominates most assumptions about advertising. Business owners all want instant gratification for the money they spend, and it's usually this desire that guides their decision-making.

A business owner's need for instant gratification can show up in many forms:

» Judging the entire effectiveness of an advertising campaign in short time periods (such as at the end of every month)

» Attempting to align the time their ads are played to the moment they receive phone calls (immediate response)

» Switching their ad schedules, stations, and messages around in the middle of the month when they feel they haven't earned enough leads

» Yelling at their ad rep when they feel they're not receiving anything for their money (my personal favorite)

While some of these seem like good things to do, it's the over-reactivity and rapid changes that often doom a campaign.

I have learned that the expectation of immediate results in advertising has substantial limits. When business owners and ad reps forget that advertising is a *human* equation, and we blindly assume that purchasing decisions happen in a neatly organized formula, we miss out on the full potential of the marketing equation.

Regardless of selling strategies, product categories, or advertising budgets, it is crucial in any advertising equation that we acknowledge that human beings are human beings. *And humans will do what they perceive to be in their best interest when they perceive that it is the right time to do so.*

With that said, the labels of today customers, tomorrow customers, and yesterday customers don't speak to the *permanent* status of the people we are speaking to. Rather, these labels speak to the current mode that any given person perceives themselves to be in for any given product. We are all today, tomorrow, and yesterday customers for different products at different times. And depending on what happens in our lives, we may quickly shift from one customer type to another.

If your refrigerator is working fine and you're happy with its features, you are not in *today* mode for a refrigerator. But if you wake up tomorrow morning to warm milk, you will instantly be in *today* mode for a refrigerator.

If a local appliance store has done a good job of building a relationship with you through their ads, you will likely consider them first. Or, if an appliance brand solidly connected with you through advertising, you might seek out their products first.

But if you've not been emotionally connected to any company, you'll likely head straight to the internet or a big-box store to start shopping for the best value or the most convenient solution.

This same exact equation is true for tires, air conditioners, mechanics, roofing companies, attorneys, and virtually every other non-commoditized product.

So, companies that have previously earned a relationship with the public through their ads and their reputation get the first shot. All others will be compared to each other largely on their perceived value and convenience.

If you quickly judge the return on your advertising by how many leads you generated this week, you're likely most focused on the today customer, and you're probably writing ads that connect with only that customer type. It's important to remember, however, that even though the today customer is a fast customer to earn, they still must be handled properly to make the sale.

A LEAD IS A PERSON WITH A NEED

My agency performs marketing services for multiple service-based companies located all across the United States. Across all industries we work in, including legal services, medical practices, and home improvement contractors, our clients ultimately want to know one thing: "How many leads am I getting?"

Generating *leads* means our clients are receiving phone calls, email inquiries, website form fills (i.e., requests), online appointments, and website live chats from potential customers.

First, I want to state that we are very happy to generate sales opportunities (i.e., leads) for these companies. Last year alone, we generated over 40,000 leads, resulting in $80 million-plus in business. However, I have learned that when we focus the conversation only around lead volume, we lose sight of the most important thing: A lead is not really something you *buy*; a lead is something you *earn*.

No magic lead vending machine is on the internet where customers can be bought by coin insertion. When a lead happens, on the other side of that phone call or computer screen there's a real-life human being who had to go through a number of complex decision-making steps to choose *you* as the company they reached out to.

The amount of processing we do as humans to make a simple phone call is amazing. First, we consult our own knowledge. In a matter of seconds, we scan through millions of pieces of information in our own minds, asking our memory, "Do I know anyone who can help me?" Then all our life experiences, friends' recommendations, exposure to advertising, and our personal business connections come crashing together to produce a *feeling* of who we should call.

The companies that have done a good job earning tomorrow customers win big in this today moment.

It's in these moments that a customer's life experience with your brand, company, and advertising can silently win the race. Your reputation within the community you serve plays a big part in it, as does the amount of consistent advertising you've aired up until this point. It's the moment when a *tomorrow customer* transitions into a *today customer.* Your business's win or loss is realized in a matter of seconds, silently in the mind of the customer.

If your business's advertising and reputation had previously made a strong connection with the person in need, you'll get that sales opportunity first, before your competitors, and before search engines enter into that part of the equation. Customers will skip Google and call you, removing all other barriers of competing at the finish line from your competitors.

RELYING ON SEARCH ENGINES AND DIRECTORIES

If a customer *isn't* aware of who might be able to help them in that moment, or if they don't trust the companies that come to mind, they'll hop over to a search engine or a directory service, like Home Advisor, to find that information.

In a matter of seconds, they'll be typing a few key words into a search bar and will immediately start scanning the options available. It's in these moments of high scrutiny that your company's website and search engine listings can come to the rescue.

But as online marketing becomes more sophisticated, it has become harder and harder to be a clear winner in these areas. In 2020, most product categories have multiple companies that have learned how to do search engine marketing well. And if your company is a winner in search engines today, there's no guarantee that it will be a winner tomorrow. In other words, winning in search engines is an ever-moving target. It can be a very profitable target to chase, but this strategy ultimately always comes with some lack of ultimate control.

SETTING EXPECTATIONS FOR TODAY CUSTOMERS

Today customers . . .

» Are usually a small group of people compared to tomorrow customers.

» Are very conscious of price and not very conscious of value.

» Need a service/product now (if they have to wait, they'll find someone else).

» Care less about building a relationship with you and your company.

» Make split decisions based on the quickest information available.

» Care less about a company being the best.

» Ultimately choose a provider who requires the least amount of energy from them.

» Are more expensive to advertise to.

» Are more likely to complain.

As you set advertising expectations for today customers, keep in mind that their quick response to your messaging usually comes with the tradeoff that they are customers of lesser quality, it is less likely you will make a profit from them, and they are harder to deal with altogether.

WHEN TO FOCUS ON TODAY CUSTOMERS

If your goal is to quickly generate business to pay bills or to move large volume in a short time period, your ad strategy will require a bigger focus on today customers. Remember, today customers are those who know they are in the market *today*. For any given category, there is a smaller percentage of people who meet this description. This is the ultimate limiting factor in earning today customers.

For some categories, there are more today customers than others. Food is a good example: Most of us are in the market for food several times a day. Advertising for today customers is relatively easy for restaurants for this reason.

But for most categories, there's a very limited quantity of today customers. Home improvement companies and professional services are good examples. No one will buy a roof, HVAC system, or replacement windows today if theirs aren't broken. Similarly, they won't hire a surgeon or a lawyer if they don't have a legal or medical need for them.

There is no hard and fast rule that guarantees how easy or difficult it will be for you to earn today customers. Your market size, number of competitors and their strength, number of years you've been in business, and your geographic location all affect the speed and volume at which you'll be able to earn today customers.

There is, however, a general relationship to keep in mind when setting expectations for your marketing strategy: The longer your product's purchase cycle, the fewer today customers there will be available and the more aggressive you must be with price and convenience to motivate people to buy. Being more aggressive can mean discounting, offering a larger selection than your competitors, promising faster delivery times, or providing a more solid guarantee.

A purchase cycle for a product category is the measure of the amount of time between when the average person has a need or desire for your product. For example, the average American may need a roofer once every 15 years. They may need an attorney once every 6 years. They may buy a vacuum cleaner once every 3.2 years. They may dine at a high-end restaurant once every 24 days. All of these examples are different purchase cycles.

Every product category has an average purchase cycle driven by the needs and desires of the people it serves. While there can be exceptions in short bands of time in the number of people in the market based on seasonality or economic factors, the purchase cycle is very consistent year to year for most products and services.

Understanding your purchase cycle is important because it helps your business set reasonable expectations. If you have a long purchase cycle (2–20 years), you must be more aggressive at pricing to earn today customers (i.e., fast), and you'll make less money with this strategy (i.e., you'll have to sell more volume).

If you have a shorter purchase cycle (less than two years), you can expect to earn today customers easier without necessarily discounting or being aggressive with your convenience.

THE LAW OF SUPPLY AND DEMAND

The law of supply and demand states that the more supply there is of a thing, the less customers must pay for that thing. Inversely, the less supply there is of a thing, the more they must pay. *This is Business Competition 101.*

Common sense tells us that in virtually every sustainable business category, there is an exponentially higher number of customers in the days, weeks, months, and years ahead than the number of customers buying *right now*. Applying the law of supply and demand tells us that because there are more *tomorrow customers* than *today customers*, then they should cost us less to earn.

In the grand scheme of your marketing, remember this:

» Short-term gain of customers = long-term pain in profit and sustainability

» Long-term gain of customers = short-term pain of marketing expense without instant results

The short-term gain of today customers comes to you seemingly easy when you focus your advertising on price, convenience, and instant gratification. But the long-term pain is that they will be less connected, less loyal, and less profitable and is the limiting factor of this focus.

The long-term pain of customers who take longer to earn happens when you speak to tomorrow's customer about your values, way of doing business, quality, and long-term partnership. However, these are the customers who will gladly pay you more for quality, refer you to their friends, complain less because they trust you, and use you again in the future.

WHY TODAY CUSTOMERS ARE MORE EXPENSIVE TO EARN

Winning over today customers usually does not get cheaper. In most markets, there's always an increasing amount of competition to earn the today buyer; you and every one of your competitors are fighting for them at the finish line. The cost exposure at the finish line is very expensive. Search engine marketing, lead generation companies, direct mail, and discount-based ads that steal from the profit margin are just a few reasons the today buyer will always be the *most expensive* customer to earn.

Even using the *best* practices in lead generation, and despite our clients continually improving their sales processes year after year, we still see constant increases in the cost for advertising for today customers. This is partly because Google, Bing, Facebook, and lead gen companies are always increasing their prices for advertising, and also because more businesses want the instant gratification of lead generation, so they are always driving up the competition in your marketplace.

As time passes, a today marketing strategy never gets cheaper and rarely becomes more efficient. This is a big downfall of relying on a today marketing strategy.

But when you need today customers, you need them. The today buyer has cash *today*. Today's buyer *will* give you money to pay your bills, hire more employees, and expand your company. Today customers *can* come at a predictable cost of advertising.

Focusing on the today customer is a good strategy when any number of these factors are true:

1. You can be the lowest cost provider and compete on price.

2. You are in an underserved market without strong competition.

3. You have a new product or solution for a common problem.

4. You don't have enough money to invest in long-term tomorrow campaigns that build relationships.

5. The value you provide is heavily built on systems and processes (i.e., it's largely scalable).

Next, I will cover the type of messaging you must use to connect with and earn today customers.

CHAPTER 10
MESSAGING FOR TODAY CUSTOMERS

» The mom whose car won't start right before she needs to take the kids to school . . .

» The young man who's so in love he can't wait another day to buy her a diamond . . .

» The homeowner whose ceiling is sopping wet after a thunderstorm . . .

These are all today customers in desperate need of today marketing to connect them with a today provider for their today needs.

Moments ago they were tomorrow customers, but their turn of events transported them into today customer mode, and now they're yours to lose.

I call them *buyers on the loose.*

Will you earn them? Or will they fall into the arms of one of your greedy competitors?

If you haven't already won them over with *tomorrow marketing,* victory hinges on your ability to write ads and website copy that connect with the customer's needs, pains, hopes, and fears that are begging to be satisfied, and the Maven Method writing process and your keen understanding of the today customer's motivations is all you need to come out on top.

Here's a quick recap of today customers:

> » They are very conscious of price and not very conscious of value.

> » They need a service/product now (if they have to wait, they'll find another provider).

> » They make split decisions based on the quickest information available.

> » They care less about you being the "best."

> » They ultimately choose the provider that requires the least amount of energy from them.

And here's a review of the Maven Method writing process:

1. Who are you really talking to?

2. What are their needs, pains, hopes, and fears?

3. How can your product meet one of these needs, pains, hopes, or fears?

4. What is the most reasonable next step you can get them to take?

APPLYING MAVEN METHOD WRITING TO TODAY CUSTOMERS

Unlike tomorrow customers, today customers generally have needs related to delivery speed, pains related to price, hopes of moving on past their pain, and fears related to choosing the wrong provider.

Talking about your company's story, along with its values and your brand, matters less in these moments. If you are using a today message, trying to drive the quickest action possible, connect your product specifically to how it saves the customer time and money and why now is the best time to buy it.

The most reasonable next step in the today customer's message is probably the sale or the sales appointment. Offer a transaction, a button for them to click to purchase the product/service, or a phone number they can call to take action.

Your business may benefit from a surge of today customers when a sudden event happens that accelerates today motivation, such as a flat tire, hailstorm, divorce, death, or other major life event. Or their motivation could have developed slowly over time, such as the desire for a vacation, a new home improvement, or a new car. Either way, there's a distinct reason they are looking for a product/service *today*.

By taking action on your message, they are proving that the time is nearing for them to make this decision. You should speak to them as if you know this, and this discussion should be part of defining "**who** you are talking to."

A TODAY CUSTOMER MESSAGE EXAMPLE
Product: Roofing

Who we are talking to: Homeowners of $250,000-plus homes who experienced the hailstorm last night in our town.

What are their today needs, pains, hopes, and fears?

- » They need to know if their roof is damaged and, if so, how they can fix it.

- » Their pain is the process and hassle of dealing with contractors and insurance companies.

- » Their hope is that their home can remain looking beautiful and hold its value.

» Their fear is choosing the wrong company that will damage their home further or do a poor job.

How can our product address one of those needs, pains, hopes, or fears?

» Meeting the need: We will perform free roof inspection so that homeowners will know if their homes received hail damage.

» Meeting the pain: Our inspection is free; we'll work with the homeowner's insurance company to save them time.

» Meeting the hope: A new roof will give their home maximum curb appeal.

» Meeting the fear: We have hundreds of five-star reviews and an A+ with the Better Business Bureau (BBB), so homeowners can trust us.

What is the most reasonable next step homeowners can take?

» Schedule a free inspection on our website now.

Putting it all together, we would write an ad like this:

If you heard hail last night, there's a good chance that your roof was damaged!

If you'd like to know the status of your roof, we want to make that safe and easy for you.

Roger Roofers is offering free hail inspections to anyone in the storm area through next Friday. We will remove the hassle of working with your insurance company and give you a full hail report, free of charge.

If there's any damage, we'll coordinate with your insurance company to get your roof replaced at no cost to you, restoring your home to its full value and curb appeal.

Roger Roofers has 832 five-star reviews on Google and an A+

rating with the Better Business Bureau (BBB). We do the hard work, we do it right, and we do it fast so you can get back to your life.

If you heard hail, get a free estimate, and make it as easy as ABC by calling 343-3434, or schedule now at RogerRoofers. com.

Do you see how we systematically addressed the world of the today customer?

- » We began the ad by immediately highlighting the today need and offering a helpful solution: "If it hailed" is how they know, and "free inspection" is how they'll get the need addressed.

- » We addressed their pain by promising easy, fast service and minimal paperwork.

- » In knowing that our client prefers larger-profile homes, we chose to address high-end homeowners by speaking about their values of "good curb appeal" and "home value." This met their hopes.

- » We overcame the fears of choosing the wrong contractor with our credibility with the Better Business Bureau (BBB) and Google ratings.

I have written very similar ads to this one that have produced millions of dollars in sales for my clients. They work because of the clarity and empathy that the Maven Method writing process provides. While every other competitor in town is busy flapping their jaws about things that don't matter to the customer (like how many years they've been in business), we speak to actual today customer needs, pains, hopes, and fears. The words make the difference!

THE DOWNFALL OF TODAY MESSAGING

I know what you're thinking. This sounds fantastic! I'm going to do this all the time in my ads!

However, this usually works less and less over time. Here's why: It feels good to talk about product and feel the instant gratification from your call to action. But understand that if you make your ads only about your product, you're greatly limiting the people who will actually listen.

Today messaging is a trade-off of quick action versus long-term recall. Look no further than your own life experience for proof of this. If you don't believe your roof has hail damage, would you listen to that ad? Would you have any reason to remember the company in the ad?

If you don't currently need tires, would you listen to an ad that was about a promotion or current sale on tires?

If your refrigerator was working fine, would you stop to pay attention in the Sunday newspaper to the current promotions for new refrigerators?

These are just a few examples, but we can find realities of this every hour of the day. When we aren't in today buying mode for something, we don't care about its price or convenience factor. So, when you are using today messaging, remember: *You are programming your ad to be forgotten by those who don't need you today.*

REASONABLE NEXT STEPS

In the Maven Method, we call the last step in messaging a "reasonable" next step. This is because it's important to remember and models the world that your customer is in at the moment of need.

Traditional direct-response ads use the phrase "Call now" and repeat their phone number about a dozen times at the ad's end. This tactic can definitely produce results and is sometimes the best option. But before you use any call-to-action tactic, consider the world that your customer is in.

» What time will they be exposed to this ad?

» Will they have time to call you?

» Where are they when they experience this ad? In their car? On their couch? At their work computer? On their mobile device?

» What are they thinking about when this ad comes across their screen? Did it occur on the weekend? On a work night? On the way to church?

» Is it reasonable that they would call you during this moment?

» Is there a better option they can take?

These are just a few of the questions you might ask when positioning your today customer ads for the best results.

When we get *empathetic* about the world that the customer is living in, we can more quickly think as if we were the customer. We know what would sound *reasonable* to us in that moment.

After asking the previous questions, you might find that there's a more reasonable next step than just asking them to call or visit your website. Examples include:

» Text message your office.

» Use your online price calculator.

» Click a specific button on your website's home page.

» Visit your location for an event.

» Place a reminder on their calendar.

» Download a free guide from your website.

» Attend a special event.

USE SOME COMMON SENSE

In my town, there's a roofing and siding company that made the decision to end all of its TV ads by obnoxiously shouting, "Callllllll Noooooowwwwwww!" Note, I've never worked with this company, and I can't speak to how successful they are with their marketing. But I was aware of this call to action, as I quite often saw the ad during the 10 p.m. news. I thought to myself, "I wonder how many people want to call at 10 p.m. to talk about roofing and siding."

One evening I was curious enough that I decided to see what would happen if I did decide to "Callllllll Noooooowwwwwww." Would anybody answer? Would they be prepared to help me?

The phone rang and rang. Finally, after about 20 rings, the line chirped a busy signal.

I didn't need what they were selling, so no business was lost in that moment. But what about the 90,000 other people who watched the ad? Some surely needed a roof or siding. What if they had called? What impression would this have made?

What if the company had, instead, offered something of value on their website, such as "You can get pricing 24/7—CreedRoofingandSidingNow.com and click 'Give me a quote' on the home page!" Surely this would have produced more sales opportunities for them than a busy dial tone. It would have been a *much more reasonable* next step for someone to take at 10 p.m.

WHEN YOU GET THIS RIGHT, YOU MAKE A LOT MORE MONEY

Several years ago my team and I discovered just how powerful the reasonable next step can be.

We were pushing ourselves to increase the amount of leads we could create for a couple of our home improvement contractor clients.

Nearly all our home improvement and professional service websites had a "Get a Quote" button as the call to action on the home page, which took the user to a form to input their name, email, and phone number. As standard practice, this email information would be sent to the client, who would contact them. This button language was getting some results, but I wondered how much we could improve it.

We decided to try an experiment. Using analytics data and search queries measured by our Google Ads campaigns, we found that one of the most common terms used around our clients' services was "price." The most used search phrases were often similar to the following:

> » "How much do new windows cost?"

> » "How much does an estate plan cost?"

> » "How much does a transmission repair cost?"

> » "How much does a new website cost?"

While some of our sites were offering a "Schedule an Appointment" or "Get an Estimate" form, we acknowledged that these weren't really answering the customer's question. *Neither of these calls to action offered any promise of an actual price,* and, therefore, we weren't offering the most reasonable next step.

We asked ourselves: "What could we say that would be more in line with the customer's next step?" It occurred to us that people who are on a website looking for pricing information *probably aren't ready* to talk to someone yet. The thought of talking to a pushy salesperson is scary to customers when they aren't confident in making a decision yet. *When a customer is in research mode, she doesn't trust you yet.*

By looking no further than our own experience with home improvement contractors, we knew that the process of having people come out to your house is not only scary, it's also a pain in the butt. Our research into personality types also confirmed this.

We then asked ourselves: "Are there people who prefer not to talk to a person?"

After researching Myers-Briggs personality types, we found that about half of Americans are of "extroversion" preferencing, and the other half are "introversion" preferencing. Extroversion-preferencing individuals get their energy from externally processing, as in talking or calling someone. Introversion-preferencing individuals get their energy from internally processing their thoughts in solitude.

Apply that research to advertising and you can quickly assume that, statistically, 50 percent of people prefer to think for themselves *before* processing their purchasing decisions!

After realizing this, we decided to try to make the language on the website of one of our clients a little more aligned with the internal thoughts of the customer. Instead of "Schedule an Estimate," which we felt was projecting the idea that a salesperson would be coming to their home, we changed the language to "Get a Price." We assumed that "Get a Price" was more in line with what the customer was already searching and hoping for—an idea of how much this product would cost them before they even met with a pushy salesperson.

And, man, were we right! **The results were immediate, and they were staggering.**

Without changing a single thing other than the button language, our client saw a 400 percent increase in the amount of leads coming from the website.

With one simple language change, we made the next step seem more reasonable. And *it cost us nothing.* It took about 48 seconds to log into the back end of his website to delete and replace three words.

And instantly he was receiving four times the selling opportunities the very next day.

We quickly applied this logic to our other websites, and the results repeated themselves. We had struck marketing gold with three simple words!

We never forgot this lesson and have since become just as obsessed about our calls to action as we are about the crafting of needs, pains, fears, and hopes into our messaging. By modeling more reasonable next steps, we can singlehandedly improve the profitability of our marketing campaigns.

No additional fancy targeting; no additional marketing budget! The *right* words, when aligned with the customer's desires, do an insane amount of heavy lifting.

After we found this trick and experienced the magic firsthand, we continued applying it to every area we thought of. Over the years, we've developed a checklist of sorts as a safety net for aligning our client's message with the most reasonable next action we want their customers to take.

These are questions you can ask to ensure that your call to action is best set up for today customers:

TODAY CUSTOMER MESSAGING PRINCIPLES

» Identify a need, pain, hope, or fear that relates to pricing and convenience.

» Connect that need, pain, hope, or fear to an outcome your product provides.

» Make it clear how taking action will save customers time, money, or hassle today.

» Make it clear why waiting to take action will cost them something.

» Offer them a reasonable next step for action.

Often, this simple objective exercise can help you shift from a *good* idea to the *best* idea in your copy. As we learned, this small shift can pay huge dividends!

After you've followed all the principles for today customer messaging, you will be equipped for success and will have best positioned yourself to receive the today customer results you want.

The icing on the cake will be the media selection that you choose. In the following chapter, I outline various media and advertising options that you will encounter, how to position each for today customer marketing, and which ones are most likely to work well for you.

As we progress to the media section, though, don't ever forget that even the best media plan will not save a bad message!

CHAPTER 11

CHOOSING MEDIA FOR TODAY CUSTOMERS

You're driving down the freeway, and you see a billboard with a giant phone number for a plumber. You think to yourself, "You know, I've been thinking about calling a plumber. I think I'll just dial him up right now and schedule some preventative plumbing."

You call the plumber for service, and he asks, "How did you hear about us?"

"I saw your billboard!" you say.

Advertising success!

Obviously, this has never happened in the history of plumbers or billboards. Why? Because the chances of someone being aware of their overflowing toilet at the exact time they're in their car and driving past that billboard are extremely slim to none. Yet at this very moment, in a sales conference room somewhere, is a hopeful plumber signing an ad contract for a billboard, and he's expecting that it will make his phone ring the day it goes up. He's expecting a today result from media that was never capable of intercepting a today customer (at least for his type of business).

You might laugh at the lack of sense in this example, but this kind of unrealistic alignment happens every day in advertising sales. Business owners expect today results with media that's very unlikely to intercept customers during their today mode of shopping.

Please know I have absolutely nothing against billboards; we use them often to get our customers well known in the towns in which they serve. And I'm not even against billboards for plumbers. However, I am saying that you should be very aware of what types of media work for the three different types of customers.

And when it comes to today customers, there are some proven winners that make easy sense. In this chapter, I'm going to review the principles of selecting the best media for a today customer result.

CHOOSING TODAY MEDIA FOR TODAY CUSTOMERS

To earn *today* customers, your goal should be to choose the media that naturally attracts the most customers buying *today*. They are people who don't have any previous preference or bond with you or other competitors in your category (meaning, they haven't been won over by tomorrow-focused advertising). They are the *buyers on the loose* who are looking for quick information and the quickest solution possible.

MAVEN METHOD PRINCIPLES FOR TODAY CUSTOMER MEDIA:

» Select the media with the largest group of people who are buying your product *today*.

» Reach them at a time and place when and where they can take action.

» Reach them as often as possible during the time period in which they are buying.

After spending millions of dollars testing and trying virtually every media type, I've learned I can always count on these four types, in this order:

1. Search engine marketing (SEM)

2. Paid social media ads

3. TV and radio

4. Targeted print

To be clear, I'm not saying these are the only things that *can* work. However, these are the only four that I've experienced the most efficient, repeatable results with over the test of many years and many millions of dollars spent. If you were my client looking for immediate today sales opportunities, I would most certainly start with one of these media types.

If you choose to test and try any media outside of these options for today customer marketing, ensure that your chosen type aligns with the Maven Method Principles of Today Customer Media by asking if it meets the principles previously listed.

If you filter your media decisions for today customers using this method, you will find a good performer for you.

Next, I'm going to share how these steps of success apply to our four go-to medias for today customers. But remember that no matter the media you are choosing, you can use these three universal principles on any kind of media and advertising equation for today customers.

EARNING TODAY CUSTOMERS WITH SEARCH ENGINE MARKETING (SEM)

Search engine marketing (SEM) is the practice of buying ads on search engine results pages, such as Google, based on the key words and phrases people are searching for.

For most of the products and services that my firm represents, SEM is most in line with the Maven Method for today customer media:

» Dollar for dollar, there are more people looking *now* on a search engine for any given solution.

» Search engines are located on computers, tablets, and cell phones, where everyone is most certainly equipped to take action.

» We are reaching people often—every time they look at a search page.

Using SEM and the Maven Method, I've been able to generate tens of millions of dollars in business opportunities per month for my clients. I've even launched some clients from selling a few thousand dollars per month out of their garage into multimillion-dollar sales revenues. Similarly, I've doubled selling opportunities for well-established businesses nearly overnight.

When you know how to intercept people who are already buying, speak to their needs, pains, hopes, and fears, it's very likely that you'll get a chance to do business with them, so long as they don't have a previously selected company in mind with which they're looking to do business.

SEM's effectiveness is largely based on the fact that your ads, and your money, aren't spent unless you've connected with someone who's interested in your product. By limiting our ad exposure only to those who are searching for our product category (e.g., "roofer in Tulsa, Oklahoma," or "dentist in Athens, GA,"), we get a much higher concentration of today customers.

SEM also enables you to quickly test different selling language and the effectiveness of your website's landing pages. It's another major reason we are able to receive much quicker and more efficient results: The ability to understand what *is* and *isn't* working within direct response allows us to make improvements to the messaging.

HOW TO BE SUCCESSFUL

» **Step 1: Be Found When People Are Searching.** With SEM, it means you're bidding on the appropriate key words and phrases for your business to be visible to those who are searching for a service you provide.

» **Step 2: Write Compelling Headlines.** You have only a couple of lines of text in a search engine ad, and there are about a dozen other links a searcher can click on besides yours. Your number one job in this moment is to affirm the needs, pains, hopes, and fears that the searcher has. Job number two is to clearly promise them that you can save them time, money, or hassle by taking action now. Discounts, coupons, and limited time offers work really well for this.

» **Step 3: Build a Helpful Landing Page.** Your landing page, or first phone interaction, *must* be filled with value for the customer. If you don't do this, someone else will, and they'll win your customer without you ever knowing! Thoroughly answer their questions instead of just trying to close the sale, or set an appointment with them to use helpful videos, case studies, reviews, and examples of your work, and give them easy access to email you with questions without you trying to force the sale on them.

» **Step 4: Provide a Reasonable Next Step.** Don't just expect that everyone is ready for a sales appointment. Instead, offer customers multiple ways to interact with your company, including via chat, email, virtual appointments, phone calls, or with a free download to continue the research process.

» **Step 5: Respond to Calls and Web Inquiries Fast.**
As always, this means being very quick to respond to
customer inquiries, emails, and phone calls. When the
customer is in *today* mode, they are not willing to wait for
you to make a connection at your convenience.

My team spends thousands of dollars daily for our clients in
buying ads on the Google Ads platform, which easily produces
10 to 15 times what it cost in sales volume. This is because search
engines are the biggest reference that everyone goes to for quick
solutions for their *today* problems.

For clarity, SEM, search engine marketing, is not the same
as SEO, search engine optimization. SEM refers to the specific
practice of buying ads on a search result page, while SEO refers
to the very broad practice of making your website faster and easier
to find in the "free" or "organic" part of Google search listings.

Both SEM and SEO can earn you visibility on a Google results
page when someone types in your business category, but SEM
is much more controllable, measurable, and is a much better
marketing tool to count on than SEO.

Both Google and Bing's version of SEM are self-serve
platforms that basically anyone can set up. That said, mastering the
art of bidding, analytics, diagnostics, and copywriting campaigns
is very complex. If you truly want to compete and achieve
profitability in your campaigns, you can learn these techniques at
MavenMethodTraining.com/book.

If SEM isn't something you want to tackle yourself, many
experts are available to help you for reasonable fees. While they
may know more *technically* than you do, never forget the five
steps of earning today customers, and always challenge your ad
professionals to employ those principles on your behalf.

EARNING TODAY CUSTOMERS WITH PAID SOCIAL MEDIA

Like paid search engine marketing, the targeting and technology behind paid social media is extremely advanced (and sometimes creepy). Even though people don't often use social media to directly search for products and services, it's relatively easy to serve ads specifically to people who Facebook's robots detect are shopping for products and services like yours (i.e., today customers).

Paid social media, such as Facebook and Instagram ads, also excel due to their ability to repeatedly reach today customers during their buying process through digital targeting capabilities.

Unlike free, or organic, postings on your business's Facebook page, when you pay for social media ad delivery, you open your business up to an entire world of targeting and creative abilities that reach far beyond posting. It's worth paying for!

The ins and outs of the social media ad platforms are always changing, but revisiting the five steps for success with today media will never fail you.

HOW TO BE SUCCESSFUL

» **Tip 1: Build Specific Targets for Each Customer.** Use the targeting abilities of the platform you're on to show ads to people who are currently experiencing the needs, pains, hopes, or fears that you can satisfy. You can do this by showing ads to people who have certain interests or occupations, who are in certain demographics, or by targeting people who Facebook knows are currently exhibiting online behaviors seeking products and services like yours.

» **Tip 2: Call Out Customer Motivators in the Headline.** In the headline section of your ad, provide a really clear reason for taking action now! Your videos, graphics, and ad copy must connect to a need, pain, hope, or fear that your ideal customer is currently experiencing and should make an offer that is either a limited-time price or availability or will remind them of a better life that they won't have if they don't take action. For example: "Get All Your Estate Planning Questions Answered in One Easy Appointment!"

» **Tip 3: Design Simple Fast Landing Pages.** With paid social media, this means that the landing page your ad links to should be rich by specifically illustrating how you can solve the need, pain, hope, or fear that was promised in the ad. Because social media visitors are usually not in research mode at the time of clicking the ad (i.e., they are in leisure mode), stick to the main point on your landing pages versus giving tons of extra information.

» **Tip 4: Ask for Form Fills Instead of Phone Calls.** With paid social media, this usually means including some sort of an online action or transaction they can complete versus a phone call. Most social media activity and response happen outside of the reasonable time to call your company, so providing a digital next step is important.

» **Tip 5: Respond to Inquiries and Social Comments Fast.** With paid social media, this means having a very helpful and quick response to comments on your ad, emails, and chat inquiries.

EARNING TODAY CUSTOMERS WITH TV AND RADIO

Though TV and radio advertising is a key tool in building *tomorrow* customers, getting a today customer's message out on these platforms can produce short-term results. Broadcast works particularly well for today customer results if you have an attractive time-limited sale or offer.

Unlike paid social media and SEM, very little targeting ability exists in broadcast media. This media excels in its ability to reach very large groups of people for much cheaper costs (i.e., per person) than you can in digital and print media. As broadcast media's name suggests, you are *broadly casting* your message to large groups of people at one time. The response and success of today-focused broadcast campaigns rely on there being enough people in those huge masses who need what you are selling.

For the same reasons we discussed earlier in Chapter 9, there is a limited number of today customers for every product and service category at any given time, which means that, by design, you'll be paying to reach a large group of people who aren't buying what you're selling today. As long as your offer is compelling enough, though, it's possible that enough people are in the audience who can and will respond to a today message.

HOW TO BE SUCCESSFUL

» **Tip 1: Buy Daytime Schedules.** The big goal is to reach large groups of people for as little money as possible during the time when they can take action. If you're a local service company with normal hours, 10 a.m. to 4 p.m. is often the best time to run your ads.

This next part is big: KNOW WHAT YOU'RE BUYING!

Your advertising salespeople can, and should, give you numbers for audience size and demographics if you ask. Don't go cheap and simply buy a bunch of "spots" in a package. Do your homework and know the spot's audience size, the basic demographics of those audiences, and what times your ad will be playing. It's definitely okay to pay more for a bigger audience, but know that you need to be running several spots per week in the same time period (with the same audience) to achieve the best results. So, don't buy programs that you can't afford to be in multiple times per week (at least three times).

» **Tip 2: Say One Thing at a Time.** Your ads usually only last 15, 30, or 60 seconds, so you must make every word count! Leave out details that don't reinforce a need, pain, hope, or fear or don't clarify what you're able to do about them, and give a very clear reason for why now is the time for the ad's audience to take action (e.g., create limited-time offers).

» **Tip 3: Close the Loopholes.** Because you only have seconds to make your point, it's important to anticipate any of the easy or too-good-to-be-true objections that will give people a reason to quickly disregard you. Tell them *why* this offer is limited by being specific: "We have only 27 left! First come, first served." This also means using the secret weapon of transparency by offering them information that is usually "behind the curtain," such as upfront pricing or a no-strings-attached guarantee. Of course, your website and phone messaging should be filled with value, as with other types of digital media.

» **Tip 4: Give a Reasonable Next Step.** With TV ads, website calls to action usually make the best reasonable next steps because most people are usually on their devices when watching the ad. On the flip side, radio campaigns are more likely to receive phone calls or text message inquiries as most people are driving at the time of the ad. In either case, make sure it's very clear what's in it for the listener when they call or visit the website (i.e., provide a tangible value or piece of information if they take action at the time you're wanting them to take action).

» **Tip 5: Be Prepared to Answer.** Be prepared to answer phone and website inquiries during the times you know your ads will play.

EARNING TODAY CUSTOMERS WITH TARGETED PRINT AND MAILING LISTS

Targeted print describes any ad you can send as a print piece to a targeted list of people. Sometimes ads are delivered by directly mailing them to the targeted list, and sometimes the ad will be located in a magazine that reaches a specific type of audience.

The strength of targeted print is in the tangible nature of the printed ad (i.e., they can hold it in their hand), and the quality of targeting available.

HOW TO BE SUCCESSFUL

» **Tip 1: Buy Targeted Lists.** Choose a list of people who you know could be in the today buying mode for your product. Direct mail companies have crazy good technology for targeting mailboxes about nearly anything you can think of, including a person's credit score, age, income range, kids in household, and brand of car they own. Use it to your advantage!

» **Tip 2: Show a Picture of the Outcome You Provide.** Make the ad's images and copy about the outcome, not the product. Don't cram your ads full of details and multiple offers; have one super-compelling point with a very clear call to action.

» **Tip 3: List the Easy Steps for Your Process.** Show customers how easy it is to get what they want by telling them the simple steps they can take to achieve their desired result. Of course, pack your landing pages with helpful information and reviews, too.

» **Tip 4: Have a Limited-Time Offer.** This is really important with direct mail! Set your offer for a limited time, and tell customers specifically how to get it by calling an easy phone number or using a website's direct URL. Don't make them go searching for the offer on the landing page when they get there—make it extremely visible.

» **Tip 5: Send Targeted Ad during Season Peak.** Because print ads aren't often seen multiple times by the same person, you're much better off sending the ad when you know there's a seasonal peak of people naturally buying.

MASTER THE METHOD, AND THE MEDIA WILL BE EASY

If the steps for success sound a little redundant, good. They should!

Media selection is scary because it's the moment in advertising when you give up your hard-earned money to someone promising you results. But you don't have to blindly trust media salespeople. Place your trust in human behavior and the simple process of being found; being compelling; and being helpful, reasonable, and responsive, and you will get results.

A few final tips when it comes to optimizing your today media campaigns:

» **Change only one thing at a time.** Optimize one platform and ensure its profitability before trying to spread your dollars out over another marketing platform. The idea that you have enough money, time, and ability to be everywhere at once is an *illusion*.

» **Know what you're measuring.** Is it phone calls? Website form fills? Store visits? Purchases on your website?

Downloads of your product guide? Know what metrics are important to indicate success, set up a system to measure them, and review them fully to avoid making knee-jerk decisions.

» **Continually optimize.** Over time, understand what messages work better and why. Make yourself a case study out of every new message you try, and look for commonalities between the winners and losers. When you know what your audiences are most likely to respond to, you can eliminate waste moving forward.

Now that we have fully profiled the today customer, what you can say to win them over, and have identified how to stack the media in your favor, it's time to take a deep look at earning a different mode of customer: the *tomorrow customer*.

In the next chapter, I outline the characteristics of a tomorrow customer and how you can curate their journey to becoming a *today customer*. Now that you've been equipped with today customer strategies, remember that your goal is to build a well-rounded marketing approach to sustainably grow your business.

CHAPTER 12
THE TOMORROW CUSTOMER

To know the value of a tomorrow customer is no different from knowing the value of a lifelong friend. You know the friend I'm talking about, right?

No matter how long ago you saw this person, whether it's been six minutes or six years, you feel the same about them. You know each other so well that you always feel at home around them and would trust their advice without question. They already like you for who *you* are.

Tomorrow customers are really no different. And your goal in earning the tomorrow customer is just that: to cause people to *like you for who you are.* Not for your current discount or website, not for your fancy targeted advertising or polished sales speech, and not even for the benefit that your product provides.

In tomorrow advertising, you're trying to make all the future customers in your service area want to do business with you because *they like you.* When that need arises for whatever it is you do, they'll think of *you* and trust *you* like an old friend they've known long before they ever needed what you sell.

My friend Lori, an attorney in a very competitive category—estate planning and elder law—is one of my favorite examples.

Through her commitment to tomorrow customer marketing, she has earned lifelong friend status with hundreds of thousands of people in the towns that surround her business.

It's worth noting that there are *very few* potential customers who care about estate planning on any given day. This is because the average person hires a service like this once or twice in their whole lifetime. Setting client appointments in this area is pretty tough as is, and today advertising is a constant battle with competitors who are all trying to earn a customer at the finish line of a 30-year buying cycle.

A few years ago, Lori committed to earning the tomorrow customer by placing TV ads every day of the week in the local news. But instead of just rambling on about her service and asking people to call for appointments, her commercials included snapshots of happy families and kids spending time with their grandparents. Each commercial showed sweet videos of granddaughters baking with Grandma in the kitchen, grandsons driving the farm tractor with Grandpa, families sitting around the fireplace at Christmastime, and in a variety of other best-life moments.

For 23 seconds out of this 30-second ad, we showed this footage with absolutely no words. Then, with one simple line at the end, Lori stated: *"You're going to leave it all to them someday. They should get every penny. Put your mind at ease with a free consultation with James Elder Law."* Daily these commercial breaks appeared, showing everyone a better life and *making them feel good.*

At first, as Lori wrote checks for her TV advertising, it wasn't always clear how much business she had earned as a direct result of those commercials. But she believed there were people who would one day need legal advice, and she wanted to be the friend they counted on when that time came.

After a while, strangers started to notice her in public, saying, "Hey, you're the one in those commercials!" She knew this was a good sign, and her business was steadily growing, but this was nothing close to the payoff she would realize a couple of years later.

As her lifelong friend status kicked into full gear, Lori's business grew faster in the next two years than it had in the previous ten years. Today we estimate that she earns nearly 50 percent of all of her town's estate planning business, while her competitors fight over the rest.

Lori's not the cheapest estate planner; in fact, she raises her prices annually. Yet she has a waiting list of people specifically wanting to do business with her and her team.

Why? *Because she's winning her customers over long before they need her.*

She didn't show up on their TV and bore them to death by talking about legal services. And she didn't use hyped-up ads to create a false sense of urgency. Instead, we created her ads using images and videos of scenes that make everyone feel good. In addition, we used simple, plain language to describe to viewers how approachable, helpful, and pleasant Lori is (much better than a stuffy, slicked-up attorney).

And by placing Lori in front of her town every day, talking about more than just her services, she slowly painted the picture of a better life for the viewers of the programs in which she advertised. She talked to them about *their* needs, pains, and hopes as they related to their families and their perfect worlds.

Would you believe that she is so admired that she actually receives letters from strangers *thanking* her for her commercials because they make their day better? It happens! That's how strong her bond has become with the public.

Over the months and years, she's not only won over more than her fair share of already existing *today* customers, Lori has moved more customers into the *today* status for estate planning faster than they would have on their own. She's the woman everyone wants for the job. They already know her, like her, and trust her because her ads introduced her as a helpful, lifelong friend type of person from days past.

Imagine for a moment what it would be like to have a business like Lori's. Imagine having a steady stream of people show up at your door *ready to buy from you.* Imagine all the energy and time you'd save in selling yourself to your customers. Imagine your business growing at record rates without having to stress over lead generation, door-to-door sales, and having to hype up your sales team month after month to meet your goals.

Does that sound like the kind of business you'd like to have? The *tomorrow customer* is *who* you need to be talking to.

Focus on tomorrow customers when you . . .

» Are in a non-commoditized business. (You don't want to earn customers by being the cheapest.)

» Have strong values that make a difference in the way you do business.

» Have strong convictions about the way you do business.

» Are willing to trade a high number of customers for fewer, higher quality, more profitable customers.

» Want your marketing to become more efficient over time.

» Have the patience to wait for your investment to mature.

» Have enough money reserved or enough cash flow to invest before results mature.

PREPARING YOURSELF FOR TOMORROW CUSTOMER MARKETING

I've never met a business owner who didn't want a business like Lori's, but I've met hundreds who weren't willing to do what it takes to get there. In addition, I've met dozens more who started the process for earning tomorrow customers and then chickened out before they could fully reap the benefits. Here's why:

» There is an ante—a minimum price to pay before it works.

» Knowing when you'll hit your stride in tomorrow marketing is never an exact formula.

» During the start-up period and until the time you reap the results, there are no clear indicators of what is and is not working. *Tomorrow marketing is largely intangible at first.*

It takes a bit to earn lifelong friend status. It's the price of playing in the big leagues.

Remember that tomorrow customers . . .

» Are a very large group of people compared to today customers.

» Are very conscious of value and less conscious about the lowest price.

» Don't need a service/product now and are willing to wait to make a purchase.

» Care more about building a relationship with an expert.

» Take their time collecting information and feelings about their purchases.

» Believe they should find the best solution.

» Are far less expensive to advertise to (i.e., there are more of them).

» Are less likely to be needy and complain.

Tomorrow customers are the customers who *aren't* thinking about your product—yet. They may not even be aware that they'll ever buy your product—yet. This is every customer who doesn't have an intention right now to spend money in your category.

Because of their lack of immediate need, you must have an abundance of confidence and commitment to win over tomorrow customers. You also must not be scared to commit time and money to them before they're ready to buy. The payoff is worth it and increases your profitability over time because you no longer have to rely on discounting and promotions to drive your everyday business. You can charge more, and the customers who're willing to pay for premium service will be attracted to you because you haven't positioned yourself as the *cheap* option.

GETTING COLD FEET

Every advertiser on the planet *wants quick results.* But it's this desire for instant gratification that often kills tomorrow customer campaigns before they ever have a chance to work. The advertiser simply *gets cold feet* and cancels the campaign because they don't see a massive amount of people rushing to their business saying, "I heard your ad! I want to buy now!"

In the first few months of a tomorrow-focused campaign, advertisers usually earn *some* business simply by a customer seeing their ad at the right place at the right time. However, the real payoff will not be evident during this time period because tomorrow-focused ads should not and do not focus on a "buy now" call to action. If they did, they would, by definition, be ignored by the tomorrow customer.

This phenomenon is just like the difference between *speed dating* and *true courtship.* If you put your company out there as a transaction, you'll attract people who are looking for a quick, cheap hookup. But if you put yourself out there as a patient, empathetic partner, you'll attract people who share your values and desire to stick with someone they trust—a *true relationship.*

When a customer hears your ad, one of three things can happen:

1. They hear you for a few seconds and then ignore you because they aren't interested in your product (i.e., a failed today marketing).

2. They hear you and are currently interested in your product, so they listen to what you have to offer (i.e., a successful today marketing).

3. They hear you and aren't interested in your product, but the other things you say are entertaining, enlightening, or otherwise valuable. So, they *pay attention* and develop a good feeling about you. **This is what happens in successful tomorrow marketing.**

Success with tomorrow marketing gets their attention even when they're not ready to buy. Covered in the next two chapters is choosing the media that will make all the difference in being able to do just that.

PRINCIPLES FOR SUCCESSFUL TOMORROW CUSTOMER MESSAGING:

» Speak to the broad needs, pains, hopes, and fears that everyone has.

» Use entertainment, humor, and emotion to earn attention.

» Keep a consistent style, flow, and feel to your ads so they build on each other over time.

The more you talk about things that matter only to someone in the market today (like price and convenience), the less *tomorrow* customers will pay attention and remember your ads.

Inversely, the broader your message, built around your beliefs and personality and with the ability to entertain them, the less urgency your ad has to push someone to buy *today*. It will, though, be heard and remembered by far more people, building future favor with your company.

PRINCIPLES FOR SUCCESSFUL TOMORROW CUSTOMER MEDIA:

» Show repeatedly to as many of the same people as possible.

» Reach them at a time and place when and where they can pay attention.

» Don't rapidly change where you advertise (i.e., commit long term to an audience).

Tomorrow customer media is all about being a *daily fixture* with as many people as possible. Just like real-life relationships, it takes regular and consistent time spent with someone before they can get to know you.

On TV, this usually means buying a schedule of ads aired during the same program every day, such as a news or syndicated program with a regular audience. For radio, this means focusing on "owning" one station at a time—being very frequent on fewer stations—versus trying to spread your ads out across several stations (in some cases you may even want to limit yourself to only one station). For Facebook and Instagram, this means creating a consistent audience whom you show your ads to repeatedly.

The principle, no matter the media, is the same, though: Repeatedly reach the same people often.

HOW TO KNOW IT'S WORKING

I'm speaking to the analytical types who are reading this book—those who live their lives and run their businesses using a spreadsheet.

First, I get it. And I am (mostly) just like you. I regularly scrutinize spreadsheets for everything from cash flow, to budgets, to lead reports, to my company's monthly growth compared to its three-year trend. *I love me a good spreadsheet.*

I love being smart about numbers. I'm usually the one in the corner doing the math.

I also believe the wise words of Peter Drucker: "You cannot manage what you don't measure."

Measurement is crucial to understanding your business's growth. *Knowing your numbers* isn't just important, it's vital to sustained growth.

But the collective impressions, feelings, and emotions of your tomorrow customers cannot be measured on a spreadsheet! The *tomorrow* actions people will take with your company also cannot be measured on a spreadsheet. Spreadsheets can measure only what *has already happened,* not what *will happen* in the future. This means that you'll need to accept the fact that you're going to have to spend some money without data to support that spending for a while. *It's going to feel like a lot of risk.* If you can't accept this, then tomorrow marketing isn't for you.

With that said, you can pick up many clues along the way that show the early signs of success in your tomorrow marketing. These are mostly *qualitative* measurements, not quantitative.

Clue 1—Increased Direct Website Traffic and Brand Searches: The more your tomorrow marketing matures, the more people will visit your website as a stepping-stone to doing business with you.

One of the easiest ways to measure early interest in a tomorrow advertising campaign is to look at the direct traffic trend on Google Analytics for your site. *Direct traffic* is a term that Google Analytics uses to define website visitors who didn't arrive to your site via a search engine, social media post, or other link referral. Direct visitors are visitors who come to you because they already know you and type in your website *directly* without the help of online advertising.

Similarly, you can use Google Analytics to understand how many people come to you from organic searches where they directly type in your name versus typing in generic terms related to your brand's category. My clients almost always see a steady and gradual increase in both direct traffic and brand searches after the launch of a tomorrow marketing campaign. Year after year, traffic for our tomorrow-committed advertisers increases by as much as 200 percent. It should go without saying that selling opportunities follow this trend as well.

An increase in the number of website visitors is an early and very good indicator that people are warming up to the idea of doing business with you. Though their action may be delayed, if you can see them on your site, you can bet that good things are coming for your business.

Clue 2—Decreased Lead Costs: The longer you commit to tomorrow customer marketing, the easier it will be to generate leads with your today customer marketing. This is because even when people use search engines and directories, your name and brand stand out as the one they like the *most* on the list. It equals a greater rate of converting searchers into visitors and buyers for your product.

Even after only a few months, my team and I almost always see a noticeable decrease in the cost of search engine lead cost for our clients due to the increased favor they earn through their TV, radio, and other tomorrow marketing campaigns (more on this in the next chapter).

Clue 3—Higher Conversion Rates on Your Website: Your conversion rate is the rate at which your website turns visitors into leads and customers. The typical business website in America converts 2 to 3 percent of traffic into leads. This means that 98 percent of website visitors leave without taking action!

Tomorrow marketing changes this *big time.*

Nearly every one of my company's tomorrow-focused advertisers has a 10-percent-plus rate of conversion. And the ones who have been advertising for more than a few years can achieve conversion rates of 20-percent-plus. This is due to the fact that visitors are won over long before they finally visit a client's website, and they're much more likely to take action because they're more comfortable doing so.

In the months following the launch of your tomorrow marketing campaign, you should see a steady increase in the conversion rate on your website because you are slowly earning a "familiar friend" status among the people in your service area.

Clue 4—Competitors Chasing You: This is one clue that definitely won't show up on a spreadsheet or marketing report. But trust me, it's real.

As your company begins to make more advertising noise, even the most established competitors in your market will become agitated. They'll wonder if they should also be doing more marketing. They'll feel the competitive pressure your ads are placing on them long before you do. Your company name will repeatedly enter into their conversations with their customers, and you'll soon see your competitors try to copy what your business is doing. They'll try advertising in the same places they see you, they'll try to combat the things you say in your ads, and they'll be reactive with their sales tactics.

Sit back and smile because this is a sure way to know that you're making progress.

Clue 5—More Repeat and Referral Business: Would you believe that tomorrow marketing also has an effect on the customers you've already earned? They also hear your ads, which reminds them of the (hopefully) positive experience they had when they did business with your company. It causes them to remember and go out of their way to endorse you more often when one of their friends needs what you sell.

Clue 6—Higher (and Easier) Sales Closing Ratios: When you are the guy or gal they've already seen and heard hundreds of times before, your business's chances of earning the sale greatly increase. It's not uncommon for our clients to report 20-percent-plus increase in their closing rates after a couple of years or so into their tomorrow marketing campaigns. Don't be surprised if even your average salespeople have an easier time closing deals and have their best years ever!

Clue 7—Faster Growth Rate Annually: By the time my company's tomorrow customer campaigns have reached a 12-month mark, nearly every client reports that they feel like they're growing faster and have the numbers to show it.

This can be subject to the amount and strength of your competition in the market, as well as how much of the current market share you already have when you commit to a tomorrow marketing campaign. But as a general rule, more and more people enter the market for what your company sells every month, and the longer you've been speaking to the tomorrow customer through your advertising, the more market share you'll earn *faster*.

A REALLY BAD WAY TO MEASURE TOMORROW MARKETING

It's nearly impossible for business owners to resist the temptation to try and get some sort of instant gratification from their advertising spending. The previous clues *can* help do that if you're not a data worshipper. However, one seemingly intelligent tactic for measuring results *simply does not work*:

"How did you hear about us?"

Businesses have an irresistible urge to put this question on their customer intake forms and train their salespeople to ask new customers to answer it. This stems from good intentions, of course, because the business wants to gauge which of their advertising expenses is "driving the most traffic." However, this question is doomed for two reasons.

The first is that the question itself prevents an accurate answer. The phrase "How did you hear about us?" implies that it was one magic ad that manipulated the customer into doing business with you. It suggests that people are machines who were suddenly programmed when they happened across a single instance when you advertised.

Ask yourself how often *one ad* made you commit to a major purchase decision.

In reality, humans aren't machines. We are emotional, constantly learning creatures who process *large amounts* of information in our conscious and unconscious minds. In addition, we make decisions based on so much more than the ads we are exposed to today.

As I shared earlier in this book, Google research shows that people consult with *more than 10 media sources* before making purchase decisions. So, it is highly unlikely it was *one* thing that brought them to you. However, because most people want to be helpful, they'll usually think of the last place they can remember seeing you, and offer that as their answer. Side note: Because most people search on the internet for your address or phone number before calling your company, they often cite the internet as how they heard about you. This leads many business owners to falsely assume that the internet wins all and that they should place all their advertising money into online marketing.

The other flaw in asking "How did you hear about us?" is that it's out of line with human psychology. While we like to think of ourselves as vastly in control of our thoughts and experiences, it's literally impossible for any person to tell you fully *why* they did something. Our opinions, biases, and preferences are largely formed in our subconscious thinking. This is a tough cookie for business owners to swallow because they want to believe that their own decisions are made in a linear, organized, predictable fashion.

Science says the opposite, however. Psychologists have found that humans largely operate off of the *adaptive unconscious*—the part of the brain that quickly makes conclusions without conscious contemplation.

Author and professor Timothy D. Wilson explains in his book *Strangers to Ourselves: Discovering the Adaptive Unconscious* that this function of our brain "plays a major executive role in our mental lives. It gathers information, interprets and evaluates it, and sets goals in motion quickly and efficiently" (Wilson 2002, 35).

In purchase decisions, all this happens without our brains being aware of it, which means your customers have literally no ability to tell you the full story about what made them take action.

A 2008 *Journal of Consumer Research* article, "Automatic Effects of Brand Exposure on Motivated Behavior," also outlined this phenomenon. The study explains the pre-exposure effect that branding, also known as "priming," has on the unconscious mind. What the researchers found is that brands have great effect on our actions even when we don't know it:

> Participants possess no awareness of the effect of the prime on their behavior or of the activation of the primed construct. Primes are often presented subliminally, showing that such effects can result even when participants are unaware of the primes themselves (Shah 2003).

So, unless you want to make decisions off of bad data, don't change your advertising based on answers to the question, "How did you hear about us?" Science and surveys say that it's just not going to be accurate.

WHEN YOU'LL SEE THE BIG RESULTS

So, I know what you're thinking: How long does it really take to see big results?

Because every market is different, every product category has a different demand cycle, and the economy is always changing, it's impossible to be completely scientific in answering this question.

As I said, *some people aren't emotionally prepared for tomorrow marketing.*

But here's what I can tell you: I've never had a client who didn't start noticing a significant impact in their business's growth within a 6- to 18-month period and life-changing results within a couple of years.

Results happen faster if any number of the following are true:

» Your ad budget is larger.

» You have fewer serious competitors.

» You have a *better* product or service (as compared to your competition).

» Your values and convictions are stronger.

» You write better ads that make you more likable.

» You buy your media with more consistency.

Inversely, the more any of these things are *not* true, the longer your tomorrow results will take to show up.

While you might not be able to control several things on this list, there are two huge ones that you can: your message and your media selection. In the next two chapters, I share the formulas and principles for success in both of these categories.

YOUR MESSAGE IS YOUR LEVERAGE

Your message's strength serves as its overall leverage point. Strong messaging can singlehandedly speed up or slow down your campaign's success. Even within a strong, competitive market amongst other established companies, your message, when crafted properly, can cut like a knife through the customer's consciousness and cause your company to be more memorable and more desirable.

CHAPTER 13
MESSAGING FOR TOMORROW CUSTOMERS

It's a Georgia spring afternoon. (Nature)

Birds are singing.

The kids are outside, ridin' bikes.

And it's the perfect time to crack open a window and let in a nice breeze.

But you can't—because your old windows don't crank open anymore.

At Easy Windows Company, we believe nothing should stop you from enjoying the spring air—especially not an old window.

That's why our windows are engineered with precision-bearing action—so smooth and easy you could open 'em with a feather.

Experience nature's best days with easy-open windows from the Easy Windows Company.

You can get a price without ever leaving your home at EasyWindowsAtlanta.com.

Easy Windows Atlanta.

Kids in Unison: *Replacement windows for Athens AND Atlanta!*

This is an ad from a tomorrow-focused radio campaign at work. We began this campaign with a few simple observations:

1. Very few people care about windows at any given moment. Statistically, 13 out of the 20,000 people hearing this ad are in the market this week for windows.

2. All 20,000 people listening to this station love their children, birds singing, and the feeling of spring.

3. We are 1,538 times more likely to earn attention if we talk about children, birds, and spring than if we talk about only windows.

This is exactly what *tomorrow messaging* is all about: talking about things that are more significant than (only) your product so that everyone becomes familiar with you over time versus just the select few who are buying today.

Imagine if we would've begun our ad like most companies:

"If you're buying windows, DO NOT shop anywhere but Easy Windows!"

Our Best Price Guarantee means we will not be beat!"

All 19,987 people not buying windows would have, at the least, immediately stopped listening and likely would've changed the channel altogether.

Yet, statistically, 13 of the 20,000 people listening enter the market for windows every single week.

And if we had appealed to them before they had transformed into *today* customers, we would now be the friendly company that they know, like, and trust.

As this client systematically advertises over time, these measly 13 customers per week will add up to *thousands* of potential customers who already know, like, and trust this client over the other options in their town.

And with campaigns like this, all the beautiful by-products of tomorrow marketing that we talked about last chapter start showing up. Sales become easier to make, lead cost decreases, profit margins increase, and your company's growth rate starts doubling and tripling.

Are you ready to make this happen in your business? All you need to understand is the key motivations for the tomorrow customer and the Maven Method writing process:

A QUICK RECAP OF TOMORROW CUSTOMERS:

» They are a very large group of people compared to today customers.

» They are very conscious of value and less conscious about the lowest price.

» They don't need it now and are willing to wait for a better solution.

» They care more about building a relationship with an expert.

» They take their time gathering information about the purchase.

» They believe they should find the best solution.

» They are far less expensive to advertise to over time (there are more of them).

» They are less likely to be needy and complain.

REMEMBER THE MAVEN METHOD MESSAGING PROCESS:

1. Who are you really talking to?

2. What are their needs, pains, hopes, and fears?

3. How can your product meet one of those needs, pains, hopes, or fears?

4. What is the most reasonable next step you can ask them to take?

APPLYING MAVEN METHOD WRITING TO TOMORROW CUSTOMERS:

Who you are talking to: Tomorrow messaging is much broader as compared to today messaging. Who you are talking to is *anyone* who could be your future customer or can influence your future customer. As you write to the tomorrow customer, keep in mind that they aren't thinking about your product now but *would be willing to* if you offered them an interesting thought that connects to their life.

Needs, Pains, Hopes, and Fears: Tomorrow customers may have a desire for your product, but it's in its early developmental stage. Depending on your product, your message may be able to move that desire into the today category a lot faster, which is a great added benefit of tomorrow customer marketing.

However, you should usually speak to the tomorrow customer as if they don't have any intention of buying or thinking about your product. Keeping this in mind, go through the Maven Method assuming *broader* needs, pains, hopes, and fears.

In tomorrow messaging, you should speak more to the needs, pains, fears, and hopes that the tomorrow customer relates more to life and human emotions in general than they do to your product. Your company story, values, and brand personality matter most in these moments.

The following example is from earlier in this chapter where we were speaking to the broad *needs* of people to be happy and comfortable in their homes and connected to their kids and nature—*very broad desires.*

"It's a Georgia spring afternoon. Birds are singing. The kids are outside ridin' bikes, and it's the perfect time to crack open a window and let in the breeze."

To the *pain* of old, non-functioning windows:

"But you can't, because your old windows don't crank open anymore . . ."

And to the *hopes* of enjoying nature:

"Experience nature's best days with easy-open windows from the Easy Windows Company."

While it was clear by the end of the ad that we were talking about windows, we brought the listener in by being more broadly interesting. It's also worth noting that we started the first few seconds of that ad with no talking at all—only nature sound effects of chirping birds, fluttering leaves, and kids laughing.

HOW YOUR PRODUCT CAN MEET THOSE NEEDS, PAINS, HOPES, AND FEARS:

If you're using a tomorrow message, try not to spook customers by letting them feel like they're trying to be sold to *now.* Rather, use the possibilities of your product outcomes to help them create a better life without overwhelming them with things that they don't care about.

In our example ad, we did this with these phrases:

That's why our windows are engineered with precision-bearing action—so smooth and easy you could open 'em with a feather.

Experience nature's best days with easy-open windows from the Easy Windows Company.

Everything we mentioned about our product features are immediately paired with how it makes the listener's life better.

WHAT IS THE MOST REASONABLE STEP YOU CAN ASK THEM TO TAKE?

The most important reasonable step in tomorrow messaging for the masses is that they *remember you* and *like you.* You can make that happen simply by being interesting and talking about things that truly matter to them.

But you should also present an action that viewers/listeners can take to advance the selling process. This can be a phone call, website action, or an invite to your physical location. For broadcast TV and social media, you'll usually have the least number of objections with a website call to action. Phone calls usually work better on radio.

The important thing is that the action is reasonable for where they are, what time of day it is, and what they most likely are doing when they hear the ad. Are they driving in their car? Are they sitting down on the couch? Are they scrolling social media at their desk? Imagine their world and what you would most likely do if you were sitting where they are.

It's also very important that you reinforce what is in it for them when they take that action. How does taking that action help them? How can you simplify things for them? How will you promise to make it easy for them?

In the Easy Windows example, we used this reasonable next step:

"You can get a price without ever leaving your house at EasyWindows.com."

It enabled people to still feel good about that company without feeling like they were about to receive a high-pressure sales pitch. To someone who was in the early stages of considering new windows, this ad would've given them a no-pressure way to explore and trust this company at a time that was reasonable for them.

While we approach tomorrow customer marketing with the expectation that we are building future sales as our primary goal, we can simultaneously make a reasonable and friendly next step for action to capture any today customers who may be ready to buy, as well as soon-to-be today customers who are ready to privately explore their options.

Unlike today-customer–focused calls to action that use a limited-time promotional hook, we use a softer, more patient invite with tomorrow-customer–focused calls to action.

Because most ads should close with a reasonable next step, it's a very good idea to develop *unique* and *specific* ways that you use consistently over time. These can become little slogan-like personality cues that help people remember your company and connect your ads together over time. They're the hooks that can greatly help your ads become unforgettable.

In the case of the Easy Windows Company, we use the same consistent voicing for every call to action, and we always sign off the ad with the owners' kids saying, "Replacement Windows for Athens *AND* Atlanta." (You can hear this full ad at MavenMethodTraining.com.)

DEMONSTRATING PERSONALITY

Tomorrow ads are especially written with the great intention to not sound like an ad at all.

Why? Because people hate ads, plain and simple.

But everyone loves personalities. If we didn't, we wouldn't voluntarily spend hours per day watching fictional TV and movie characters.

So, when you need to earn the attention of large groups of people, you are much better off being a personality than an ad, right? The first step in making your ads more appealing is to remove *any* and *all* hype, clichéd advertising words and phrases, or anything else that remotely makes your ad sound or look like an ad.

And to make it even more memorable, you should be very intentional about the personality you create with your voices, sounds, words, images, and style of delivery. For example:

> » Think of Tom Bodett for Motel 6: *Noticeably slow and relaxed.*

> » Think of the guy from the Jimmy John's ads: *Noticeably fast and excited.*

Both are very memorable spokespeople because their personalities are exaggerated to make us *feel* the feelings the brand wants us to feel. For these reasons, millions of people per day happily listen to the ads of these brands and develop a long-term set of emotional responses to them.

Personality costs absolutely nothing to incorporate into your ads, but it can make a difference of millions of dollars over time.

Listen to the Easy Windows ad at MavenMethodTraining.com/book, and you'll quickly hear how we accomplished this with their ads. Tyler, the owner, delivers the ad in his very natural Southern accent, with a natural pace and meter (i.e., no fast talking).

We included sound effects that transitions the listener to a blissful, spring outdoors scene. Tyler speaks directly to the listener as if he were sitting in their kitchen having a glass of sweet tea with them.

We used some really unique phrases like:

"Our windows are so smooth and easy, you could open 'em with a feather."

Finally, we included the cute little voices of his kids, which create an emotional response because everyone smiles when they hear cute kids saying grown-up things.

The details of the ad—his delivery, tone of voice, subject matter, and the scene we set with sound effects—make the ad very *sticky* (hard to forget). Compared to the high-octane shouting ads that every radio station is plagued with, his ad stands out as 30 seconds of fresh air.

In this process he *proves* he's different without saying, *"I'm different,"* which nobody would believe anyway.

Tyler's style—the style of this ad—and his promise are altogether *different* from a company that is shouting out prices, specials, and today calls to action.

Within a couple of weeks of this ad airing, Tyler's customers and many of his friends and family were joking with him: "Can I really open your windows with a feather?" *His personality had already resonated and made him a memorable company.*

Anybody can do this. You don't have to be considered a creative person to develop these personality tactics in your advertising. Most of them require very little artistic skill at all, actually.

All you need to do is be *unlike* the stereotypical overhyped, overproduced loud words and voices that plague all bad advertising and *more like* an actual person.

QUESTIONS TO ASK YOURSELF

How do you want to be perceived?

- » High pressure or easygoing?

- » Interesting or boring?

- » Serving others or self-serving?

- » As a salesperson or an expert?

- » Authentic or fake?

- » Approachable or elite?

Do the following things reinforce how you want to be perceived?

- » Your voice's tone

- » How fast you talk

- » Your body language

- » Your language and vernacular

- » How you dress

- » The colors you wear

- » Your hairstyle

- » The spokesperson's age

- » Your fitness and shape

- » Your accent

- » Your hobbies

- » The scene in which your ad is set

The most important things are that you *choose* these things with intention and that you commit to doing the same things over time.

To learn more tactics for making your ads more memorable, see our course "15 Ways to Make Your Ads Stand Out" at MavenMethodTraining.com/book.

TAKING A STAND FOR (OR AGAINST) SOMETHING

Like your personality, the values and beliefs you stand for can make you very memorable to tomorrow customers.

Why? Because people feel drawn to people who see the world as they do.

It is a human tendency to form tribes. We do this with our sports teams, churches, political parties, car brands, music we listen to, and even the type of coffee we drink. When we are placed in a room of strangers, our first tendency is to find and network with people who share our interests, values, or beliefs. We are wired to feel safer when we're in like-minded company.

You can create the same connection with people via your ads by cluing them into what you're about. Our Easy Windows Company example clued people that we are about nature and enjoying the outdoors with the entire setting of the ad. We took a stand when we said:

> *"At Easy Windows Company, we believe nothing should stop you from enjoying the spring air—especially not an old window."*

You can take a hard stand by demonstrating your convictions on just about anything, including:

» A promise or commitment you make to your customers, no matter what

» How you'll make it right if you somehow fall short on your promise

» Why you only sell _____ kinds of products

» Why you'll never _____ (insert a specific promise)

» Why you contribute to a cause, nonprofit, or mission

» A specific process or way of doing business that you'll never deviate from

» Sports teams, hobbies, and lifestyles that you share

The stronger your conviction in any moment, the more you'll attract people like you and repel people who aren't like you. It can be a really powerful tactic!

It's important to note that what you stand for or against must be something that's unique and something that's non-negotiable for you to deviate from (even if it costs your company business). People will not believe your conviction if it's an easy thing to commit to, such as "Customer satisfaction guaranteed or your money back!"

Select something specific you can commit to and stand for it as if your life depends on it. Or pick something to stand against and fight it as if it were the big bad wolf trying to blow your house (and your customers' houses) down.

PUTTING IT ALL TOGETHER: TOMORROW MESSAGING

By now, you should see the clear differences in how to execute tomorrow customer messaging. Here's a checklist you can use to ensure that your tomorrow messaging is in check:

» Have I talked about broad desires that appeal to most everyone?

» Have I connected those desires to something my product can provide?

» Have I talked in a way that demonstrates my brand's personality?

» Have I kept my brand language, visual elements, and voice consistent within all my ads?

» Have I taken a stand for something?

With these principles in hand, you're ready to put your tomorrow message out into the world!

In the next chapter, we discuss tomorrow media principles with a detailed look at how to align and set up your advertising investment with a media delivery that helps compound the effect of your tomorrow messaging over time.

CHAPTER 14

CHOOSING MEDIA FOR TOMORROW CUSTOMERS

You wake up.

You shower.

You get dressed.

You brush your teeth.

You drink coffee.

You go to work.

You go to lunch.

You go back to work.

You go home.

You rest. . . .

You basically do these things at the same time every day, right?

That's because you, like billions of others on this planet, are a creature of habit.

And in between those activities, you likely watch the same handful of TV programs, listen to the same radio stations and podcasts, drive by the same billboards, flip through the same magazines, and visit the same websites.

Humans are predictable. And it's that predictability that enables us to build tomorrow relationships with complete strangers. By *intercepting* the habits of the tomorrow customers' everyday lives and consistently showing up on their radar, you can become a lifelong friend with them long before they ever need your service. But you must have the right media selection to pull it off.

CHOOSING TOMORROW MEDIA FOR TOMORROW CUSTOMERS

To earn *tomorrow* customers, you should choose media that repeatedly reach large groups of people. It's the repetition of your relevant tomorrow message that puts you in long-term favor with them, earning more and more of these customers as time goes on.

MAVEN METHOD PRINCIPLES FOR TOMORROW CUSTOMER MEDIA:

» Repeatedly show up to as many of the same people as possible.

» Reach them at a time and place when and where they can pay attention.

» Don't rapidly change when and where you advertise (i.e., commit long term to an audience).

After spending millions of dollars testing and trying virtually every type of media, I've learned I can always count on these four to deliver:

1. TV ads

2. Radio ads

3. Paid social media ads (Facebook and Instagram ads)

4. Billboards

These four media types tend to be the *most efficient* at repeatedly reaching large groups of people, which is the thing that matters most. If you choose to test and try any media outside of these options for tomorrow customer marketing, ensure that they align with the Maven Method Principles of Tomorrow Customer Media by asking the following:

> » Is this truly the largest group of people I can repeatedly reach for my budget?

> » Am I reaching people at a time and place when and where they can pay attention?

> » Can I commit to reaching them for the long term?

If you filter your media decisions for tomorrow customers through this method, you *will* find a good performer for you.

Next, I'm going to share some easy steps for success with each media. Whenever you run into challenges, however, know that these three principles will always serve you well!

EARNING TOMORROW CUSTOMERS WITH TV ADS

TV is a powerful media for building tomorrow customers for one simple reason: You can reach massive amounts of people at once. If your business is local or centered around a specific town, there's often no better way to reach large amounts of people regularly.

When compared to other media, TV's strengths are as follows:

> » Dollar for dollar, you can reach people for less money. It's not uncommon for my company's team to reach 2 to 10

times more people for the same ad budget on TV as we do radio or Facebook.

» While it's very possible to earn tomorrow customers with radio, TV offers the benefit of visual connection by placing you and your employees in your ads.

» TV is usually a "leisure" media, where large groups of people are voluntarily paying attention.

Using TV advertising, I've been able to increase annual sales revenue for my clients by as much as 500 percent. I've also used TV to launch new businesses to well over $1 million in revenue their first year.

HOW TO BE SUCCESSFUL

» **Tip 1: Buy Ads in Programs That Repeat Daily.** Because humans are creatures of habit, they'll generally watch the same programs every day. Repetition with those audiences will earn your company lifelong friend status sooner than if you're reaching the audience only once weekly.

Regular news programs are a very good option for reaching a consistent audience. Syndicated programs, reruns, and advertising during specific sports team programs are also a good way to reach the same people with repetition.

It's very wise to avoid "broad rotator" schedules, which are schedules that randomly place your ads at different times of the day.[1] Media reps love to sell these as discount spots and tout all of the extra value you get

---

1 The only exception to this rule is when buying cable programming. Because cable programs have a much smaller average audience size per program, you'll often have to buy a wide schedule of spots all day on a station to reach a suitable amount of people.

with "more spots for your money." But unless you have a core schedule that's repeatedly reaching the same people, it's very difficult to build a relationship with your audience because they'll only see your ads randomly (not consistently).

» **Tip 2: Fill One Program at a Time.** When building your ad schedule, it's important that you buy spots for one program at a time. Buy four to five spots per week for one program before you add another to your schedule. If you can't afford to buy four to five spots in a specific program, buy a smaller, more affordable program. If your audience sees your ads only a couple of times per week, it will take a lot longer for them to get to know, like, and trust you!

» **Tip 3: Advertise (All) 52 Weeks per Year.** When you skip weeks, you lose the connection with your audience. This can be especially troubling early on in a campaign. Regardless of the seasonality of your business or what else is going on, you'll have results much sooner if you commit to advertising no matter what.

When your competitors aren't advertising is the time for you to pick up ground!

In addition to making a bigger impact by committing to 52 weeks of advertising, you'll also be able to negotiate better deals with your media companies.

» **Tip 4: Keep Fresh Ads Rotating.** Studies have shown that after a person has heard the same message more than 10 times, the impact of the message begins to decline. This usually occurs for the average person in your audience after six to eight weeks of showing your ads in a program that you are on four to five times per week. Changing your ads out monthly, even if you only make minor adjustments, keeps your impact fresh. You can also mitigate against ad fatigue by airing several ads in rotation with each other.

Just ensure that your production style, words, and phrases are consistent so that your audience can tell it's you in the different ads.

» **Tip 5: Ask for Freebies.** If you're committing to a consistent schedule for the entire year, you can expect (and ask) your media company to give you extra spots, sponsorships, or promotions at no extra charge. Media companies *love* being able to predict their revenue, and because media advertisers aren't consistent, you should get some extra love with your long-term commitment.

Example TV Media Buys

Station	TV Program	Spot Rate	October Ads Per Week 10/1	10/8	10/15	10/22	Monthly	November Ads Per Week 10/28	11/4	11/11	11/18	Monthly	December Ads Per Week 11/25	12/2	12/19	12/16	12/23	Monthly	RTG M35-64	TOTAL IMPACT POINTS	CPP	Total
CBS	Sam News	$185	5	5	5	5	$3,700	5	5	5	5	$3,700.00	5	5	5	5	5	$4,625.00	4.1	102.5	$45.12	$12,025.00
CBS	6am News	$400	4	4	4	4	$6,400	4	4	4	4	$6,400.00	4	4	4	4	4	$8,000.00	6.1	122	$65.57	$20,800.00
CBS	Noon News	$250	5	5	5	5	$5,000	5	5	5	5	$5,000.00	5	5	5	5	5	$6,250.00	5.7	142.5	$43.86	$16,250.00
Totals:			14	14	14	14	$15,100	14	14	14	14	$15,100.00	14	14	14	14	14	$18,875.00		367	$133.72	$48,075.00

Of all the media options, TV usually requires the biggest initial investment simply because the audience sizes are so much larger.

It's important to know that if you can't afford to use TV media the right way by being in programs four to five times per week, you should wait until your ad budget allows for it. Starting small almost never produces enough impact for your ads to be noticed enough. Although media reps will try to sell you a starter "small" schedule, you're much better off to wait or to choose another tomorrow media to start with. In fact, radio can be an excellent option for slightly smaller budgets.

BUYING RADIO FOR TOMORROW CUSTOMERS

Radio also is a great media for repeatedly reaching large groups of people. As compared to (most) TV stations, radio typically reaches a smaller geographic area, usually 30 to 50 miles around a centralized city, versus 75-plus miles with broadcast TV. If your service area is smaller and more metro-driven, radio can be a great option to reach more people who are only near your main city.

On radio, people tend to listen to the same couple of stations multiple times per day. So, reaching the same audience repeatedly means advertising on the same station repeatedly, multiple times per day.

HOW TO BE SUCCESSFUL

» **Tip 1: Buy at Least 30 Ads Per Week.** Unlike TV, people listen to the radio multiple times throughout the day in short bursts. Because of this, at any given hour per day there are far less people listening than will add up over the entire week or month. For this reason, your ads must air several dozen times for the average listener to hear it even a few times.

To avoid your message getting lost in the noise, an average station listener needs to be exposed to your message at least four times every week (known in radio lingo as a *4.0 frequency*).

While every market and every station vary a little in audience behavior, there's a general formula that almost always ensures that you achieve enough repetition:

30–35 spots per week Monday through Friday between the hours of 6 a.m. and 7 p.m.

Your media salesperson will have software to project the exact frequency of your schedule and how many spots will be required for a 4.0 frequency, but as a general rule you should plan on buying at least 30 spots. If your budget won't allow for this frequency, look for a smaller or more affordable station.

» **Tip 2: Go Deep with One Audience Before Adding Another.** While a 4.0 frequency should ensure that you aren't getting lost in the noise of other ads, adding more spots will deliver results much faster.

As a general rule, you could air as many as 60 spots per week before you're overdoing it. If you don't have the budget to fully saturate on another station, it's often a better idea to just add spots to your schedule on your current station(s).

» **Tip 3: Advertise (All) 52 Weeks per Year.** Just like with TV, you don't want to skip weeks. Be there every week to build a solid relationship with your tomorrow customers. Don't let them forget you!

» **Tip 4: Don't Buy 60-Second Ads If You Don't Need To.** Many reps will try to sell 60-second ads for slightly more than 30-second ads. While sometimes this is a great option if your message requires 60 seconds, it's actually more important that you have *more spots* versus *longer spots*. Don't force a 30-second ad to be a 60-second ad if you don't need the extra time to make your point!

» **Tip 5: Change Your Ads Every Four Weeks.** To avoid fatigue with the same message, the average ad schedule should have new ads every four to five weeks. You can also have multiple ads in rotation at a time to avoid fatigue, but you probably shouldn't air the same ad more than 120 times.

Example Radio Media Buys

Station	Radio Daypart	Net Rate	October				Total Monthly	November				Total Monthly	December					Total Monthly	RTG M35-64	TOTAL RATING POINTS	CPP	Total
			10/1	10/8	10/15	10/22		10/28	11/4	11/11	11/18		11/25	12/2	12/19	12/16	12/23					
97.3	6am-10am	$75	10	10	10	10	$4,000	10	10	10	10	$3,000.00	10	10	10	10	10	$3,750.00	3.5	175	$21.43	$9,750.00
97.3	6a-7p	$65	15	15	15	15	$3,900	15	15	15	15	$3,900.00	15	15	15	15	15	$4,875.00	3	225	$21.67	$12,675.00
97.3	3p-7p	$100	10	10	10	10	$4,000	10	10	10	10	$4,000.00	10	10	10	10	10	$5,000.00	4	200	$25.00	$18,000.00
Totals:			35	35	35	35	$10,900	35	35	35	35	$10,900.00	35	35	35	35	35	$13,625.00		600	$9.04	$35,425.00

EARNING TOMORROW CUSTOMERS WITH BILLBOARDS

While it is very difficult to build a deep relationship with tomorrow customers using billboards alone, they can be a very great complement to your radio and TV campaigns. Placing billboards in the right places can be a very affordable way to remind tens of thousands of people of the feelings they've experienced with your brand.

TIPS FOR BUYING BILLBOARDS

» **Tip 1: High Visibility Wins.** Small billboards in crowded areas rarely earn enough attention to make an impact. Commit your budget for bigger, brighter, less crowded billboards rather than talking yourself into a smaller, more affordable placement.

» **Tip 2: Use Seven Words or Less.** Statistically drivers can't comprehend more than seven words at 55 mph. This is not a story-telling media!

» **Tip 3: Use Stark, Simple Graphics.** Don't go too intricate or "pretty" with your designs. Stark colors and unexpected images greatly improve the chances of getting attention.

» **Tip 4: Use Catch Phrases and Images from Your Other Ads.** Create a strong brand personality by using the same language everywhere you advertise. Just like a famous Hollywood character, the catchphrases and language you use can create a memorable connection with your audience.

» **Tip 5: Use One Call to Action.** Choose either your phone number, your location, or your URL. You don't have room to do more than one.

BUYING PAID SOCIAL MEDIA FOR TOMORROW CUSTOMERS

Much of this chapter has been written with local businesses in mind, but local TV and radio are usually not effective media for nationally focused or e-commerce companies.

One of the great strengths of paid social media audiences is their ability to create specific audiences regardless of geography. Reaching the same person repeatedly is achieved by the targeting technology that exists in the platforms (like Facebook and Instagram).

Paid social media is also an awesome tool for following the people who are in between today and tomorrow customer modes because you can target your ads to those who Facebook and Instagram know are in a buying cycle based on the websites they have visited or by retargeting visitors from your specific website.

TIPS FOR BUYING PAID SOCIAL MEDIA

» **Tip 1: Create Frequency by Retargeting Engaged Viewers.** To create perpetual frequency with the same people, use a customized audience setting on your social media that follows the same people who have stopped and looked at your ads. This can be a great tool to ensure that you're continually building your relationship with the same people.

» **Tip 2: Use Both Video and Graphics.** Facebook and Instagram allow you to have multiple ad types in the mix. Because some users prefer reading and others prefer watching, it's a good idea to incorporate both graphics and video in your ad sets.

» **Tip 3: Use Website Retargeting to Push In-Between Customers Over the Edge.** By installing a Facebook retargeting code on your website, you can follow people who have started to show interest in your company and show them ads that will finalize the relationship and connection needed before they buy.

» **Tip 4: Use Look-Alike Audiences.** In addition to retargeting your actual website visitors, you can tell Facebook and Instagram to find people who resemble your website visitors or past customers (via their email addresses). These platforms often see patterns and similarities in your ideal customers that you can't and can magically show ads to people who are more likely to pay attention.

» **Tip 5: Analyze Your Creativity with Engagement Stats.** Facebook and Instagram judge how popular your ads are based on how many people stop scrolling to read them, hit the play button, or interact in other ways. Analyzing these statistics can be a great way to see which of your ads are more powerful.

Learn advanced tactics for buying Facebook and Instagram ads at MavenMethodTraining.com/book.

REMEMBER IT'S ALL ABOUT ACHIEVING FRIEND STATUS

While there are big nuances to each type of tomorrow media you might buy, the principles remain the same: Repeatedly show up to as many of the same people as you can, reaching them at a time and place when and where they can pay attention, and commit to reaching them for the long term.

A few final tips when it comes to optimizing your tomorrow media campaigns:

» **Fill one glass at a time.** Saturate one platform or audience before adding another. As your budget grows, you can add additional platforms.

» **Don't abandon audiences just because you've been there for a long time.** Once you've earned lifelong status with your tomorrow customers, which happens a year or so after being consistent, your job is to maintain that friendship. This means that your media plans should look similar year after year, with big changes occurring only when you add money to your budget to reach more new people.

Now that we have fully profiled the tomorrow customer, looked at what you can say to win them over, and identified how to stack the media in your favor, it's time to take a deep look at earning a different mode of customer: the *yesterday customer*.

In the next chapter, I outline the characteristics of a yesterday customer and how you can curate their journey to doing business with you.

CHAPTER 15
THE YESTERDAY CUSTOMER

You've decided you're going to do it. You've worked hard and got the cash. *You're finally going to buy your dream car.*

You go to the dealer, write out a check for $100,000, drive it home, park it in the garage, and never take it out again.

How insane would that be? Well, if you're like most businesses, you're probably doing that with your customers.

Let's say you attain 200 new customers this year (not including repeat and referral customers). And your marketing budget is $100,000. It makes your cost per new-customer acquisition $500.

New customers are dadgum expensive.

But as soon as they buy from you, you "park them in the garage" and never do anything with them again. Yesterday customers are the *biggest missed opportunity* in marketing.

While this chapter will be the shortest chapter of the book, it can make you more money than any of the others.

Today and tomorrow customers command the most attention of the marketing world. Certainly in the world of the family business, owners wake up eager to earn more—*more than they had yesterday.*

While yesterday customers may be in "today" or "tomorrow" buying mode, they . . .

» Are much more willing to listen to you if you provided them a good service.

» Want their purchase decision to be continually justified.

» Feel good knowing they have a "person" to go to when a problem arises.

» Feel good when their friends and family use the same provider they did.

» Feel good being the expert guide for your future customers.

Traditional wisdom tells us that winning business is a game of earning new customers, stealing market share, and bringing new people to the category.

However, once again, traditional wisdom is failing us.

THE EASIEST CUSTOMER

New customers require an exhausting amount of energy, patience, time, and money to win over. Existing customers need only a reminder of what you've already done for them.

I've spent my career learning how to make ads work better and how to buy media more efficiently, but neither of those things has produced near the profits that yesterday customers have.

Regardless of what marketing style you used to earn your customer in the first place, it's remarkably easier for both you and your customer now to do repeat business with each other versus each of you finding new relationships.

Yesterday marketing is where you stay married to your customer, where you develop a lifelong relationship of providing value to each other. Your bond is too strong to be broken by transactional offers from other companies. Your trust is too deep for your customers to seek out another provider.

Can you think of someone in a business that you have this kind of relationship with?

> » Your mechanic?
>
> » Your doctor?
>
> » Your veterinarian?
>
> » Your lawyer?
>
> » Your dentist?

Can you imagine what would need to happen for you to go seek out someone else?

Mark and Julie, my insurance agents, would *literally have to die* before I'd go shopping elsewhere. It's because they exhibit all the behaviors of a healthy, long-term relationship. Early on, they provided me regular communication about rates and always let me know they were checking for better ways to serve me, even when I wasn't thinking about it. *They didn't have to do that.* Yet, every month or two I'd receive a *just because* email from them checking in.

They had a mutual respect for and an understanding of my needs and fears. I wasn't a large customer by any means; I had a cheap car and a starter house to insure. I didn't even buy life insurance policies from them for several years, but they were consistent in keeping up with me, probably their smallest customer.

Because of their regular communication, it was easy to see that their desire was to see me succeed. They added value and support by asking me questions about my business, giving advice, and contributing to my understanding of risk management.

Mark and Julie are master yesterday marketers. They have my business for life, as well as the business of dozens of friends and family members I've sent their way.

THE CHEAPEST MARKETING

You might have noticed something in my example of Mark and Julie's yesterday marketing to me over the years: *None of it required advertising.*

Short of the cost of their time to call me, a few stamps, and their email service, they've paid nothing to keep me as a customer for life. None of this effort has required sophisticated targeting, media negotiating, great copywriting, or aggressive discount offers. It just required that they be intentional about communication.

Yesterday marketing can be executed by a variety of different platforms:

- » Email

- » Social media (paid and organic)

- » Text messaging

- » Direct mail

- » Customer appreciation events

- » Phone calls

- » Loyalty clubs

While I'll dig into each of these in the following chapters, you'll find that most tactics for yesterday customer marketing are remarkably unsophisticated. In fact, yesterday marketing is so simple and so affordable that *there is virtually no reason not to do it.*

THE MOST PROFITABLE CUSTOMER

By the time you've spent money to earn a customer, you're at your peak investment in marketing for that customer. If you earned that customer via *today* marketing strategies, you might have paid several hundred dollars to generate a lead or their contact information. If you earned the customer via *tomorrow* marketing strategies, you've paid by investing patience and money in branding campaigns. Either way, the first time you do business with a customer is *the most expensive* interaction you'll ever have.

But when new-customer acquisition strategies are effective and profitable, too many companies accept the first transaction as "mission accomplished."

Direct-response marketing has trained us to be okay with a *never-decreasing* percentage of our revenue being dedicated to marketing.

Yesterday customer marketing can greatly reduce the amount of money you have to spend to sustain and grow revenue!

As customer loyalty legend Fred Reichheld stated in the article "Prescription for Cutting Costs" for Bain & Company on Bain.com:

> In financial services, for example, a 5% increase in customer retention produces more than a 25% increase in profit. Why? Return customers tend to buy more from a company over time. As they do, your operating costs to serve them decline. What's more, return customers refer others to your company. And they'll often pay a premium to continue to do business with you rather than switch to a competitor with whom they're neither familiar nor comfortable.

Because yesterday customer marketing can save you money in marketing and advertising while simultaneously generating revenue of the sale, it's by far the most profitable type of marketing you can engage in! While most things we do to improve our businesses are singularly pointed at either cost-saving or revenue-generating, *yesterday customer marketing does both at the same time.* And as Reichheld points out, for most companies, a tiny increase in yesterday marketing serves as a huge leverage for increased revenue.

On top of the sheer profitability of yesterday marketing, we must acknowledge that after the first transaction, we very rarely can say "mission accomplished" because the customer isn't done! Average customers don't maximize spending until several months or even years after their first purchase.

According to another Bain & Company study, "The average repeat customer spends 67% more in their 31st-36th month of their relationship with a business than in months 0-6." (For more info, check out "The Value of Customer Loyalty and How You Can Capture It" [https://media.bain.com/Images/Value_online_customer_loyalty_you_capture.pdf].)

YESTERDAY MARKETING IS MORE THAN MARKETING—IT'S AN ATTITUDE

We all enjoy yesterday customers when we get them. But how do we do it on purpose? How do we make it more than a happy accident?

Fred Reichheld is the inventor of the Net Promoter measurement system. Many of the biggest brands in the world leverage this tool to measure customer satisfaction—including Apple, American Express, and Intuit. He reminds us that "without trust, there can be no loyalty—and without loyalty, there can be no true growth." With that said, it's imperative that you understand that yesterday customer marketing is useless if you don't have a deep dedication to the outcomes and well-being of your customers. Remember, marketing is always a *human* equation, not a technology, targeting, or media equation.

Every principle of the Maven Method is amplified in yesterday customer marketing:

» Have a very clear picture of who you are speaking to.

» Focus on the needs, pains, fears, and hopes of your customer.

» Connect the needs, pains, fears, and hopes of your customer to an outcome your product can provide.

» Give your customer a reasonable next step for action.

If your company culture focuses only on *what you can get* from the customer, yesterday customer marketing will not work for you. This is because yesterday marketing requires an attitude of communicating *even when you know no sale will result immediately*.

Too many bloodthirsty sales managers under pressure to meet sales deadlines neglect yesterday marketing for this reason. It's why this has to be an *attitude*, not just a *tactic* that you adopt.

Because the yesterday customer isn't measurable in the short term on a spreadsheet, efforts in the yesterday department are seldom considered more than "a nice thing to do." And even when companies have strong dedication to their customers, they often fall short of yesterday marketing because yesterday customers aren't seen as immediate opportunities, or immediate money.

My agency sees this in nearly every company we meet with. When a new client reaches out to us, they're typically asking us to help them earn new customers; that is, to help them with advertising and media. When business owners ask us to help grow their company, they never expect that focusing on their existing customers is how they might accomplish this. They show up to our first meeting expecting us to say, "You need this TV campaign, this billboard, and this digital marketing plan."

Yet very early in our strategy meetings, we dig deep into yesterday customer marketing. Leaders usually answer that they would "like to do more loyalty marketing," but they never find the bandwidth in their efforts to do anything about it. When we point out the cost to them of acquiring a new customer versus the cost of getting their (sometimes 10,000-plus) past customers to do business with them again, it's very clear just how misunderstood yesterday customer marketing is.

To fully understand the potential of yesterday customer marketing for your business, let's take another look at some principles from earlier in this book dealing with your customer purchase cycle.

SETTING EXPECTATIONS FOR YESTERDAY CUSTOMERS

Your business (product) category, how long you've been in business, and the number of people you've served in the past ultimately determine the speed and direct-response potential of yesterday marketing.

If you are a service company, yesterday marketing may not cause someone to desire doing business with you. Open heart surgeries, transmission repairs, and commercial real estate agents will be needed only when they're needed. Inversely, restaurants, lawn service companies, and massage therapists can create the desire instantly with a simple email offer. How much you can expect in direct repeat business from regular communication is still in line with the customer purchase cycle math discussed in Chapter 9: Every product category has a finite amount of people who are already buying.

I have online retail clients who generate millions of dollars of repeat business each year just with email marketing and social media.

Remember my client Kevin in the boating industry who was skeptical about the effectiveness of email marketing. We managed to pull together a list of a few thousand past customers who had never been emailed before, and within one send we generated over 100 new sales leads for him.

An office product company my company consulted with saw $600,000 in new sales generated from a couple of simple email sends.

Surprises are never-ending in how much business we're able to generate when we finally start yesterday marketing. But direct response from your yesterday marketing is often the *least* of its uses.

Many of you may be reading this thinking, "My customer only does business with me once in a lifetime." If you are selling caskets, I may have to agree with you. But even long-purchase-cycle products and providers, such as HVAC, roofing, windows, car transmissions, plastic surgery, home builders, and divorce attorneys, have huge potential for yesterday marketing. Even when your customer may not personally buy from you again, their friends and family will. Consider your yesterday customers a permanent billboard for tomorrow customers for you. With their past experience with you in their memory, they happily contribute to new-customer opportunities for you.

Most of us have been lectured on the power of referrals and even believe in it. But *how* and *why* they work is often unmeasured. We fail to fully visualize the mathematic power and leverage of yesterday customer marketing.

Yesterday marketing works so well because the opinions of your past customers are drastically more persuasive than any other advertising you could do.

According to Nielsen Research, word-of-mouth is the most trusted form of advertising: "Ninety-two percent of consumers around the world say they trust earned media, such as word-of-mouth or recommendations from friends and family, above all other forms of advertising."

MAKING WORD OF MOUTH HAPPEN

Many businesses grow for years by only word-of-mouth marketing. However, very few can tell you *how* they control it or make it happen. Doing a good job and letting their customers endorse them seems to be the beginning and end of their word-of-mouth strategy.

But what if, like other forms of advertising, we could make it happen more often? What if we could, on purpose, use word-of-mouth marketing as an advertising tool?

You can. You just have to keep regular communication going. While that seems like common sense, once again it's not common practice. You need to spend more time talking to the yesterday customer!

WHY IT WORKS

Trust and credibility are the ultimate gatekeepers of future customer decisions. With new customers, getting past these guards is a *very* tough thing to do. It's what drives up the cost of our customer acquisition; we spend tens of thousands of dollars on advertising to lift the weight of skepticism from the public's perception of us.

However, with past customers, the weight of skepticism has already been lifted. Assuming you did a good job, all future messages you send the customer after the first sale are automatically considered trustworthy.

What's remarkable about your past customer's trust is that it can be transferred automatically to the friends and family of that customer. Your advertising explodes like rocket fuel when it's ignited by the positive opinions of your past customers.

All that it requires is that you keep the spark alive in your past customers—don't go dark on them. When you remind them of who you are and of your continuing support for their outcomes, the positive emotions associated with their experience with you will radiate from them, making your ads ring true and your sales presentations go down easier than a fresh glass of lemonade.

If you did a good job, the customer's guards are happy to wave you through the gates of influence. But if you did a bad job, they will, of course, ban you for life. Either way, your ultimate credibility has been established after the first transaction.

The point is this: Yesterday customer marketing is powerful because it reduces the skepticism in the customer's mind. Your message makes it directly into consideration on the vehicle of their past experience with you. The message and the media you choose will be the fuel in making this happen!

CHAPTER 16

MESSAGING FOR YESTERDAY CUSTOMERS

"Eddie Van Halen's Secret Weapon for Rip-Your-Face-Off Solos"

"4 Cozy Restaurants That Are Perfect for Getting the Family Together"

"Make Your Car Shine Like the Last Time It Left Here."

Had you bought an electric guitar, the first subject line would have spoken to the inner teenager inside you longing to be a rock star.

Had you purchased an estate plan, the second headline would have spoken to the core of your value system.

Had you used a body shop, you'd immediately remember how good your car looked when it was "new" again.

All three of these are examples of yesterday customer messaging. Yesterday messaging tactics should be executed with the assumption that you have some sort of means of connecting with those who have done business with you in the past.

Most yesterday campaigns contain an email and social media component, but these principles can also be applied to direct mail, direct interactions, phone calls, text message marketing, and even customer appreciation events.

When creating messaging for yesterday advertising, remember these key characteristics of a yesterday customer.

Yesterday customers may be in "today" or "tomorrow" buying mode, but they . . .

» Are much more willing to listen to you if you provided them with good service.

» Want their purchase decision to be continually justified.

» Feel good knowing they have a "person" to go to when a problem arises.

» Feel good when their friends and family use the same provider they have.

» Feel good being the expert guide for your future customers.

Remember the Maven Method messaging process:

1. Who are you really talking to?

2. What are their needs, pains, hopes, and fears?

3. How can your product meet one of their needs, pains, hopes, or fears?

4. What is the most reasonable next step you can ask them to take?

WHO YOU ARE TALKING TO

Talking to a yesterday customer is like talking to a friend, someone you already know, because you do. Imagine going on an adventurous vacation with a complete stranger. Before you go, you know nothing about each other. But after going through the journey together, you feel a bond with each other and are no longer strangers.

The journey with your past customer is the same: They've gone through the experience of buying something with you by their side, so you can talk to them differently than with new customers. *Yesterday marketing is the continued lifetime dialogue you have with this person.*

Because you know this person so well, you can clearly speak to them better than any other form of advertising can. You know their preferences and why they ultimately chose you as their provider. As a collective whole, the way you do business, the way you talk, your sales process, and what you value will produce consistencies in the type of people who do business with you. So, even though you might not be talking to them individually, you can assume that all the people on your past customer list are similar in at least some ways.

Use your voice to continually *remind the customer of every reason they chose you in the first place.*

NEEDS, PAINS, HOPES, AND FEARS

Speaking to needs, pains, hopes, and fears will require you to use tactics from both today and tomorrow advertising modes. In a sense you have two types of yesterday customers: *yesterday today customers* and *yesterday tomorrow customers.* Meaning, you can assume that some of the people on your list are ready and willing to buy again, and some are back in future-buying mode. As discussed throughout this book, today customers are earned with offers that save them time and/or money. Tomorrow customers are earned by being the company that builds a favorable relationship long before the need arises.

In yesterday marketing, you do both at different times. How much of each you should do depends on your product category.

If you are a service-based company with a long buying cycle and no "add on" products to sell after the transaction, you might make the majority of your messaging focused in tomorrow mode.

If you are a retail or hospitality company with a short-term buying cycle, your audience may be very open to continuous weekly calls to action to do business.

SPEAKING TO THE YESTERDAY CUSTOMER'S TOMORROW NEEDS, PAINS, HOPES, AND FEARS

When you are confident that most on your list of past customers won't be doing repeat business with you any time soon, the best need you can speak to is the need for them to have an expert in their back pocket.

Their pains relate to having to spend money on your product again before they are ready or to the product not delivering what it should.

Their fears relate to you not being there for support when they need it.

Their hopes relate to knowing that they've made the right decision and to feeling good when they can help one of their friends in the future by recommending you.

By doing all these things, you are primarily reminding them of what a good company you are so that they'll go out of their way to recommend you to a friend.

Here are some examples:

» An HVAC company sends monthly care tips for maintaining your system and saving energy.

» A roofing company sends safety tips for hanging Christmas lights.

» A window replacement company sends tips for cleaning windows.

» An estate planning attorney sends advice for having tough family conversations.

» A barbecue grill store holds an annual cook-off for their past customers.

» A home improvement contractor sends an offer for a steak dinner to any of their past customers who refer them business.

» A divorce attorney sends out regular advice on how to talk to kids about separation.

» A real estate agent sends out the latest interior and exterior design trends for keeping your home at its maximum value.

SPEAKING TO THE YESTERDAY CUSTOMER'S TODAY NEEDS, PAINS, HOPES, AND FEARS

If your product is a consumable product or a product that needs continual accessories or generates upsells or additional experiences, you can very easily speak to their today needs, pains, hopes, and fears. If your product is related to entertainment, a hobby, or a lifestyle, you should especially speak to their today desires!

Their needs are related to getting more value out of the product you sold them. In the case of retail and restaurants, their needs are related to repeating awesome experiences at your location.

Their pains are related to disappointments with your product or frustrations with getting the most out of it.

Their hopes are related to being happy and justified in choosing you as their provider.

Their fears are related to realizing that they made the wrong decision in buying your product or service—it wasn't worth it.

While some of these may seem trivial or inapplicable to your product category, remember that the point of the Maven Method messaging process is ultimately designed to help you lay out all your options and speak to one core desire at a time and to prevent you from making pointless noise in your communication—even to yesterday customers who already like you and are probably willing to listen to you.

Here are some yesterday customer examples:

- » An online performance car parts company sends out a special on a suspension kit package.

- » A restaurant sends out a special for a wine-pairing dinner.

- » An apparel company sends out an email for the latest spring fashion trends—a call to action to buy.

- » A high-end barbecue grill company sends out emails on must-have accessories with a coupon to come to the store.

- » A roofing company sends out a special for gutter cleaning.

- » An estate planning attorney sends out a call to action to update wills and trusts.

- » A yoga studio sends out a special class invite—a call to action to sign up.

Yesterday messaging on the whole will skip a lot of the energy that you need to consider in today and tomorrow messaging. Your earned business with your existing customers has done this for you. You must always remember that your goal is to continually connect and be their preferred provider for your product category!

Next, I discuss the media options available to you for yesterday marketing and how to get the most out of them. Keep the Maven Method messaging principles in mind as you study them.

CHAPTER 17
CHOOSING MEDIA FOR YESTERDAY CUSTOMERS

Media for reaching yesterday customers is drastically different from the media needed to reach today and tomorrow customers for one main reason: The audience you're reaching is largely your own, and you don't have to pay for it via advertising.

Yesterday media is remarkably cheaper for this reason. In some cases, yesterday media can be completely free.

Most of the cost associated with yesterday media is related to the tools that are used to administer and reach yesterday customers, including:

- » Email marketing software
- » Paid social media reach (i.e., boosting posts and retargeting)
- » Text message marketing services
- » Direct mail—postage and printing
- » Customer appreciation events—entertainment and food cost
- » Phone service
- » Loyalty club software

By and large, these tools cost pennies on the dollar compared to buying TV, radio, magazines, billboards, targeted social, and other digital advertising.

One of our clients generated over $2.5 million in sales from her email list last year, reaching nearly 80,000 people per week, and her entire email software costs were less than $4,000.

For some of our service-based companies with smaller lists, we generate $100,000-plus in opportunities per year with a *free* email service software.

Email lists, in particular, are an extremely overlooked asset for owner-operated companies.

My friend Robert owns a high-end retail store. At first he was skeptical of the value of email marketing compared to broadcast. "I just don't see how it can be that big a deal," he said one afternoon in a strategy meeting.

"Robert, do you know how many people the average radio spot reaches in our medium-sized market of Springfield, Missouri?"

"I dunno. Five thousand people?"

"Yep. The biggest station in town reaches about 5,000 at peak time. If you advertise throughout the week, you'll reach a bigger total audience, but every spot that airs reaches 5,000 *max*." I quickly added, "And do you know how much you'd pay for that radio spot?"

"A hundred?"

"About $125, *actually*," I said.

"What's your point?" he barked, not yet ready to be convinced.

"Do you know how big your email list is?" I asked.

"I dunno. A couple thousand?"

"Twelve thousand people!" I shouted. "Congratulations, Robert. You have your own freaking radio station!"

For the last 30 years, Robert has been one of the most consistent and wisest advertisers I've ever met. He was exactly right to be skeptical of new marketing tactics; he's seen a lot of shiny objects come and go over the years.

Robert is old school, but he's very smart. He hired a team of marketing and salespeople and gave them the freedom to try new things. Over the last couple of years, they have collected a great deal of customer information in the form of emails and a social media following. Putting this into perspective for him, by comparing those numbers to radio advertising that he knew very well, turned the lightbulb on. We could reach an audience that already liked him, wanted to do repeat business with him, and who would cost him 1,000 times less than the radio spots he was also buying. It was *doubling* his reach potential.

If you have the dedication to collecting customer information, you can build *massive* momentum in your communication. The greater your previous customer list grows, the greater your growth potential becomes.

The following media are the mainstays of loyalty and yesterday customer marketing. Our team has repeatedly used these platforms to create repeat business to the tune of tens of millions of dollars.

EMAIL MARKETING

Email marketing is an instant, nearly free media for keeping yesterday customers engaged. Would you be surprised to know that, after nearly three decades, email is still the most powerful of all yesterday media?

Many shiny objects over the years have tried to knock email off its throne. Young and upcoming marketers often try to claim that email is a dinosaur or that it lacks sophistication. But there are two realities of email that can't be challenged:

1. It is extremely inexpensive.

2. It has unprecedented message delivery rates.

IT'S INEXPENSIVE

Whereas social media platforms, advanced targeting, text messaging, direct mail, and other platforms have a premium cost associated with reaching your yesterday audience, email management software can handle most service-business lists for less than $100 per month. For some marketers' needs, a free plan with Mailchimp.com may even suffice.

But regardless of what end of the spectrum you're paying, one thing is certain: The return on investment is extremely high. For most businesses my company works with, one repeat or referral sale per month would more than pay for the expense and time factor associated with email (though we often see $100,000-plus per month results from our email marketing efforts).

UNPRECEDENTED MESSAGE DELIVERY

With nearly every other platform of reaching yesterday customers, you are *borrowing* someone else's platform. Facebook gets to decide who's important enough to end up in *its* newsfeed. The USPS gets to decide the dimensions and cost of reaching *its* mailbox addresses, and phone providers get to decide if it's legal for you to contact *their* subscribers.

But your email list is *yours*. Short of you violating spam practices, you're free to send your messages at will. And if you are providing value to your audience, they'll let you stay in constant communication with them for a very long time!

Common objections to email tend to include "I don't want to annoy people" and "Won't people just delete my messages?" To these objections, my team says, "Get over it." So what if someone deletes your email? They still had to read it first! Have you kept every piece of mail you've ever received?

No.

But did you get the message before you tossed it in the trash?

Yes.

If you need any further proof, consult the industry. According to a recent study by ExactTarget, 77 percent of Americans say they prefer to get their offers via email over any other platform. And this preference has actually *increased* in recent years.

Why?

Email is easy. People use it for multiple areas of their lives—school, work, personal, finances, paying bills, getting news—and as a central hub for all their online activity. The 2018 Adobe Consumer Email Survey found that the average person spends 2.5 hours per day on email!

Bottom line: Email isn't going away. It's a universally habitual form of communication, and you can use it with great efficiency to keep yesterday customers buying from you.

SOCIAL MEDIA FOLLOWING

Yesterday customer marketing is one of the best uses for a social media following. As I've discussed in other chapters, your social media following (i.e., the people who choose to receive your content) can be a disappointing media to acquire new customers simply because the numbers acquired are often small. For example, Facebook's average reach for a business page is usually less than 5 percent of your total following size. So, even if you have 10,000 likes on your Facebook page, you'll likely reach only a few hundred of them at a time when you post. That said, Facebook, Instagram, LinkedIn, Twitter, and even Snapchat, can be fantastic platforms to keep your past customers talking with you and talking about you to their friends.

And even when your message reach is throttled by the social media algorithms, your truly engaged brand followers—your *superfans, insiders,* and *brand ambassadors*—will most likely see your messages. Serve them well!

Let your organic social media following be the behind-the-scenes club that gets to geek out with you and be in the know about things before anyone else. And yes, give them special promotions and offers that no one else does. Treat your social media as more of a customer loyalty tool than a customer acquisition tool, and you will find success.

DIRECT MAIL

Direct mail is expensive, but when used correctly it can make a big statement.

If using a past customer address list, you can expect to spend $0.50 to $10-plus per person when sending direct mail. Costs vary based on postage, list size, and, of course, how much it costs to print the piece you need to send them.

Lower-quality and smaller-sized print pieces, such as post cards and enveloped letters, will keep you on the lower-cost end. High-impact pieces can add up very quickly.

My team reserves direct mail for event-driven promotions so that the audience has a tangible reminder they can hang on a refrigerator or bulletin board. We also use direct mail when we want to make a personal connection, such as a birthday or anniversary card, often hand-signed by the owner of the company for whom we're marketing.

TEXT MESSAGE MARKETING

Text message marketing platforms are great platforms for shorter offer-driven messaging. Like email marketing, text message marketing is typically managed through a third-party software. Cost varies depending on your list's size, but most services will send texts for around a penny per message.

Gathering text message lists is usually done best in response to an offer or at the point of sale. Having a sign-up list at your cash register or asking a customer to join your list for a coupon or offer can help you build this list over time.

PHONE CALLS

I'm always amazed at how many sales teams ignore the power of the good old-fashioned phone call. No, I'm not talking about a fancy automated calling system or robo dialer. I'm talking about calling your best and favorite customers, out of the blue, to check on them. Let them know you care about them. Let them know about something new going on in your industry, an event you're hosting, or something else helpful for them.

If you or your sales team did this once a month by taking two hours to call your top 20 customers, what kind of effect do you think it could have on sales? Do you think there's at least one person on that list who may need to buy something from you? Could the friendly check-in cause them to recommend you to one of their friends or family members? Or if you're already providing an ongoing service, would that gesture increase your chances of retention?

This is possibly the least sophisticated marketing activity you could do but very likely one of the most powerful. All it requires is your time and dedication.

CUSTOMER APPRECIATION EVENTS

Hosting customer appreciation events is one of my favorite ways to double down on yesterday customers for one simple reason: You can build a lot of goodwill in a short amount of time.

A two-hour lunch event, evening mixer, or seminar sends a signal that you're committed to your customers' success. It provides a natural venue to have conversations that wouldn't happen otherwise. And while you're being the generous one, you'll likely find your past customers will find new reasons to spend money with you.

My favorite example of this is one of my company's attorney clients. Once a year, she hosts a barbecue at her office. It's nothing fancy and doesn't even require a ton of planning. She spends maybe $500 on the whole event, but regularly her past customers set up follow-up appointments with her, which result in thousands of dollars of revenue!

You can go big by hiring a speaker, band, or other entertainment, or you can go simple by catering some local barbecue. No matter what you do, don't forget that gathering your customers together once in a while pays major dividends!

TODAY, TOMORROW, AND YESTERDAY WRAP-UP

I have discussed the three types of customers in depth. I've explored how to focus on each type of customer to meet your growth goals. I've discussed how to speak to each of these types of customers. And now I've discussed how you can reach each of these types of customers. *You now have the knowledge to build a world-class marketing plan.*

With this information, knowing *what to do* and *when to do it* will no longer be a guessing game based on instinct; your plans can systematically address business growth with confidence and efficiency.

What has become the Maven Method—everything I have taught you up to this point—took me several years to learn. But more importantly, it took sacrifice from my clients, my family, and my colleagues.

We now know that success in marketing isn't about finding the best media or even the best message. It's about using the proper tools and words at the proper time to achieve the goal you need to achieve.

When I finally developed these tools, my entire career changed. With this systematic approach to categorizing marketing and knowing how to speak to different customers at different points in their journey, I could quickly cut through the chaos in any room and provide solid marketing advice. Because I could explain exactly why and how a plan was going to work, my clients began to see me as much more than a media salesperson—I became their consultant. I began to earn opportunities to share what I had learned with larger groups of people.

It took years of a hard-knocks education to prepare me for the next year of my life. It was the year I would learn more about business than I'd ever learned. And it all began when I met Cindy.

CHAPTER 18
BUILDING A LEGENDARY BUSINESS

It was a Friday afternoon, and I was exhausted and frankly ready to call it a week. But I had promised to meet Cindy, and she wasn't going to let me reschedule.

She's the most determined person I've ever met.

I had met her a few weeks before at the internet marketing class I was teaching. After the event, she was adamant that we meet. I thought this was just another meeting with just another business owner to talk about marketing. But little did I know that, from a corner of a small-town café in Republic, Missouri, I was about to learn the most important business lesson of my life.

Cindy ordered chicken tenders. I ordered a cheeseburger.

I started the meeting with the question I learned from one of my marketing heroes, Tim Miles: "So, what are you trying to make happen?"

She laughed and remarked, "Well, I'm hoping you can tell me."

"I have to confess, I'm not really even sure what exactly you do. Can you start me from the beginning?"

"I'm in the rhinestone business."

"Rhinestones, eh?"

"Yep. Going on 25 years now."

192 ~~~ THE MAVEN MARKETER

By this point in my sales career, I had met hundreds of business owners of every shape and size. I'd come across people who made money in the most interesting of ways. But rhinestones was a new one. What in the heck could I do to help a rhinestone business?

Trying not to sound dumb, I asked, "And how is the rhinestone business these days?"

"Crazy as always," she said. "Always growing."

"That's good to hear. What does growth look like in the rhinestone business?"

"Well, we're going to be up about a million this year," she said nonchalantly, "but I think we can do better."

"Wow," I said. "A million dollar increase sounds like a lot. I know a lot of people who'd be satisfied with that."

"I'm not one to be satisfied," she said with a smile.

"So, what do you think you could be doing better?" I asked.

"Well, I've never done any marketing in my business."

"Wow," I said with genuine surprise. "No marketing at all?"

"Not really. That's why I've been trying to get with you."

I chuckled and said, "I'm afraid I might be the least-qualified person. I'm not really even sure what a rhinestone is."

"Let me show you." She pulled out her laptop and navigated to her website.

"Crystals, rhinestones, beads—people put them on costumes, make jewelry and all sorts of things with them," she said.

I watched in fascination as she navigated through the pages of her website to show me all her products.

"You sell all of this?" I said.

"Yep. We keep about 30,000 different products in stock. People all over the world buy them."

"Holy smokes. All over the world?"

"Oh yeah. We shipped to over a hundred countries last month."

The more questions I asked, the more I began to see this was far from a *regular* business meeting with a *regular* business owner. I began to see that Cindy had built an extraordinarily successful company. She was selling millions of dollars per year. I didn't know anything about the rhinestone and crystal industry, but it was crystal clear that she was dominating it.

Cindy didn't look like what you might imagine an e-commerce mogul to look like. She wasn't dressed in a fancy suit or working from a high-rise downtown office building. Her business and 30,000-plus products were completely housed in her *house*. But the more the conversation unfolded, it was clear that's exactly who she was—*a complete badass.*

I was confused just as much as I was fascinated, thinking to myself, "This chick is a superstar. What could she possibly need me for?" and "Did she really say that she had built this without any marketing?"

I decided to just come right out with it.

"Okay, I have to stop you," I said. "Are you really telling me you built a business like this without any advertising or marketing?"

"Uh huh," she said.

"How does that happen?" I asked with genuine curiosity.

"Well, we just take care of people. They tell more people, and then they tell more people."

"What kind of people?" I asked.

"Mostly moms. They buy the rhinestones to put on their daughters' dance costumes. That's how I got started."

"By being a mom?"

"Yeah," she said. "My daughters wanted pretty costumes, but we couldn't afford to buy them. So I learned how to make them on my own."

Cindy went on to explain that in the early 1990s, it was very hard to find the supplies to make costumes for dance and beauty pageants. The rhinestones and crystals were only sold to big companies in large quantities. She and other moms couldn't afford to buy premade costumes, and they couldn't afford to buy thousands of dollars in materials.

So she took matters into her own hands. She bought the large quantities and sold them to other moms at prices they could afford. In her local community, she became known as the rhinestone hookup. Word spread, and pretty soon she was selling to other groups of moms in other towns.

She went on to tell me how she made her own catalog with Polaroid pictures and the library copy machine. She would mail them out to dance studios with an order form, and people would mail orders back. She and her daughters would count out the crystals and rhinestones on their kitchen table and ship them out.

"Then, I decided to get a website," Cindy said. "I didn't really even know what the internet was at the time, but it sounded like a good idea."

"Ha! Looks like that was a good choice."

"I've always trusted my gut," she said. "That and hard work have gotten me to where I am."

"So that's your secret?" I asked in amazement.

"Yeah, that and I suppose one other thing," she said.

Then she said the thing that completely stopped me in my tracks.

"I helped people in a way they needed to be helped."

It was clear. She had built a legendary business by staying true to this one principle. She was the epitome of the American dream: *She saw an opportunity to help people, and she took it.*

She didn't wait around for anyone to teach her or tell her it was okay. She didn't copy someone else. She didn't have investors, a business plan, marketing team, or employees. But she had one irreplaceable, unmistakable ingredient that drove her to multimillion-dollar success: *strategy! A strategy to serve people in a way they needed to be served.*

Despite lack of resources and all other odds against her, she *won* due to this one simple thing.

I was inspired. But I was honestly a little daunted by the fact that marketing had nothing to do with her success.

"Cindy, I have to tell you, I've never seen anything like this. You've built an amazing company."

"It can be bigger," she said. "I need a marketing plan."

"Ha! It looks like you're doing just fine without one."

Cindy went on to explain how running the business took up every hour of her day. She had a couple dozen employees, thousands of orders, millions of pieces of inventory, and dozens of vendors to tend to every day.

"Marketing is always the last thing on my list," she said. "I want you to make it the first."

After only a half-hour of meeting with me, Cindy offered me a job to come work with her company. Just from talking to her across the table, it was very clear to me that she was a person who knew how to get what she wanted.

"Cindy, I really love what I do. I'm not sure I'm looking to change jobs." (I was doing really well in advertising sales by this point.)

"Tell me what it would take," she said persistently.

"Well, can I have the weekend to think about it?"

"That's only fair," she said. "But I don't want to wait around. I need to know if you can help me or not."

We agreed to talk the following Monday. I had a lot to process.

Over the next couple of days, I must've told her story 20 times. I was fascinated by her success. I was blown away at how such a simple formula equaled such massive results. The thought kept replaying in my head: "Serve people in a way that they need to be served."

I wanted to be around people like her. I wanted my own version of Cindy's success. And with her story ringing in my head all weekend, I woke up Monday morning knowing exactly what I needed to do.

"Cindy, I can't take a job with you," I said over the phone, "but I do have another idea."

"I'm listening," she said.

"I think it's time for me to start my own business. Will you be my first client?"

"I can settle for that," she laughed. "Bring me a proposal this Friday."

I had no idea what I was getting myself into, but with Cindy as my inspiration, I took action and started my own consulting company that week. Cindy became my first client, and to this day, she's the one who taught me the most important thing about business:

When you start with a strategy to serve people in a way they need to be served, you will be successful.

Over the next few years, with a little bit of marketing, Cindy's sales nearly doubled.

It was the biggest success I had as a marketer. But can I be honest with you about something?

It was also the easiest success I had as a marketer.

Because of Cindy's original strategy, nearly every marketing activity produced results. Her core strategy of serving moms in the way they needed to be served created massive amounts of goodwill and word-of-mouth marketing for her. She is literally a legend in her industry because she helped a group of moms who previously had no other option but to buy expensive premade costumes.

Her core strategy of serving moms also drove her to expand her product offerings to include things she heard people needed. Early on, she made very big, uncomfortable investments in the supplies her dance moms needed so that she could offer the product in smaller quantities that everyone could afford.

Her core strategy of serving moms drove her approach to customer service and availability. Though she literally has tens of thousands of customers, it's not uncommon when someone calls and asks to talk to her. And if she's not in a meeting, she takes the call for even the smallest of customers.

Are you beginning to see why she grew so large without marketing?

Her strategy did all the heavy lifting. Her strategy had built a legendary business long before marketing was ever in the equation!

As I went on to consult and got other businesses, it became clearer: Solid strategy is the *key* ingredient for success.

Without strategy, nothing in marketing matters.

Cindy's story opened my eyes to this fact, and over the next couple of years I learned how to teach other people what she had done. Ultimately, it became the foundation for my success as a consultant and eventually for the company I would create.

Today every person on my team and every client we ever agree to work with know that business growth does not happen due to messaging and media. It happens because a solid strategy has been set into place first.

The message and media simply amplify a solid strategy.

Now I know strategy is the first thing that should be addressed in any conversation about business growth.

And now it's time to discuss how to put strategy first in your marketing so that you can have the same kind of leverage that made Cindy such a smashing success. If you create a solid core strategy and make it the first step of your marketing, all things become easier in your growth.

Finally, in the next chapter, I lay out the Maven Method from start to finish so that you can do *on purpose* what I found to be true by accident.

CHAPTER 19
STARTING WITH STRATEGY

After the revelation in that small-town café, I was completely enamored with what I had seen in Cindy's business. I wondered, if she grew to multimillion-dollar status without any advertising, could others do the same?

And, if so, what is marketing really good for?

The more I looked to my successful clients, the more the answer became clear: Behind every marketing campaign that I had seen success with was much more than good messaging and media. *There was a solid business strategy.*

Now, that might seem like an obvious statement; business strategy isn't exactly a new concept. But business strategy is very seldom part of the advertising conversation.

As I had experienced buying and selling advertising, and as millions of business owners are experiencing at this moment, media salespeople and creatives make the advertising go straight to message and media. Nobody stops to ask, "Are we building this campaign on a solid business strategy?"

Trillions of dollars per year are spent in the broken system of advertising with trigger-happy ad sellers and ad buyers blindly assuming their big idea is on point.

The media salesperson spends their time talking about the strengths of their product.

The business owners who want to advertise spend their time contemplating, "Is this advertising going to be worth the money I spend on it?"

Yet, nowhere in the conversation does anyone stop to take a look at the *big idea*.

The ad salesperson flaps his jaws until the buyer says, "Okay! I'll try it!"

And the salesperson says, "Great, you want to buy my ads! Now tell me what you want them to say."

At that point, the business owner tells the salesperson everything he thinks needs to be included in the ad, and within a couple of weeks they're running thousands of dollars' worth of ads completely left to chance. When these ads don't deliver unicorns and rainbows as promised, the media and the message get blamed for the wasted money, and the broken system continues. The broken system wastes the dreams of so many would-be successful marketers because no one stops to examine the real deciding factor—business strategy.

As I put this realization to test, I saw just how much the success of my campaigns was not all *my success*. I realized that all the companies that had experienced great results with advertising were already going to grow. Just like Cindy's, they were built on a solid *conviction* of how to do business. And like Cindy, the company owners had solid convictions about who they *served* and *why*. In short, they all had a certain obsession with their customers that led them to serve that customer in a unique and superior way. Recall a few of the examples I've used in this book:

» Bill was hell-bent on getting customers' cars back to them fast.

» Keith was deeply motivated by the money he saved people with his windows.

» Mark was deeply concerned about saving people from buying insurance they didn't need.

Their advertising merely made the world aware of what was already true.

The advertising did not make them great. *They made the advertising great.*

On the flip side, every campaign I had struggled with to help a client have success in advertising was built on a flawed strategy. Their business *wasn't* that great. They were mostly companies that weren't worth advertising, or at least what they wanted to advertise wasn't in line with a deeply felt need in the public they were trying to serve.

I thought of the businesses I had tried to help but failed:

» Sam's furniture store was located in a bad part of town trying to sell overpriced furniture.

» Scott's restaurant had mediocre food and horrible service in a hard-to-find location. He was in it for the party of owning a restaurant.

» Dan's contracting business was constantly not delivering on its promises, and he had no passion for his quality of work. He was in it only for the money.

I began to see something else about all my unsuccessful campaigns: The owners of those companies were singularly focused on money or personal gain, *not the outcome they provided for their customers.*

The companies I had success with certainly felt the effects of good advertising. They noticeably grew, and they were confident that marketing had something to do with it.

It didn't take long for two things to become very clear:

» Marketing cannot make up for a weak strategy.

» Marketing speeds up good strategy.

The companies that grew using my marketing were already growing at a healthy rate because they had a healthy strategy. Marketing was just gas on their fire. I noticed that the struggling companies and many that eventually went out of business had the following in common:

» They didn't have deep convictions about how they should serve their customers; they were merely "selling widgets" or charging fees for services.

» They were chasing money, not focusing on better outcomes for those they served.

» They didn't pay attention to the competitive landscape they were in and had no drive to become a better option.

I also noticed the following commonalities of my clients who were thriving:

» They had a distinct reason for being in the business they were in—they were trying to make a difference for someone.

» They viewed money as a by-product of serving people.

» They focused on being better at either quality or price than their competition.

After repeatedly observing these commonalities in successes and failures, I concluded that strategy can be boiled down to three key ingredients:

» Your vision

» Your values

» Your vows

Vision, values, and vows make your company's story easy to tell and your product/service easy to sell. Your vision, values, and vows will determine the success of your advertising. Every failure I had in marketing could be traced back to at least one of these ingredients being flawed.

BUILDING YOUR STRATEGY

Like everything in life, becoming good at something is easy when you have an example to follow. My examples to follow came from the businesses that had long stood the test of time before me. After studying hundreds of companies, the concept of vision, values, and vows became more and more real.

So, how do you build a winning strategy that is ready for marketing?

1. **Declare your vision:** What world are you trying to create?

2. **Declare your values:** What do you stand for?

3. **Declare your vows:** What are you going to do about it?

DECLARING YOUR VISION

Most people think of vision as this big, ambiguous, corporate kind of thing that you see in grandiose mission statements. But vision is really much simpler than what people make it.

Vision is simply *the world you're trying to create.* What world are you trying to bring to life with your product or service?

For my friend's company, Bill Wilson's Auto Body, it is a world where soccer moms get their minivans back in time for Saturday practice.

For Cindy, it is a world where moms can afford costumes for their daughters.

For Tyler, it is a world where people are more comfortable in their homes.

For my company, it's a world where business owners don't waste money on marketing.

Most businesses we work with don't necessarily have these statements written down, but it's very clear that they are being driven by their visions. Watch them work and look at what they've built, and you'll quickly see they have a *very* clear picture about the outcome they're trying to provide for their customer.

However, vision is bigger than just a statement.

Leaders with a strong vision have an almost unrealistic outcome they are striving for. The vision being bigger than themselves is what makes it an attractive vision.

You may remember the ambitious words of Steve Jobs: "I want to put a ding in the universe."

When you hear a statement like that, often the first reaction is to laugh. Then you realize that people like Steve Jobs meant it. *He wasn't joking around.*

You then start to wonder if the guy is crazy. *And he most certainly was.* The world was drawn to his craziness. People want to see what's going to happen with a vision that bold. It's how followers are created.

Legendary architect Daniel Burnham may have said it best when he declared, "Make no little plans; they have no magic to stir men's blood."

Napoleon Bonaparte's statement perfectly explains why he is regarded as one of the greatest commanders in history: "Impossible is a word to be found only in the dictionary of fools."

Their visions drove them to do extraordinary things, and so can yours.

YOUR PISSED-OFF MOMENT

Entrepreneurs are usually exceptionally talented people. Their abundance of talent often makes them unaware of just how strong their convictions are. Where the rest of the world sees excellence, they feel that what they do is obvious and not all that great. For that reason, it's often hard for them to state their vision; they are so in tune with it that they don't know how to describe it.

But I've found there's one question that almost always bring out the heart of their vision. It's a question I ask within the first five minutes of my strategy engagements with clients:

"What was your pissed-off moment?"

When you got crazy enough to start your business, what were you trying to change about your world? Or the world of a person you love? What made you so mad that you had to go out and do something about it by starting your own business?

For me the answer was so obvious. My pissed-off moment was the failure of my family's company. I was trying to change that for other business owners.

What about you? If it's not immediately obvious to you, spend some time reflecting on the bigger meaning of your work. Ask yourself these questions:

- » What would mega success look like in your wildest dreams?

- » Whose life are you really wanting to change?

- » They're naming a scholarship after you; what did you do to deserve it?

- » A time machine just dropped you off 20 years in the future. What do you hope has changed?

- » Your grandkids are talking at your funeral about your life accomplishments. What do you want them to be able to say?

Consider this simple format for your vision statement: A world where (ideal customer) can (hope or need) without (pain or fear).

Remember strong visions are . . .

» Based on a better life for your ideal customer or someone you're serving.

» Bigger than the function of your product or service.

» Ambitious—not "easy."

Strong visions should scare the hell out of you. They should even make you wonder how you're ever going to achieve them.

JFK's historical impact wouldn't have been nearly so profound had he stood before Congress and declared, "We want to make advancements in aerospace." Instead, he declared with complete conviction: "We choose to go to the moon!"

No one knew how he was going to pull it off. Nobody knew exactly what would happen on the journey, but the nation was stirred. Rapid innovation resulted, and unity in a common goal was the undeniable by-product. *His larger-than-life declaration drew support from millions who never knew they cared about space.*

It's that same kind of bold declaration that will make your company attract the masses. When you show up in a room with complete clarity and conviction on the better life you want to provide for your customer, the rest of the world will feel it, too. Like a glittering star, you will attract others who want the same thing you want. You will be *the one* who takes them there.

Cindy's vision was a world where moms could give their daughters the best costumes without spending a fortune. Her answer to the vision questions went something like this:

» **What would mega success look like in my wildest dreams?**
Her "mega success" was helping as many moms as she could— completely reinventing a subcategory of her industry.

» **Whose life do I really want to change?**
She was changing the life of moms like her.

» **They're naming a scholarship after me; what did I do to deserve this?**
Cindy's name would most definitely be worthy of a business school's scholarship in her honor because she saw a problem and gave every ounce of her being to solving it. The by-product was an astoundingly profitable business.

» **A time machine just dropped you off 20 years in the future. What do you hope has changed?**
Cindy is always thinking 20 years into the future: How many more people can I provide to? How many new people can I bring to this art?

» **Your grandkids are talking at your funeral about your life accomplishments. What do you want them to be able to say?**
Her kids and grandkids will most definitely remember her for the lifelong example she showed them about commitment and hard work.

Put these questions to test, and it won't take you long to get face-to-face with the vision component of your strategy.

DECLARING YOUR VALUES

Like vision, your values have tremendous power to make your company attractive.

Values are your self-imposed rules. They're what you stand for, what you stand against, and what you believe about the way business should be done in your category.

In his wildly popular TED Talk, and later in his internationally best-selling book, *Start with Why,* Simon Sinek famously said, "People do not buy what you do. They buy *why you do it.*"

Sinek explains that companies with a strong conviction—a strong reason for why they do what they do—are naturally more attractive. They naturally talk about things that matter. And they are naturally preferred by those who share the same vision.

He also uses the world-class example of Apple computers. When compared to other computer companies, even ones of great size like Dell, it's easy to see the difference. Both are large, capable companies. But Apple is by far the stronger brand and by far the stronger company because they understand the world they want to create—they understand their *why*.

Apple's *why* is centered in challenging the status quo—constant innovation in design and technology. With that attitude, Apple instantly attracts artists and businesspeople with that same vision.

Apple has become more than a technology company that makes computers; it has become a statement of identity. Look around in your local coffee shop at everyone whose computer is sporting an Apple logo, and you'll know that they paid 50 percent more for their device than a PC equivalent. And they did it because Apple . . .

» Stands against conformity.

» Stands against mediocrity.

» Stands against ugliness.

» Stands for intuitive and easy-to-use devices.

» Stands for fun.

» Stands for creativity.

» Stands for innovation.

Entrepreneurs are naturally wired for vision, but as we pursue our business journey, we often forget how powerful it is to express our values—the convictions that brought our vision to life. This isn't to say that not expressing our values leads to violating our moral standards. Most of us have the same standards of honesty, customer service, doing the right thing, etc.

But very often we fail to *lead* with the convictions that led us to our way of doing business. When the chaos of running our business sets in, we become temporarily motivated by other distractions like customers, team members, and money. Before we know it, the passion that drove us to start our business is buried. The feelings that we couldn't stop thinking about at the conception of our company fall to the bottom of our energy tank.

Pretty soon, we've forgotten what got us into our business in the first place. And we forget to put that in our ads.

If you wish to build a good strategy—a magnetic force that will attract customers without marketing—you *must not* let this happen to you. And if it has happened to you, you need to take a walk in the woods and find those convictions again.

Go back to your pissed-off moment:

- » What did you believe you could do better?

- » Who was failing the customer you wanted to serve?

- » Why are you a better choice than your competitor?

- » Did you vow to offer a better option? A cheaper option? A faster option?

- » Did you invent an option that was never available before?

- » What do you stand for?

- » Whom do you stand for?

- » What will you always do, no matter what?

- » What mountain are you willing to die on for your customer?

- » What do you stand against?

» Whom do you stand against?

» What will you never do, no matter what?

If you don't have strong answers to these questions, I have a really strong suggestion for you: *Get into a different business.*

Without these fundamental value convictions, you have no fundamental selling strategy. You will forever build blah ads, develop blah customer connections, and you will never be a strongly preferred business in your category. While that may work for you for a while, your death sentence will be the competitor who comes along with a deeper conviction than you.

If you don't believe me, go take a stroll down the haunted halls of your nearest shopping mall. Walk the empty aisles of JCPenney and Sears—once giants in their category, now hanging on by mere threads of their decades-old carpet. Drive by the run-down building in your town that used to be Kmart.

The most whimsical advertising in the world couldn't save these companies because they've long lost their values. They don't even know why customers should shop with them, so how could anyone else?

Ad people scramble to try to save the day with entertaining campaigns. Though they may get laughs at the water cooler and some likes on Facebook, they will have little effect on the company.

Why?

The company has no conviction. It has no *values.*

Remember Kmart's "Ship My Pants" campaign? It was hailed as one of the greatest TV campaigns of the early 2000s. Media everywhere declared its success by how many millions of views it had on YouTube. People laughed, and you'll still find the ad at the top of "Top 10 Ads" blogs. Now go ask the former employees of Kmart how well it worked.

As Kmart continued the implosion of 2,000 locations down to a few dozen stores, marketers had some explaining to do. How did one of the most viral ads of modern marketing fail?

After all the hype wore off, strategy experts agreed: Kmart's death sentence had nothing to do with clever advertising. It had already been secured by its lack of strong values; it stood for *nothing* of substance.

> "But among the myriad of issues with Kmart, none are quite so damaging as the fact that no one really knows what the brand stands for, or how it's supposed to benefit its customers. Compared to its main competitors, Kmart has failed dismally in this area. We believe that all successful companies—Walmart and Target included—know precisely how they provide value for customers. They make a deliberate choice about their 'way to play' in the market, guided primarily by what those companies do uniquely well: their distinctive capabilities," wrote Paul Leinwand, the global managing director for Capabilities-Driven Strategy and Growth at Strategy&, PwC's strategy consulting business. (Source: CheatSheet.com)

You can make people laugh, but you can't make them believe in something you don't even believe in.

MAKE YOUR VALUE STATEMENTS

Knowing your values is very important. But being able to communicate them to others is crucial.

As originally taught to me by Wizard Academy, one of the best ways to communicate your values is to make a statement about what you believe.

Take the questions from your pissed-off moment, and develop concise statements that communicate *specifically* and *uniquely* what you stand for.

These statements should not be generic. "We believe in great prices and customer satisfaction" does not inspire anyone, because everyone believes in these things. Instead, you need to go deep. Take a stand for or against something, *especially* if that something will potentially cost you customers for taking that stand. Remember: "Make no little plans; they have no magic to stir men's blood."

Ben and Jerry's takes a strong stand for fair trade, and they proudly declare how they've paid $3,416,775.91 in fair-trade premiums to their sugar, cocoa, and vanilla farmers from whom they source their ingredients.

Apple proudly declares: "Technology is most powerful when it empowers everyone" on a page where they share all their commitments to making their devices accessible for those with disabilities.

Henry Ford believed every working American household deserved to own an automobile, which defined his commitment to revolutionizing the automobile manufacturing process.

Cindy believed that moms should be able to afford beautiful costumes for their daughters; she created a way to make that happen by selling sparkly rhinestones in smaller quantities that didn't require huge expensive orders.

Do you see how each of these beliefs is backed up by a direct action that the company takes to make them true?

Your value statements should also be a clear statement that proves *why* you do the things you do.

EXAMPLE VALUE STATEMENTS

Your value statements should draw an unmistakable line in the sand that attracts the people who see the world as you do and likely repels the ones who don't. Here are some great examples:

> » "We believe democracy only works when it works for everyone." (Ben and Jerry's)

> » "We believe you should outsource your weakness." (Duckett Ladd CPAs)

» "We believe life is too short for fast food." (Pine View Farms)

» "We believe teachers should be lifelong learners." (Carroll School)

» "We believe the Bible should be taken seriously, but not always literally." (The Venues church)

» "We believe your website should never be held hostage by nerds." (Frank & Maven)

Make your own list of convictions, get your team on board with them, and display them to the world on your website. Don't be surprised if you magically start attracting better customers!

DECLARING YOUR VOWS

Vision and values focus on your beliefs and intentions.

Vows are about your actions.

What are you going to do about the world you want to create and believe in? What features will you bake into your products and services to make your vision and values real?

Vows are the "features" that people read on your label. They are the distinct actions you take to prove you are who your values and vision say you are. Vows can be any of the following:

» How you price yourself

» The amount of selection you offer

» Your availability or amount of stock you keep on hand

» How fast you can deliver a product

» A commitment to a way of delivering your service

» The amount of time you give each customer

» The level of transparency you provide

» The added value you provide

» How you hire people

» A non-negotiable deliverable

» A guarantee of any kind

It's likely that your vows already exist in your company. It's also likely that they were driven at one point in time by your vision and values.

Most companies just forget to speak them with conviction. And when it comes to advertising, instead of leading with a powerful vow, they instead choose to talk about unimportant things that are disconnected from their vision and values. How often have you been bored to death with empty-hearted statements like "customer satisfaction guaranteed," "certified professionals," or any number of the following flaccid claims:

» "Over 50 years of combined experience"

» "12 convenient locations to serve you"

» "Lowest price guarantee"

» "Upfront and honest"

» "For all of your _____ needs"

It's not that these things aren't true (probably); it's just that nobody cares.

Behind every advertiser flapping his jaws about these sugarcoated hype statements is a deeper story that needs to be uncovered. That deeper way of doing business is your *vow*.

The *vow statement* is always offered in close proximity to a declared value or vision. A vow statement says something like this:

We believe you're smart enough to choose the best option for you. That's why we don't require a high-pressure in-home sales pitch. You can get prices right from our website.

Is it not clear that, by making that vow, the company is trust-worthy, transparent, experienced, honest, and a worthy provider of their customers' needs? Yet, they didn't have to say any of those overused, half-hearted words that nobody really believes.

Vows, when backed by your values and vision, *show* the customer instead of *telling* them. *Anybody can tell people something.* But nobody believes it until you actually show it to them. Let's look at some other examples.

Bill Wilson's Auto Body Shop:

» Bill's vision is a world where soccer moms get their minivans back in time for Saturday practice.

» He stands against wasted time, inconvenience, and excuses.

» His vow is to get his customer's car back to her two days faster than anyone else.

Mike and Gina's Roofing Company:

» Their vision is a world where homeowners and insurance companies are treated fairly.

» They stand against misinformation, out-of-town companies that won't be around to fix problems, and inferior products that won't hold up.

» Their vows are to never replace a roof that doesn't need to be replaced (even if they can convince insurance to pay for it), to be in business for generations to come, and to only use shingle products that have strong manufacturer warranties.

Lori's Estate Planning Firm:
  » Her vision is a world where families have those hard conversations before times of loss.

  » She stands against bad advice and people taking advantage of the elderly while in nursing homes.

  » She vows to always be available for people in need, even if she has to go to their home to have the appointment. She also vows to give everyone the proper information they need with a free consultation (other attorneys charge for this).

Cindy's Rhinestone Business:
  » Her vision is a world where every mom can afford to support her daughter in dance.

  » She stands against overpriced and hard-to-get products.

  » She vows to make over 30,000 products available in smaller, more affordable quantities.

Do you see how the vow statement for each of these is much more powerful than just throwing out a hype statement? Do you see how customers get a clear idea of who they're dealing with?

You can amplify the strength of your entire marketing by taking the time to align the vision, values, and vows that you declare. Write out your vows that are driven by your vision and your values. Declare the things you will *do* about what you *believe*.

When you take the time to connect what you offer to why you offer it, your customer quickly feels like they know you. When they feel they know you, they naturally trust you. When they trust you, they buy from you.

After working with hundreds of companies, I can tell you that most of the time the answers to these questions exist. You just have to dig a little beneath the surface and believe that your convictions are more important than you probably thought they were in the past.

STRATEGY AND THE THREE CUSTOMER TYPES

One important thing to remember before moving forward is that different visions, values, and vows speak differently to today customers, tomorrow customers, and yesterday customers.

After declaring your vision, values, and vows, you might see that your business may be overwhelmingly positioned to serve (and sell) to one type of customer more than another.

In the next chapter, I discuss "flipping the script," and how to start every one of your marketing activities with a strategy so that the message and the media fall into place. But before I do that, it's important to acknowledge that, just like the message and media tactics discussed, your strategy will have three different "modes" of customer.

Visions, values, and vows that position you for *today customers* are related to the following:

» **Price.** You believe in saving them money.

» **Speed.** You believe in delivering the product faster.

» **Convenience.** You believe in shortening the selection process.

Visions, values, and vows that position you for *tomorrow customers* are related to the following:

» **Relationships.** You believe it takes time to earn good customers. "It's okay if you're not ready to buy today. We want to add value anyway."

» **Quality.** You believe in delivering the product at a higher quality (even if price is higher).

» **Commitment.** You believe in an undying standard of follow-through or guarantees.

Visions, values, and vows that position you for *yesterday customers* are related to the following:

» **Added Value.** You believe in continuing to help your customer after the sale.

» **Support.** You believe in lifelong support of their purchase.

» **Tribal Inclusion.** You believe your product is a community of its own.

While your visions, values, and vows shouldn't ever really change, you might select different parts of them to focus on at different times. Furthermore, using the guidelines discussed you can quickly see which kinds of customers you are most passionate about serving or selling to.

Of the examples used throughout this book, many of the companies' visions, values, and vows were in line with *today customers*, but just as many were more aligned with *tomorrow customers*. This is not an indication of how successful or easy you will be at marketing; multimillionaires have been made on each strategy.

The important thing to remember is that no strong communication and no strong marketing can be built from weak strategy (i.e., vision, values, and vows). This is the largest truth I've ever found in advertising.

Every time I've struggled to produce consistent results, I could trace the problem back to a vision, value, and/or vow that wasn't being properly communicated. Inversely, many of the owners my company works with who have strong visions, values, and vows built their companies and personal fortunes to multimillion-dollar status.

It took me years to perfect the method for putting strategy *first* in marketing. Today, my agency refuses to begin any work without first having an in-depth strategic planning session with prospective clients. We literally turn away business or companies who just want the end product without investing the time and money into strategy.

>   » Want us to write your ads? Schedule a strategy session with us.
>   » Want us to build your website? Schedule a strategy session.
>   » Want us to negotiate your media? Schedule a strategy session.

Yes, it costs considerable time and money for us to do this with you. But it's the only way we can be sure that we will achieve the result you want, and we are only interested in having successful clients.

Too much time in the world of advertising is spent directly on the media and the message, as if either one is the secret to winning. Strategy is left to chance and is often not considered. But when the message and media aren't aligned with a company's vision, values, and vows, customers don't really feel anything. The customers who do respond find misalignment in what they were promised and what was delivered.

Don't be Kmart, pretending to be more exciting than you actually are.

Don't be an average jaw-flapping advertiser, boring people to death.

Instead, dig beneath the surface, and declare your visions, values, and vows to your customer, then speak them with conviction!

If you get these three steps to strategy down, you might even be able to build a multimillion-dollar company like Cindy did without spending a penny on advertising. Her vision, values, and vows made all the difference.

At the very least, however, getting serious and in touch with your vision, values, and vows will build you a strategy that drives incredible results through your advertising, sales, and profitability.

CHAPTER 20
THE MAVEN METHOD

I went from being bad at buying advertising to being bad at selling advertising, and then to being accidentally good at it sometimes, to finally figuring out the process to nail it with predictability. That was the decade-long journey I took to be able to offer the methodology I'm about to lay out in completion. If you've made it this far in the book, I hope the lessons and stories I've shared will skip you past the pain of learning it on your own.

Of course, this journey was formative, and necessary, to my career as a consultant. Though it was very painful at times, costing my family and my friends greatly, I now see that this is why I had to go through all of that—so that you don't.

I was so defined by the roller coaster of ups and downs and the frustrations I had that when I began my company, I decided to symbolize them in our logo:

Our logo's squiggly line represents that journey.

I believe that as entrepreneurs and experts, we all must experience a similar distraught and up-and-down battle in our respective fields. Without this journey, we can hardly be called experts. But I don't believe you have to personally experience that to be good at marketing.

Do you see the straight line going through the squiggly line in the logo? It represents the straight path I want you to take—the shortest path to your goals and your dreams.

The past 19 chapters of this book shared with you the lessons I learned. The next two chapters will tell you, finally, how to put them into action.

As you see by now, the typical approach to advertising, the one that I took, is completely backwards. Because the idea of advertising is often introduced to us by the media sales world, we often let the media dominate our conversation. This was my first failure in marketing.

And when the media doesn't lead the conversation, we go straight for the message—an idea for a cute or catchy ad—and we let it dominate our focus in marketing. But almost never do we focus on our deep convictions in marketing first (i.e., vision, values, and vows).

The world has trained us that good marketing means funny ads, flashy technology, big budgets, and sophisticated customer attribution measurement, not the business owner's deep feelings about the service she provides. But the world is wrong.

It's time to insert the universal magic of human connection back into our advertising. It's time to start saying what matters from a place that matters. It's time to start letting your business strategy direct your message, and your message direct your media. I urge you, from this day onward, to make things remarkably easier for yourself by flipping the script using the Maven Method.

In any marketing activity, the Maven Method approaches strategy first, message second, and media third. Every. Single. Time. In this order.

The following steps are the playbook that my team and I have used to achieve wildly profitable results for the companies that have hired us.

No matter what we're working on, no matter the industry, client, or scope of project, we filter *everything* through this process. It enables us to produce advertising that is more than busy work—it's a business outcome.

No matter if you're planning your annual advertising expense, buying a new type of advertising, or planning a new social media campaign, stop and go through this process first.

Throughout this book I've given you the lessons and the bits and pieces that built this method. But here is the method start to finish:

STEPS FOR STRATEGY: WHAT'S THE BIG IDEA?

1. DEFINE YOUR BUSINESS OUTCOME

It's a question that a staggering number of advertisers never stop to ask: What is the business outcome that you want?

Seriously. What are you expecting as a result of this marketing endeavor that you're about to embark on? What do you want out of this ad? This investment? How do you specifically plan to go about getting that outcome?

As we covered early in this book, too many campaigns are started with the objective of "getting your name out there." As you know by now, nobody does business with you because your name is "out there."

If you know your goal needs to be bigger than just making noise, then why are you doing this in the first place? Set some goals for growth using your experience in your own business, by looking at your competitive landscape, and by asking yourself, "What is reasonable?"

Remember the lessons about market share and customer buying cycles when considering the timeline you expect these results.

Remember that if your product has a short-term buying cycle, like food, entertainment, or services people buy often, you can expect results much faster.

And remember that if your product has a long-term buying cycle, like home improvement, professional services, or large luxury items, the world will not rush to your door to buy them just because all of a sudden you're advertising.

Define your business outcomes using these questions:

» Define revenue growth as $ _____ by _____ date.

» Define other goals as _____ by _____ date.

» At your average transaction price, how many customers do you need to achieve this goal?

» Are there enough current customers in the market to achieve this goal? Or will you have to create (inspire) new ones?
  • If you wish to steal a market share, how aggressive are your competitors? How many customers do they already hold captive? Will you compete against them with a bigger budget? Or a better strategy?
  • If creating new customers, why aren't they currently buying your product? Does what you offer simply require awareness to be desirable?

2. DEFINE WHICH TYPE OF CUSTOMER YOU NEED TO INFLUENCE TO ACHIEVE YOUR DESIRED OUTCOME

Every business outcome is driven by a human being or group of human beings who need to be influenced to do business with you. Depending on your timeline, pricing strategy, and approach to doing business, you need to deliberately choose which of the three types of customers you want this specific marketing campaign to speak to.

To be clear: You *can* and *should* have multiple campaigns that can each speak to different types of customers. But in any given marketing activity, you need to choose the *one* that specific activity is designed to influence.

Each marketing activity and media you spend on should have a clear primary customer you're expecting results from, and there are only three types of customers: the today, tomorrow, and yesterday customers.

Will you meet your business objective by intercepting customers who are already buying today?

If so, you build your message and media plan to compete on price, convenience, or speed of delivery. Your customer acquisition costs will be higher in the long run, and you'll always be fighting against your competitors for leads and sales. Even though the today customer is more expensive to acquire in most categories, the selling opportunities may come sooner if you are competitively positioned.

Or will you take a long-term approach to earning a larger number of future customers?

In all long-term buying cycle products (e.g., home improvement, professional services, and large purchases), tomorrow customers are much cheaper to earn in the long term. Very few may buy today, but if you use your ads to build a relationship with them long before the sale, you'll perpetually earn more and more customers each month you advertise.

After a couple of years of these campaigns, you should think of today and tomorrow customers like the stock market. Working with today customers is like day-trading: provides quick results but with high risk and high stress. Tomorrow customers are like mutual funds: provide slower gains, are more predictable, and often provide a larger outcome.

Or will you meet your objective by influencing your past customers?

The cheapest and easiest customer to earn business from is often the yesterday customer—your past customers. Every company can and should focus on (basically free) yesterday customers, but your ability to get new (repeat) business from them will depend on your products and offers.

For products and services with long-term buying cycles, yesterday customer marketing may be limited in its direct-response ability. However, consider adding extra upsells and value ads that you can use to receive monthly revenue. Also consider the extremely valuable possibility that you can earn referral business from your past customers. Often just keeping regular communication via email marketing will keep your customers ready and willing to promote your company to their friends and family.

When choosing your business objectives, consider: Am I more prepared to meet this goal from a today, tomorrow, or yesterday customer?

- » **Today Customer**—Focus on competitive price, speed, and convenience to earn customers who already need what you sell right now.

- » **Tomorrow Customer**—Focus on relationships, quality, and commitment to customers who aren't buying yet but will choose you when they're ready.

- » **Yesterday Customer**—Focus on adding value, support, and tribal involvement for your past customers so that they do business with you again.

Once you've decided which customer you want to influence to meet your objective, look deep into the strategy you've built and pull out the vision, values, and vows that will speak to them.

3. DECLARE YOUR STRATEGY

In the previous chapter, I discussed the importance of strategy. It should be clear in this chapter that strategy should always be considered *before* message and media. With your customer type in mind, answer the following. Note, you might have different answers for today, tomorrow, and yesterday customers. You should define an individual strategy process for each type of customer and each additional audience you're hoping to do business with.

For example, you might have two target audiences with two completely different demographics. You might also have a product that works really well for today customers and one that works really well for tomorrow customers. You should copy the following questions and keep a separate strategy for acquiring each.

» **Declare Your Vision:** What world are you trying to create for this customer?
- A world where (ideal customer) can achieve (need/hope) without (pain/fear).

» **Declare Your Values:** What do you stand for? Against?
- We stand for:
  - Promise
  - Promise
  - Promise
- We stand against:
  - Promise
  - Promise
  - Promise
- We believe:
  - Belief Statement
  - Belief Statement
  - Belief Statement

» **Declare Your Vows:** What are you going to do about it?
- Our (product/service) will (insert vow/benefit) for (ideal customer).

- Our (product/service) will (insert vow/benefit) for (ideal customer).
- Our (product/service) will (insert vow/benefit) for (ideal customer).
- Our (product/service) will (insert vow/benefit) for (ideal customer).
- Our (product/service) will (insert vow/benefit) for (ideal customer).

STEPS FOR MESSAGE: WHAT WILL YOU SAY TO CHANGE BEHAVIOR?

With a clear strategy, your core message becomes remarkably easier to produce. This is mostly an activity of sizing up your audience and offering them the things (from your strategy) that you think will be most beneficial or appealing to them.

Just like in planning your strategy, you can and probably will have multiple customers you are speaking to who all have different needs. In this case, you should repeat the following steps for each different audience you are speaking to.

This message process works for literally any kind of message you are trying to develop: TV, radio, newspaper, social media, website landing pages, search engine ads, email marketing, and even one-on-one emails with a customer (or your team).

These questions force you to be very in tune with the person you hope to earn as a customer. The goal is to get so specific about who you are talking to, even down to assigning them a name, that you can speak to them as if they were a long-lost friend. This step requires a little imagination, but these questions paired with common sense and experience in your industry are all you need to know to develop a solid message. Refer to Chapter 4 for in-depth examples of how to write to each type of customer.

» **Who are you talking to?**
- Avatar name
- Age, gender

- Location
- Lifestyle
- Political views
- Describe a day in their life
- Where do they shop?
- What bands do they listen to?
- What do they like to do in their free time?
- Who and what do they admire?
- What brands do they admire?
- What is their perfect world?

» **What are their needs, pains, hopes, and fears that you're addressing?**
- Needs (customer's void):
  ○
- Pains (inconveniences they face):
  ○
- Hopes (long-term aspirations):
  ○
- Fears (what they don't want to lose):
  ○

» **How can my vision, values, and vows satisfy those?**
- We meet their need by (value proposition).
- We make it less painful by (value proposition).
- We encourage their hope by (value proposition).
- We overcome their fears by (value proposition).

» **What is the most reasonable next step for action?**
- To have them know, like, and trust us more.
  ○ Make a lasting impression with our personality
  ○ Deliver our message with consistent tone, language, and value propositions
- To have them take an immediate action with us.
  ○ Call.
  ○ Email.

- ○ Visit our location.
- ○ Shop our website.
- ○ Text message us.
- ○ Fill a form on our website.
- ○ Download a guide.
- ○ Schedule a virtual appointment.

STEPS FOR MEDIA: WHERE WILL YOU DELIVER YOUR MESSAGE FOR MAXIMUM IMPACT?

As we've discussed throughout this book, media is often regarded as both the problem and solution to struggling marketing campaigns. But now you know that media can do only one thing: *Put a message in front of a potential customer.*

No matter the targeting, technology, or efficiency behind your media plan, if your message doesn't sell, the audience isn't buying.

All that said, picking a good media plan is all about spending the least amount of money to place your message in the place it's most likely to be acted upon (even if that action is to enter into long-term courtship with you before their time of need). Knowing this, keep the following considerations in mind for choosing your media plan:

» **Budget:**
- Can you afford to buy enough exposure on this platform for people to notice?
- This will vary by market size, geography, and competitive landscape. Consider how loud your competitors are compared to you, and be realistic about whether you can compete with more repetition or relevance in your messaging. A competitor with a big budget *can* be beat with a smaller budget if their reputation and messaging are weak. But you do *not* want to bring a knife to a gunfight with a small budget if your competitor is stronger.

- See MavenMethodTraining.com/book for in-depth tactics on how to buy and negotiate each media.

» **Are your message and strategy focusing on today, tomorrow, or yesterday customers?**

- Your media selection should heavily depend on how focused you are on today, tomorrow, or yesterday customers.
- If you are advertising for today customers (quick transactions), your goal is to intercept as many shoppers as possible.
  - Targeted media like search engines, direct mail, and targeted digital media work best for service and retail-based today customers.
  - Outdoor media and other broadcast *can* work for today customers for commodities, food, and entertainment because so many people are already in the market for these products.
- If you are advertising for tomorrow customers, your goal is to speak to as many people in the general public as possible. Targeting is less important than the sheer number of people who could be future customers. You want to show up consistently, several days a week, in their viewing and listening habits. To create long-term recall, buy media that enables you to be in front of them four to five times per week (known as frequency).
  - If your company serves one particular geographic area, broadcast media like TV and radio usually reach far more people for your dollar. You can often reach them for a fourth or fifth of the cost of digital media to reach similar-sized audiences.
  - If your market or service area is much larger than a localized town, print, targeted social media, or cable TV advertising may be a better option for tomorrow customers. Don't forget the rule of

being present four to five times per week with each of these customers.

- Yesterday customers can very easily be reached by most companies using a few simple platforms.
  - Email marketing is extremely valuable.
  - Social media posts typically reach less people than email, but they are also valuable.
  - Direct mail, text message marketing, and customer events are also great platforms for reaching yesterday customers.

» **What is the easiest media to use to ask for your reasonable next step by the customer?**

- **For today customers:**
  - Search engines and paid social media ads offer some of the highest capability in getting quick action.
  - Use ads that direct people to lead forms, virtual consultations, phone calls, or online chats.
  - If using broadcast for today customer acquisition, radio typically works better advertising phone calls to action than advertising website calls to action.
  - If using TV for today customer (direct response) acquisition, website calls to action often work better than phone calls to action.
  - For promotions and limited-time offers, print and magazines often work well in communicating urgency.
- **For tomorrow customers:**
  - Your goal is to be remembered, and being remembered can happen only with repetition and relevance. Buy media that enables you to achieve at least a 4 frequency with your audience on a weekly basis and up to an 8 frequency per week, budget permitting.

- Buying TV and radio schedules every week of the year enables you to get multiple and consistent exposures with your audience. Advertise consistently even when your season is slow in order to maintain and strengthen the relationship with your future customers. If you go off the air, they'll forget about you, and you'll have to start all over!
- Remember that if your sales cycle is long, you are often building relationships with people you won't see or hear from in months or years. But they are still your future customers if you stay committed to them!

When buying media from a local print or broadcast media partner, remember that you can negotiate on rating points and added value. While relationships with your media reps are very important, the media itself is a commodity.

Compare apples to apples as much as you can. Also remember that you can almost always get a better deal by negotiating annual schedules—committing to 52 weeks of a consistent schedule.

Rates for self-serve digital media platforms like Google Ads, Facebook, and Instagram ads are almost always driven by competition and the ad platform's algorithm at that particular time. In almost every case, digital platforms will reward you by airing ads they believe are more relevant (i.e., quality) for their users. The reward comes in the form of charging you less or delivering your ad to more people for less money.

Bottom line: Choose the right media that is in line with your message and strategy.

PUTTING THE MAVEN METHOD INTO ACTION

My team and I created a Maven Method workbook that you can fill out and repeatedly use over and over: see MavenMethodTraining. com/book. This workbook walks you through all the steps listed here. Use it to get clarity for any marketing decision you have, and avoid wasting time and money on the wrong things.

I'm confident that with the Maven Method in hand, you can forever take the guesswork out of advertising and grow your company by multimillion-dollar figures.

	Strategy	Message	Media
⌇	Focus on vision, values, and vows related to:	Connect vision, values, and vows to customer desires by asking:	Choose the most efficient platform by asking:
Today Customers	Price Convenience Hassle	Who am I talking to? What are their needs, pains, hopes, and fears? How can my product satisfy one of those? What is the most reasonable next step for action?	Where can I target people buying right now?
Tomorrow Customers	Commitment Quality Relationships		Where can I talk to the largest group of people daily?
Yesterday Customers	Added Value Support Tribal Bond		Where can I continually communicate with my past customers?

CHAPTER 21
PUTTING THE MAVEN METHOD IN ACTION

As I stood on the balcony in Hawaii that day a decade ago and heard the words that would crush all my plans and my family's hopes and dreams, I believed I was largely to blame. I thought I wasn't smart enough. I thought I wasn't experienced enough. I thought that, for as much as I loved it, I must not be cut out for marketing.

I wish I would have known that marketing isn't this mystical creature most of us make it out to be. I wish I would have known that, despite all the marketing world has done to complicate it, the only thing that's required for awesome marketing is to be *human*.

I now see so many things that I would have done differently with our family company. It is long gone, though, and I have a wildly growing business of my own now.

But I still wonder, "What if . . . "

» What if I could go back and start from the beginning?

» What if I hadn't wasted all that money trying and testing new things all the time?

» What if I had had clarity on the three types of customers?

» What if I had known how to speak to the customer I wanted to earn, instead of just making noise?

» What if I had known that I could have been successful with any of the media I spent our money on if I'd only used it correctly?

I will never know the answer to that. But I'm hoping you can help me find the next best thing. Take these lessons that cost me and my friends dearly. Follow the steps I learned the hard way. Don't lose another night's sleep. Don't tell yourself you're not smart enough to be good at marketing. Don't settle for years of 80-hour workweeks. Don't gamble the money you and your family have worked so hard for.

Put it to absolute use.

Kick it into Maven mode.

Scale up your company to make the impact you've always wanted.

Every time you are faced with a new advertising investment, consult the Maven Method.

Every time someone presents you with a new enthusiastic commercial idea, consult the Maven Method.

Every time you are stuck on ideas for how to grow your business, consult the Maven Method.

And most definitely, when you don't feel like you're making a big enough impact, consult the Maven Method.

Like a cheat sheet, you should quickly run through the questions:

» What are my business objectives by doing this?

» What type of customer am I hoping to earn?

» Have I declared my selling strategy?

» Do I have a solid message that connects that strategy to the customer's desires?

» Is this the best media to deliver that message?

My team and I get to experience the joy every day of watching companies grow faster and stronger. Many of our clients who were extremely small are now dominating the markets they serve. They are hiring people, leading with strong vision and values, and making meaningful vows to their people. Many have become millionaires in the process.

Getting to be a part of that is truly a dream job, and I want you to have the same results. I want you to confidently hold the keys to problem solving, optimizing, and compounding your marketing efforts. I want you to never feel like you've thrown away money. And I want to keep you from falling to the bottom, where I found myself nearly a decade ago.

So, I am happy to share with you the Maven Method and my stories, and am grateful for the time my team has sacrificed to pull it all together, because I know you can succeed.

You can be a confident marketer. You can be amongst the wise. Your journey to marketing your way to a legendary business starts here, but you are not alone.

After growing dozens of companies beyond seven figures, my team and I have vowed to do this for as many companies as possible. *We don't want to impact dozens. We want to impact millions.* That's why I'm taking everything my company knows and teaching it to every business we possibly can.

I love the agency my team and I have built, but we'll only make the impact we want to make if we teach others how to do what we've done. This book is our first step—to be a guiding light for anyone lost in the waters of marketing.

But Maven Method training goes so much deeper. We're teaching in-depth courses for exactly how to build your marketing strategy, write million-dollar ads, and buy media like an absolute pro. With these tools, you can continue making your company everything you want it to be.

In the process, we'll be doing the same for ours: *Creating a world where every business can grow with confidence.*

I hope that when you finish this book, you take these lessons, and go do just that.

Cheers to you and all your future success!

ABOUT THE AUTHOR

Brandon Welch is the President, Founder, and Chief of Strategy of Frank & Maven, a strategic marketing and communication firm.

Drawing from lessons learned in his family business, Brandon developed a method to help companies avoid the expensive trial and error that plagues the marketing process, and systematically inspire customers into action.

His first book, *The Maven Marketer,* is a collection of the principles and tactics he uses to guide his clients across the United States through multimillion-dollar growth. This clear and concise roadmap is a go-to guide for anyone wanting better results from advertising and marketing.

Outside of work you'll find Brandon cooking, making music, flying airplanes, and telling dad jokes. He and his high school sweetheart live in Southwest Missouri with their four beautiful children.

For advanced training on

- Marketing Strategy
- Lead Generation
- Media Buying
- Writing Profitable Ads

visit:
MavenMethodTraining.com

MAVEN METHOD

ACKNOWLEDGMENTS

To Valerie, for being my rock, my voice of reason, and my best friend.

To Jude, Jovi, Anna, and Archer for reminding me to imagine and play every day.

To Mom and Dad, for relentlessly believing in me, and giving me an education that couldn't have been earned any other way.

To Ben, Emily, my Grandmas, Grandpa, and Aunt Lucille for always being there.

To Grandpa for teaching me everything I've ever needed to know about sales, people, and showing up.

To Janet for being my mentor, my friend, and my mother-in-law; to Terry for having my back no matter what; and to both of you for raising the girl of my dreams.

To Taylor for being my constant sounding board, forever consigliere, and brother from another mother.

To my team at Frank & Maven, who shaped this book and inspire me to be better every single day: Caleb, Megan, Janet, Val, Tanner, Carter, Wendy, Shay, Mike, Joel, Emily, and Leslie.

To Caleb and Ciera for being a constant source of truth and guidance.

To Phillip and Devin Wright for teaching me how to bring people together.

To Kent and Kim for giving me a shot, and for the countless times you let me keep my job when I screwed it up.

To Jimmie for being my Jimmie.

To Roy H. Williams for pushing me off the ledge, being a beacon of light in my most defeated hour, and for teaching me everything that matters about advertising and communication.

To Daniel Whittington, Jeff Sexton, Mark Fox, and everyone at The Wizard Academy for teaching me what no other school in the world could.

To Tim Miles for being a constant role model as a consultant, author, and ad guy. To Randy Mayes for being my mentor, my friend, and always helping me figure it out.

To Bill Perkin for being my Yoda.

To Marcus Crigler for always having a brilliant idea.

To the members of The Round for constantly bringing me new perspectives and for your unwavering honesty.

To Ashley Mansour for giving teaching me the power of mindset, making me a better writer, and finally getting this book off my list.

To Debbie Enlow for helping me polish and process this thing, and for your always-solid perspective.

To Cindy and Ron Wilson for believing in me before anyone else, and for letting me be a part of what you've built.

To all of my clients over the years who have been crazy enough to trust me, welcome me into your homes, share your dreams, and allow me to be a part of the incredible work that you do.

Special thanks to Duane and Amanda, Mark and Julie, Keith and Lori, Tyler and Ashley, Randy and Dee, Chris and Erica, Kent and Tom, Bill and Julie, Mike and Gina, Jessica and Lori, Tim and Jennifer, Keith, Amanda, David and Amy, Carrie, Brian and Lynn, Klaus, Steve and Brad, Ben and Stephanie, Nick G., Bev, RD, Kenny and Aaron – You guys literally made this book possible.

To the countless friends, colleagues, and neighbors that I have been blessed with. I could not do this without your support and friendship.

SOURCES AND FURTHER READING

Baveja, Sarabji Singh, Sharad Rastogi, Chris Zook, Randall S. Hancock, and Julian Chu. "The Value of Online Customer Loyalty and How You Can Capture It." Bain & Company, Inc., April 1, 2000. https://www.bain.com/insights/the-value-of-online-customer-loyalty-and-how-you-can-capture-it.

"The Brain Forgets in Order to Conserve Energy." ScienceDaily. Lund University, October 27, 2015. https://www.sciencedaily.com/releases/2015/10/151027082317.htm.

Emberson, Lauren L., Gary Lupyan, Michael H. Goldstein, and Michael J. Spivey. "Overheard Cell-Phone Conversations: When Less Speech Is More Distracting." SAGE Journals. *Psychological Science*, September 3, 2010. https://journals.sagepub.com/doi/abs/10.1177/0956797610382126.

Fitzsimons, Gráinne M., Tanya L. Chartrand, and Gavan J. Fitzsimons. "Automatic Effects of Brand Exposure on Motivated Behavior: How Apple Makes You 'Think Different.'" OUP Academic. *Journal of Consumer Research*, March 4, 2008. https://academic.oup.com/jcr/article-abstract/35/1/21/1847975?redirectedFrom=fulltext.

"Global Trust in Advertising and Brand Messages." Nielsen, April 2012. https://www.nielsen.com/wp-content/uploads/sites/3/2019/04/global-trust-in-advertising-2012.pdf.

Hendrick, Bill. "Why People's Cell Phone Conversations Annoy Us." WebMD. WebMD, September 22, 2010. https://www.webmd.com/brain/news/20100922/why-peoples-cell-phone-conversations-annoy-us#1.

Hesslow, Germund. "The Brain Forgets in Order to Conserve Energy," October 26, 2015. https://www.lunduniversity.lu.se/article/brain-forgets-order-conserve-energy.

Johnson, Caitlin. "Cutting Through Advertising Clutter." CBS News. CBS Interactive, September 17, 2006. http://www.cbsnews.com/news/cutting-through-advertising-clutter.

Leinwand, Paul, and Cesare Mainardi. "Why Can't Kmart Be Successful While Target and Walmart Thrive?" Harvard Business Review, December 15, 2010. https://hbr.org/2010/12/why-cant-kmart-be-successful-w.

"Maslow's Hierarchy of Needs." Wikipedia. Wikimedia Foundation, January 20, 2021. https://en.wikipedia.org/wiki/Maslow%27s_hierarchy_of_needs.

Murphy, Nikelle. "Why No One Cares About Kmart Anymore." Showbiz CheatSheet, February 15, 2017. https://www.cheatsheet.com/money-career/no-one-cares-kmart-anymore.html.

Nelson, Amanda. "25 Mind Blowing Email Marketing Stats." The 360 Blog from Salesforce, July 12, 2013. https://www.salesforce.com/blog/email-marketing-stats-blog.

"Nielsen: Global Consumers' Trust in 'Earned' Advertising Grows in Importance." Nielsen, April 10, 2012. https://www.nielsen.com/us/en/press-releases/2012/nielsen-global-consumers-trust-in-earned-advertising-grows.

Oppong, Thomas. "Depleted By Decisions (How Your Brain Makes Choices That Sabotage You And What to Do About It)." Medium. Personal Growth, June 1, 2018. https://medium.com/personal-growth/depleted-by-decisions-how-your-brain-makes-choices-that-sabotage-you-and-what-to-do-about-it-b6cb5065f8f1.

Pine View Farms. Accessed January 29, 2021. https://www.saskmade.ca/collections/pineview-farms.

Rasmussen, Anders, Riccardo Zucca, Fredrik Johansson, Dan-Anders Jirenhed, and Germund Hesslow. "Purkinje Cell Activity during Classical Conditioning with Different Conditional Stimulus Explains Central Tenet of Rescorla–Wagner Model." PNAS Proceedings of the National Academy of Sciences of the United States of America. PNAS, October 23, 2015. https://www.pnas.org/content/early/2015/10/22/1516986112.abstract.

Reichheld, Fred. "Prescription for Cutting Costs." Bain & Company, Inc., October 25, 2001. https://www.bain.com/insights/prescription-for-cutting-costs-bain-brief.

"Rethink Email: Earn a Place in Your Customer's Inbox with Personalization." ExactTarget. Salesforce Marketing Cloud. Accessed January 29, 2021. https://brandcdn.exacttarget.com/sites/exacttarget/files/mc-earn-a-place-workbook-personalization.pdf.

Sinek, Simon. "Start with Why: How Great Leaders Inspire Everyone to Take Action." Amazon. Portfolio, December 27, 2011. https://www.amazon.com/Start-Why-Leaders-Inspire-Everyone/dp/1591846447.

Story, Louise. "Anywhere the Eye Can See, It's Likely to See an Ad." *The New York Times*, January 15, 2007. https://www.nytimes.com/2007/01/15/business/media/15everywhere.html.

The Venues. Accessed January 29, 2021. https://thevenues.org/about-the-venues.

"We Believe Democracy Only Works When It Works for Everyone." Ben and Jerry's. Accessed January 29, 2021. https://www.benjerry.com/values/issues-we-care-about/democracy.

"We Believe Statements Generated by Carroll Faculty & Staff." Carroll School. Accessed January 29, 2021. https://www.carrollschool.org/dyslexia-news-blog/blog-detail-page/~board/carroll-school-news/post/we-believe-statements-generated-by-carroll-faculty-staff.

"We Believe." Duckett Ladd CPAs and Advisors. Accessed January 29, 2021. https://duckettladd.com/we-believe.

"We Believe." Frank & Maven. Accessed January 29, 2021. https://frankandmaven.com/we-believe.

Williams, Roy H. "The Wizard of Ads: Turning Words into Magic And Dreamers into Millionaires." Roy H. Williams Marketing. Bard Press, May 1998. http://www.rhw.com/youll-laugh-youll-cry.

Wilson, Timothy D. "Strangers to Ourselves: Discovering the Adaptive Unconscious." Amazon. Belknap, May 15, 2004. https://www.amazon.com/Strangers-Ourselves-Discovering-Adaptive-Unconscious/dp/0674013824.

"The Zero Moment of Truth Macro Study." Think with Google. Google, April 2011. https://www.thinkwithgoogle.com/consumer-insights/consumer-journey/the-zero-moment-of-truth-macro-study.

Made in the USA
Middletown, DE
15 June 2022

BOLD

Essential Leadership for Transformative Change

CHRIS LAVICTOIRE MAHAI

Out of the Ordinary Media
Bloomington, MN

Printed in the United States of America.

Library of Congress Control Number: 2018940570

Cover design by Carla Januska, SmartHive, http://smarthive.com

Out of the Ordinary Media

CONTENTS

ABOUT THIS BOOK

We live in a world where the pace of change and innovation is accelerating, even if we think it can't possibly go any faster. Where winners and losers find themselves spotlighted every day. Where the performance gaps continue to widen. Where the definition of competitor keeps morphing. We live in a time when those organizations capable of pivoting quickly to seize an opportunity stand in stark contrast to those lumbering along.

> "Boldness happens on the ground... our mission has to flow through the fingertips and brains of everyone on the ground. At every interaction point. You have to see it in action, not in slogans on coffee cups!"
>
> — President, Private University

We also live in a time of rising consumerism and rising customer experience expectations. We observe how big data, artificial intelligence, and digital innovations challenge, disrupt, and destroy traditional business models every day.

In other words, we live in a time of transformational change. Whatever your business or industry, wherever in the world you call home, you are affected. You feel the pressure to transform because it touches everyone: business-to-consumer, business-to-business, and business-to-business-to-consumer.

This book is about BOLD leaders in existing organizations – leaders who can see well beyond their current business, who see the potential available to them, and who both appreciate and relish the transformational challenge to win.

These leaders will not sit by and let their organizations be the next to fall. We have defined them as the "BOLD leaders essential for transformative change." They will invent the future starting from the position they are in today. They are leaders who view market dynamics opportunistically, who are excited by the challenges, who can imagine the possibilities and translate them to their colleagues, and who will assemble teams to drive the needed changes to successful conclusion. And then they will do it again.

Focusing on BOLD leaves out many other kinds of important leaders. For example, this is not a book about:

- Singular iconic figures that show up now and again: Steve Jobs, Henry Ford, and Walt Disney as past examples. Jeff Bezos, Warren Buffet, Elon Musk, Sergey Brin and Larry Page, Oprah Winfrey, Steven Spielberg, and Howard Schultz as current examples. These dynamic individuals are fun to read and learn about, but they are also never really the likely answer to MOST organizations needing to drive significant, meaningful change.

- Start-up entrepreneurs: Pure innovators are the ones stirring the pot and building new concepts, business models, and entities to take down or replace existing ones. Often by the time their new concept becomes successful, these entrepreneurs (or their investors) have brought in other managers and leaders to scale and develop the organization, and they move on to the next exciting idea. These figures are energizing. They are extremely important to the dynamics of a healthy marketplace, and they get heavily profiled in many books – but not here. In fact, some of the people who work with and for these start-up entrepreneurs are likely the BOLD leaders we are discussing. These are the people capable of taking the founder's original idea, then growing and morphing it well beyond anything first imagined, enrolling many of their colleagues along the way.

- Managing-the-current-state leaders: These great and indispensable leaders make sure the world works. They include operating leaders, marketing professionals, sales drivers, technology masters, and team leaders of all kinds. They bring their creativity, disciplines, and organizational skills to current challenges. They ensure that the power comes on, factories produce as they should, shipments move, marketing campaigns hit benchmarks, stores open, and customers are served. Here again, many great books by outstanding scholars of leadership already cover the characteristics of this broad array of leaders.

BOLD leaders, the kind that are discussed in this book, are rare. Rare, we have come to believe, because they must first be born with a set of characteristics (nature) that creates the potential for them to be BOLD. And then they also need the right opportunities to develop and refine their capacities (nurture) to drive transformative change. Thankfully you don't need – and likely couldn't handle – an organization full of these BOLD leaders. But you do need a strategic few, and you need them in those areas most critical for future success.

This "nature versus nurture" distinction is important for organizations that may look around and feel they lack the BOLD leadership they need. In the pages that follow, we define the profile. We then share the required – born with – characteristics that shape them. Finally, we highlight the behaviors you witness and themes that emerge when you have the opportunity to interview, study, and work with them.

So, while this book is *about* BOLD leaders, it is *written for all* leaders. Why? Likely, if you picked up or downloaded this book, you already know you're facing some big choices that require changes to the way you operate. If you fit the BOLD definition, you need to work with all kinds of effective leaders to accomplish big things. If you don't have the BOLD profile but need to drive important changes, understanding BOLD leaders – how to find, develop, support, and work with them – will benefit you and everyone around you. These concepts will prove useful to anyone leading an organization, particularly in times of great change.

If you see yourself as a BOLD leader when reading this book, we have some ideas to help you confirm your capabilities and focus your personal development to enhance your BOLD gifts. Keep reading here and visit AveusBOLD.com for additional ideas and tools.

For those of you who (let's assume!) exhibit wonderful, competent, and highly effective leadership, who build strong teams, who keep the operation running smoothly and on time, and who deliver results, yet don't possess the chemistry of the BOLD leaders we describe, we offer ideas and tools in the book and at AveusBOLD.com to:

- Find, work with, support and empower BOLD individuals within your organization so you can enjoy the benefit of their abilities, and

- Practice and develop some of these transformational leadership abilities within yourself.

This book reflects a deep understanding of who these folks are, and are not. Once we had identified them, we worked to understand them. We have confirmed our conclusions over the past couple of years, and this work continues.

People make things happen. That's not news. But what kinds of people, for which kinds of change?

BOLD leadership is messy. It is hard, and it isn't always pretty. The actions taken by BOLD leaders don't always work at first and may need adjusting. This process is hugely rewarding for those compelled to BOLD leadership. Yet at the same time, it can be lonely work. It requires a certain kind of individual.

BOLD character and orientation, we believe, cannot be taught. You either have it or you don't. People recognize the uniqueness of these leaders and crave the opportunity to be involved with their work, to be led by them when given an opportunity. As one person we interviewed said, "BOLD leaders, of the Aveus rubric, are a rare and wonderful thing. If you meet one, hang on to them!"

Throughout the book, the descriptions, themes, analyses of the characteristics, and quotes from our interviews, we aim to reveal the essence of these BOLD leaders. For those of you who are BOLD leaders, *BOLD* should read familiar and provide insights into what you feel and experience. For others, *BOLD* may help explain what you observe as you interact with these leaders.

It is important to note that this book comes out of the work we do at Aveus. We are not psychologists or organizational development specialists who study leadership and management as a profession. We have high regard for and have learned much from the psychologists and OD specialists with whom we have worked. Because we love change done well, we have also read, studied, and researched this topic independently and as a team.

Specifically, our interest in BOLD leaders comes directly out of our own hands-on experiences with large scale change efforts. We have done this work in corporate and entrepreneurial roles as well as consultants working side by side with clients. *We come to this subject as business minds,* first thinking about what needs to happen, and then how to make it happen.

Aveus is a boutique consultancy that, in shorthand, works with BOLD leaders to successfully solve big, messy challenges. Our mantra is "Make change rewarding." For nearly two decades, we have worked around the world and across industries, company sizes, types, public, private, and not-for-profit organizations. Our team has been filled with people who have deep experiences from their careers on the client side of the desk. As I often say, we know what it is like to live with a decision.

BOLD is a brief book intended to start conversations, ideally between leaders and especially inside organizations facing significant change challenges and desires. **And the book is only the beginning** of the resources we have created to nurture this conversation and aid in the identification and development of more BOLD leaders, fully capable of driving transformative change.

At the companion website AveusBOLD.com, you will find all kinds of additional information, including:

- A self-assessment that you can take, confidentially, and at no cost

- The methodology behind our research and creation of the BOLD assessment

- Ideas for business leaders who want to identify and develop BOLD leaders

- BOLD leader interviews from the past few years and new ones added regularly

- A private community where BOLD leaders (who assess as BOLD) can meet, share ideas, ask questions, and support and collaborate with one another

Enjoy!

BOLD UNCOVERED

Business upheaval is constant as shifts occur in markets and industries. Household names and Fortune 500 giants of yesteryear don't make the list today, having been consolidated, dwarfed by the rise of other companies, or disappeared entirely. Remember American Motors? Brown Shoe? Studebaker? Detroit Steel? Zenith Electronics? National Sugar Refining? At one time, all were at or near the top of their industries. Today if these companies spark a memory at all, it is one of nostalgia. They remain frozen in time but not present in the market today.

Meanwhile, companies like IBM and GE have stayed relevant by reinventing themselves in significant ways over the decades. They keep evolving and they continue to win over time, although not always the darlings of analysts in "real" time who are impatient for immediate realized results. While not at the tippy top of the Fortune 500 list (ranked #32 and #13, respectively in 2017), they remain powerhouses in the marketplace.

"I saw the galvanizing power of purpose."

— Senior Corporate Strategist, Global Services

Companies that dominate markets and corporate lists today have been around for a while, yet their industry leading growth has occurred in just the past 20 or so years. These companies clearly understand the importance of continual innovation and transformation. Take a look at the Fortune 500 Top 3 for 2017:

- Walmart: #1 on the list for five years running. The company has been around since the 1960s, but it took 30 years for Walmart to hit $100 billion in revenues. From there it has only continued to soar. Today, Walmart flirts with $500 billion in annual revenues.

- Berkshire Hathaway: Many people only know this company's founder, Warren Buffet. His little firm grew up and still resides in Omaha. Over time, it has made the steady climb to #2 at $234 billion in annual revenues.

- Apple: Some project Apple will be the first company to reach a $1 trillion (with a T) valuation. But as recently as 1997 when Steve Jobs returned to the company, Apple had only $7 billion in revenues and was losing money. Many thought Apple wouldn't survive Jobs' death in 2011. Today, under Tim Cook's leadership, Apple sits at #3 with $216 billion in very profitable revenues.

These top spots hop around a bit from year to year. But what companies at this level have in common is a clarity of purpose that extends beyond a mere company bio. Over years and decades, they take BOLD actions to refresh who they are and expand beyond the company of today.

A CONCLUSION BEFORE WE BEGIN: BOLD IS ESSENTIAL LEADERSHIP FOR TRANSFORMATIVE CHANGE

It says so right there on the book cover! At the end of our preparation for writing *BOLD*, and at the end of the book in "One Closing Thought," we conclude that a single question stands above all others in determining success or failure: Was a BOLD leader driving the needed changes?

Tons of books exist about leadership, learning to lead, and even driving change. They can be very useful. But when the topic is specifically about transformation, the data is clear: Over our careers (think 20-30-40 years), ***more change initiatives fail to some low or high degree than succeed***.

Experts provide much research on the reasons why change initiatives fail. In our consulting practice, we often see the factors that contribute to those failures in action. We also observe how certain tools, methods, and practices (ours and others!) can drive transformative change and ensure a higher level of success.

So there's hope! Still, until you do one thing, failure to some degree is way more likely than success.

That one thing? Place a BOLD leader at the helm of your initiative – and support them.

STUMBLING UPON BOLD

Our interest in this topic started in our own portfolio. Aveus was formed in the midst of the "dot com" bubble, so we were born into a transformative time for business. Starting with our earliest clients, we have had opportunities to see and support many interesting and challenging transformations, some of which worked far better than others.

Then in 2014, we had a "take stock" conversation about our first 15 years of existence. With a wide range of work under our belts as change consultants, we felt it important to reflect on our portfolio of work.

First, a little context: Our own "galvanizing purpose" has always been about making change rewarding. We help clients transform and achieve the business results they seek, and ideally more.

We asked ourselves how often we achieved and exceeded that purpose. Then we labeled the really successful clients and projects in our portfolio "fabulous work," which meant:

- The work exceeded the client's original expectations and goals.

- The transformation they undertook as a result of that work proved fundamental to their future, sustainable success.

- These clients grew stronger. They built internal capabilities that helped them continue to evolve and adapt.

We then used this "fabulous" lens to review results from roughly 140 clients over the 15-year period. Our work included large, mid-sized, and small clients. It spanned public and private companies, large non-profits, and national associations. It represented well-known names and those relatively unknown and new. It included companies headquartered in North America, Europe, and Asia across pretty much any industry you can name: healthcare, financial services, consumer goods, technology, medical and technical devices, professional services, and manufacturing.

Through our sorting process, we determined that much of our portfolio counted as good, solid, respectable work. Yet it didn't cross the "fabulous" threshold. Among those that did stand out, we found no commonality by industry, size, location, or type of problem.

Instead, an interesting insight emerged: 100% of the projects and organizations we agreed met our "fabulous" criteria had at their helm a clearly identified client leader with certain special characteristics. These were the very characteristics we began referring to as "BOLD"! We always understood the importance of having a strong client partner leading the work. But now, the requirements of those leaders had started coming into clearer focus. We had the realization that without the right leader to help ensure an organization fully engages, lasting, transformative change rarely emerges.

At the time, our definition of BOLD was somewhat squishy. In discussions, we kept circling some basic traits. But other than our impressions, we really had no solid way to describe these rare leaders. What we did know was that (not surprisingly), we wanted a future full of more fabulous clients! "Is it possible," we wondered, "to identify BOLD leaders within client organizations before work starts, so we can increase the chances of our clients achieving fabulous success?" Just like that, the conversation turned to: How do we define and identify BOLD leaders?

STUDYING BOLD

Our first idea was simple enough: Let's talk to some of them – see if we are on to something. See if we can tighten up our definition. Let's start with those we already know are the types of leaders we are thinking of. Then we can network our way to others based on referrals. We set a goal to talk with 100 BOLD leaders. We knew some would turn out to NOT be BOLD (by our early definition). But we knew we'd learn from those conversations, too. And so, we began. Today we are long past 100. The interviews are really energizing and the feedback from our willing subjects positive... so we keep going!

BOLD can be such an overused or exaggerated word that we have, at times, contemplated abandoning it. But based on our work and research, we believe it is precisely the right word. BOLD is the correct adjective for the rare leaders capable of driving significant, rewarding change for their organizations and customers – and shaping or reshaping the marketplace along the way.

Early in our process, one of the leaders we interviewed coined the phrase "Aveus (BOLD Leader) Rubric." In March of 2015, in a blog post titled "What is a BOLD leader?" we listed out some of our early thoughts trying to describe this BOLD leader, including:

BOLD leaders...

- Never settle for the status quo. There is always opportunity.

- Are unable to let a needed change go unaddressed.

- Will walk head-on into both positive and negative stress situations and conquer them.

- Know every decision or action is not immediately effective. New concepts take refinement and, in some cases, rounds of revisions to get to the right outcome.

- Stay to see the results of their work.

- Are positive – with moments of self-doubt that they push through.

- Make very (and we mean very) strategic decisions about where and how they invest.

- Rely on top talent and are choosy about who surrounds them.

- Are team-oriented. They are "we" people interested in success broadly, not selfishly.

- Anchor their decisions in what is right for the customer.

- Often feel lonely within their organizations. They are acutely aware of the change burden that others do not see or fully understand.

But we still didn't have a clear, crisp, testable definition or something we could use to screen and identify for BOLD characteristics. Now we believe we do and will share what we have learned in the chapters ahead.

VALIDATING BOLD

By the time we had reached 100 interviews, we had the qualitative validation we were looking for. (Some might say our thousands of notes were quantitative!) But our task was far from complete. All we knew was there existed a segment of leaders who are relatively rare, and who are essential for significant, transformational change.

What we needed was a testable methodology for identifying them. So we enlisted the help of a friend of Aveus, Ali Shirvani-Mahdavi, MIT PhD, who has lots of field experience of his own to draw upon.

Ali did extensive research, working with us to design a testing approach. After many rounds of debate, research, and review, we know today we have the simple tools an organization needs to identify BOLD leaders. *For those really interested, a more complete description of this methodology can be found at AveusBOLD.com.*

Over time and through this research, we have been able to simplify and clarify the defining characteristics of BOLD leaders.

In "BOLD Defined," we lay out the characteristics that must be present for someone to be considered a BOLD leader under the Aveus definition.

The chapters "Believe," "Open," "Learn," and "Do" that follow are a collection of quick-read essays that bring the BOLD leader to life, based on themes heard repeatedly in our interviews.

In "BOLD: A C-suite Conversation" we have a "top of the shop" conversation with CEOs, board members, and other C-suite executives who, while quite talented, are not themselves BOLD under this rubric. These executives find themselves in key positions to quash or force BOLD leaders out, thereby losing the benefits of their contributions. OR, they can unlock the potential of the BOLD leaders working for them and benefit from their ability to deliver important, positive, future-oriented changes for the organization.

"BOLD Leadership Unlocked" speaks directly to BOLD leaders, people who know they are BOLD and assess as BOLD. This section can help these leaders recognize and start developing, stretching, and applying their talents.

We leave you with "One Closing Thought," which sums up why we believe this conversation is needed in any organization facing significant challenges externally and internally.

It is time to define BOLD leadership.

Meet BOLD leader Ben Freakley, Lieutenant General (Ret), Senior Advisor to The McCain Institute for International Leadership and former Eagle Scout.

"I've thought about this a lot; these rare leaders," he said.

- First, they are self-disciplined. You cannot lead others if you are not disciplined yourself.

- They are values-based.

- The essence of BOLD leadership is trust. If people trust you, they will do their very best for you.

- BOLD leaders are confident, not reckless, with an incredible work ethic.

- They are optimists. They believe in what they are going to do.

Ben reflected, "I've known a few defeatists. People want to be around people that believe we can get it done. I've never understood what a leader gets out of being grumpy all day!"

Read more of my conversation with Ben at http://aveusbold.com/blog/

BOLD DEFINED

You've guessed it: **BOLD is an acronym**! Through our research, we have refined our list of the behaviors these rare leaders demonstrate consistently. Grounded in a set of core characteristics, BOLD behaviors merge in various ways to create BOLD leaders – those rare leaders able to drive *successful* transformative change. Later in the book we'll talk about why that word "successful" is so important, and not at all common, in transformational situations.

BOLD stands for the behaviors these leaders exhibit.

B – Believe

O – Open

L – Learn

D – Do

BOLD is also a definition.

One day I called someone who had been referred to me as a BOLD leader. I started with a question we ask all our interview candidates: "Do you see yourself as a BOLD leader? And if so, what does that mean to you?" The interviewee pointed me to the dictionary and said, "Originally when you invited me to this interview, I thought no. But then I looked up the word. If 'beyond the usual limits of conventional thought or action; imaginative' fits your definition, then yes."

> *"Beyond the usual limits of conventional thought or action; imaginative."*
>
> *—Entrepreneur and Chief Sales Officer*

We looked up the word, too. You will see many definitions of the adjective "BOLD" if you consult your dictionary of choice. Here's a short sample from www.dictionary.com:

- not hesitating or fearful in the face of actual or possible danger or rebuff; courageous and daring:

  ◦ *a bold hero*

- not hesitating to break the rules of propriety; forward; impudent:

  ◦ *He apologized for being so bold as to speak to the emperor.*

- necessitating courage and daring; challenging:

  ◦ *a bold adventure*

- beyond the usual limits of conventional thought or action; imaginative:

- *Einstein was a bold mathematician; a difficult problem needing a bold answer.*

- striking or conspicuous to the eye; flashy; showy:

  - *a bold pattern*

BOLD is a word that has evolved greatly over time. In today's world, it often gets associated with personality (and not always in the most positive way). Take the synonyms "brazen," "forward," or "presumptuous": "How bold of her to assume she was invited!" or "He is so bold, everything he does is over the top." BOLD gets overused and frequently exaggerated for dramatic effect: "To boldly go where no man has gone before," to quote Captain Kirk in the opening sequence of any *Star Trek* adventure.

At times, we have contemplated abandoning the word for these reasons. We have played with other options. But all words have their strengths and drawbacks. In the end, we know from our work, interviews, and research that BOLD is precisely the right adjective to describe the rare change leaders we profile here. We focused on the fourth dictionary.com definition listed above, as it most closely describes the characteristic necessary for matching the transformational change challenges we observe. Beyond that dictionary definition, however, there's an important organizational context and risk orientation to consider as well.

Taking all these definitions and this context into consideration, and sorting through hundreds of pages of interview notes, we have concluded that the BOLD leader we have in mind can be defined as follows:

OUR DEFINITION

A BOLD leader is someone who thinks and acts beyond the existing organizational limits, is imaginative, and is willing to take risks to get rewarding results.

Many of the leaders we interview are referred to us by someone who named them a BOLD leader. These leaders often come into the conversation reluctant, even a bit shy about accepting the idea that they exhibit this type of leadership. In fact, this reticence has proven to be an early distinguishing (and endearing!) characteristic of BOLD leaders. They are not at all brash, presumptive, or self-oriented. They are all about results, imagination, risk taking and action. They do what they do as much for others as for themselves. In testing this definition, we have found it precise enough that individuals can quickly scan their memory banks and successfully identify candidates.

WHY IS DEFINING, UNDERSTANDING, AND FINDING THE BOLD LEADER SO IMPORTANT?

If your organization faces a major challenge or you have more opportunity than you can handle today, you need a BOLD leader (or several) to get you successfully to the other side. It is really that simple.

Like "BOLD" and "leader," the words "transform," "transformative," and "transformational" get thrown around a lot. For our purposes, here's another dictionary definition for the scope and kind of transformation we mean:

- a change in the form, structure, capabilities, conditions, even a change to the character and substance of the organization.

Put differently, transformation is about the future state and performance of the organization appearing differently than the current state (status quo) across multiple dimensions. Going back to our Aveus BOLD rubric, transformational situations involve a clear intent to move the organization beyond existing limits. They also require the infusion of creative – perhaps even formerly untried, discarded, or feared – concepts into the fabric of the organization. Only then can the potential and strengths of the organization evolve dramatically beyond its current state.

WHY MATCHING BOLD LEADERS TO TRANSFORMATIVE CHANGE IS SO IMPORTANT

Aveus has been in the change business for a long time now. But change results can fail or fall flat for a variety of reasons. When we see breakdowns in strategic implementation of some big, well thought out initiative, they occur first and foremost because the organization failed to appoint and support the right change leader – a BOLD leader. Let's underline that last point. You need to find them AND support them.

When the support doesn't follow, an organization's results fall short of desired or required benchmarks. The organization fails to effectively evolve. Too often, the strategic direction itself and investments are attacked as wrong-headed. Failures fall hardest on those who tried but found themselves ill-equipped for the task at hand. In the worst cases, good people, and loyal team members become scapegoats for poor decisions that put them in an unwinnable situation.

On the flip side, success always involves the leadership of those with the right makeup (and a backbone of steel). These leaders see what others can't. They pursue their goals with tenacity. They know talent and how to leverage effective teams. And they command the support of the organization, pushing forward until they land the winning results.

A NATURE VERSUS NURTURE DEBATE

As we started this work, we had that age-old debate about whether BOLD leader skills and capabilities could be taught and trained. Can BOLD managers and leaders be made? Or must they be born with core ingredients that create the opportunity for them to be BOLD?

Reading much of the literature in the field of leadership, one comes to an overwhelming conclusion that leadership skills can be taught. And we believe that. We can, and we bet you can, look at the array of leaders around you – people on your team, friends and colleagues, customers, and business acquaintances – and identify many examples of leaders who have grown more effective and successful through personal development, training, and work experiences. Many critical skills can be nurtured as leaders mature.

However, when it comes to BOLD leaders truly capable of navigating complex transformational challenges, we have concluded they are born with a set of distinct characteristics. Nature gives these individuals a leg up in their potential to become BOLD. Certainly, their capabilities benefit from education and experience as well.

Knowing BOLD leaders are born and then developed – not made – we wanted to learn more. How do they see themselves? What drives their work ethic and their people orientation? What informs the philosophies that inspire them to take on daunting, often long-term and lonely assignments, successfully bringing others along with them?

In the next chapter, we share how these BOLD leaders show up in the world. We believe when you read about them, you will be able to recognize a few that you've met across your career. First, we'll unpack the "born with and developed" characteristics that make them so unique.

SO, WHAT ARE THE "BORN WITH" CHARACTERISTICS THAT DISTINGUISH BOLD LEADERS?

Through our study and research, we whittled a very long list down to just four standout characteristics. *(More information about these characteristics and assessing for them can be found at AveusBOLD.com.)* Life and work exert influence, but at their core these leaders possess four defining traits:

- **Curiosity**
- **Confidence**
- **Empathy**
- **Trust (being both trustworthy and trusting!)**

Over the past few years of research and conversations, four characteristics consistently stand out. BOLD leaders are those who are motivated by their innate **curiosity** to tackle new and intractable problems. They are **confident** in their ability to find the solution that works for both their customers and organizations. They are **empathetic** to their customers and to the strengths and weaknesses of their colleagues. They work hard to be the **trusted** leader the organization will follow.

In conversations with BOLD leaders, they affirm that they've "always been this way." No one had to teach them to be curious. They couldn't help but be that way. They were always confident, whether overtly or quietly. Empathy is instinctive – they don't have to think about it. And they are a trusted and trusting bunch, careful with their trust but oriented to demonstrate it, earn it, and give it.

Let's dig deeper to better understand the importance of these characteristics in BOLD leadership.

Curiosity

Curiosity is an always-present, unquenched desire to look beyond what exists today and to acquire new knowledge and sensory experiences that motivate and guide next actions. Curiosity is the foundation of the BOLD leader's exploratory behavior. There are always new ideas, approaches, and avenues to explore. While curiosity without purpose can devolve into fickleness (one interest today, another tomorrow), BOLD leaders demonstrate a disciplined application to a particular challenge. That's why the first thing to look for when selecting a leader to tackle a transformational situation is someone who clearly demonstrates their skill in using curiosity to drive ideas and actions. These leaders have a track record of creative results that have taken them, their teams, and their organizations to new places and levels of performance.

> *"It's always most interesting when it is still a little foggy out the window but starting to clear."*
>
> — CEO and President, Senior Care

Confidence

Confidence can be enhanced – or sadly, destroyed – under certain circumstances. Methods to increase confidence can definitely be learned. In a BOLD leader, intrinsic confidence has a high bar. Beyond a trained and practiced skill, BOLD leaders begin with a deep assurance in their inherent abilities to find and successfully implement new, effective solutions. Quite simply, they have an unwavering belief in themselves. Certainly, they have momentary doubts. But they are just that: momentary.

> *"Walls are just part of the day job that you have to break through."*
>
> — *CEO and President, Social Services Non-Profit*

The BOLD leaders we know carry their confidence with grace and generosity, rather than arrogance. As a result, they build confidence in others as well. Because these leaders are also "other-oriented" and recognize they can't do everything themselves, they have the ability to assemble a highly capable, confident team that won't quit until the desired result is achieved.

Empathy

Empathy starts with the ability to identify with the feelings, thoughts, or attitudes of others. Empathy discussions in leader and management circles are very popular these days, and for good reason. Empathy is the starting point for understanding and solving issues – or for introducing new options to customers, employees, and other stakeholder groups. With the rise of the customer and employee experience disciplines and the growing popularity of design thinking, new methods of developing empathy are coming onto the scene. BOLD leaders, born with a natural gift for empathy, are a step ahead in applying it to transformation situations where many stakeholder interests collide. Empathy requires deep work to go beyond traditional research insights and feedback from a target population. BOLD leaders start with empathy and infuse it into their work as they proceed. They do this by gathering information and experiences so they can truly walk in the shoes of the people impacted by the planned transformational changes they are designing and implementing.

> *"First, I come from a place of total empathy for the consumer or end user.... I start there."*
>
> — *Retail Executive and Entrepreneur*

Trust

Trust is a loaded concept. It grows through a continuous series of conscious and unconscious assessments (both positive and negative) we make about a person or a situation. Do the actions of this person consistently build trust or diminish it? Does this situation feel stable or precarious? Often just bringing up the concept of trust in a business context can be stressful. But why? There's a lot to unpack to truly get underneath what increases or decreases trust within an organization. BOLD leaders have a natural ability to create, extend, and assess trust in others.

> *"I read people and then dial my use of emotions up or down to fit the situation as needed, in order to lead, follow, and develop trust...."*
>
> — Senior Industry Partner, Investment Banking

Do a search and you can find many trust models, including ours. They all attempt to get underneath the concept of trust to something actionable. Over the years, we have refined how we talk about trust. We break it down into three elements: capability, reliability, and motive.

- Capability: Does an individual have the requisite skills for the assigned task? Example: I love my husband, but I'd never trust him to do my taxes. He literally is not capable of that request. (And neither am I!) As we discussed earlier, the success of any transformation initiative hinges on the leader to be BOLD. Here, that means "capable."

- Reliability: Does the person consistently do what they say they'll do? If they miss their own deadlines, fail to inform and update constituents as changes occur, or exclude others, their credibility sinks. And that's a problem. BOLD leaders in transformational efforts know that the intention and intended outcomes are clear, but the path is not. Remember, they are in a discovery process. They build trust by informing and engaging others, and by sharing the learnings (good and bad) along the way. They are reliable.

- Motive: Does the person put decisions that benefit themselves ahead of decisions that benefit others? If so, they are self-oriented. You've likely seen a self-oriented executive who cares more about how they appear, how they benefit, and/or how their staff serves them. They will never be a BOLD leader. The motives of BOLD leaders consistently orient toward better outcomes for others. They build trust in large part because they are other-oriented more than they are self-oriented. In other words, they first consider the impact of their decisions and actions on others before they think about themselves. Their motives inspire others.

Let's move on and see how curiosity, confidence, empathy, and trust show up in these BOLD leaders.

BOLD LEADERSHIP IN ACTION

Like all effective leaders and managers, BOLD leaders make use of many skills and abilities. Yet the core skills of the rare BOLD leader (who they are, how they think, how they develop and hone their skills, and how they act and interact with others) come from an intermixing of the *curiosity, confidence, empathy* and *trust* they are born with and strengthen over time.

"Bold leaders of the Aveus rubric are a rare and wonderful thing. If you meet one, hang on to them!"

— North American President, Global Services

In the next chapters, you will find a collection of essays emanating from our interviews that bring these BOLD leaders to life. As you read, we feel confident you will recognize some of these behaviors you've seen in certain people that stand out in your own life and your own experiences.

BOLD reflects the rare leaders we have met who:

- **B = Believe** These true *believers* understand the power of purpose. They act, learn, shape, and test their way forward. They hold out for nothing less than rewarding results.

- **O = Open** Passionate about discovery, better ideas, and new information, these leaders approach everything with an *open* mindset. They demonstrate this behavior in how they evaluate talent, assemble teams, and share success.

- **L = Learn** Curiosity and empathy are exceptionally strong in BOLD leaders and guide the ways these *learners* discover new, creative ways to move forward. This willingness to learn also informs their confidence by reinforcing the fact that they can find answers in the unknown.

- **D = Do** From our experience, transformations rarely fail for lack of desire or ideas. They fail because the levels of urgency or discipline required for successful execution don't last long enough to achieve the intended outcome.

Transformational initiatives require *doers* at the helm who know how to find their way through uncharted territory, bringing people and organizations with them. They don't quit until they get great stuff done!

In the "Believe," "Open," "Learn," and "Do" chapters that follow, we provide a series of short essays to bring a sense of these leaders to life. They are not superheroes. They make mistakes and have to adjust and make another run at their intended outcomes. Transformations or major change initiatives are typically long and arduous. The secret to success isn't completely knowable at the beginning, so at times the actions and intended results don't always make sense to people around the BOLD leader. But they remain steely focused on what they intend to achieve.

BOLD leaders have this core – and rare – ability to set a vision, enroll others, pursue progress doggedly, and never quit until they reach the outcome or event that they've been pursuing.

We recognize that these characteristics and behaviors may all sound familiar. Even obvious.

Don't all leaders do these things?

Well, no, they don't.

As we said in the first chapter, many company managers and leaders are great at other kinds of situations, but they fail in the tornado of a major change challenge. The BOLD leaders we describe actually get stronger in these situations and increase their performance over time.

We believe for most leaders and managers in companies today, these BOLD individuals – rare as they are – will be familiar to you. If you have ever worked with a BOLD leader, you likely cherish that relationship.

If you apply the BOLD definition, you will know almost instinctively who fits and who doesn't. The short essays that follow will hopefully help you quickly relate and say, "I've seen [insert name of BOLD leader] do that!" Or perhaps you will recognize, "I do that and want to do more of it!" Or as an executive needing to drive a major change, you may think, "I need to find someone like that!"

Let's meet some BOLD leaders.

Meet BOLD leader Glen Gunderson, President and CEO of the YMCA of the Greater Twin Cities.

Because Glen so clearly pays attention to those around him, sees their abilities, and has the capacity to decide what fits, I asked him what has stood out in the BOLD leaders he has learned from.

- An indomitable spirit.

- Impatience with politics.

- Focus: an intensity that is clear in how they use their time.

- "All their levers and actions are FORWARD!"

- Thinking about the "potential" with far less emphasis on the practical.

- "While younger (or less capable) leaders cow-tow to others, BOLD leaders don't.

And so, we got to a fundamental question: "Are BOLD leaders born or made?" Glen observed, "I do think the wiring is something a BOLD leader is born with; the switches, however, can be altered and developed."

Read more of my conversation with Glen at http://aveusbold.com/blog/

BELIEVE

BOLD leaders demonstrate common behaviors grounded in their personal *curiosity, confidence, empathy, and trust.* They carry and share a clear vision and sense of purpose at all times. They value exploration when answers are unclear. They view short-term obstacles and lessons from failures as opportunities to expand possibilities and discover new routes to success. These leaders are laser-focused on their goals, they **believe** in their personal and team abilities to achieve them, and they never retreat even when everything doesn't go according to plan.

Believers are:

1. Unsatisfied with the status quo
2. Visionary and playing the long game
3. Customer oriented
4. Growth oriented
5. Innovative and entrepreneurial in ways that transform
6. Investment oriented and willing to place smart bets on strategic priorities

How do these attributes show up in BOLD leaders? Let's find out starting with the status quo, since believers are happy to leave it behind.

UNSATISFIED WITH THE STATUS QUO

What is the status quo anyway? Dictionary.com calls it "the current state or condition."

Much of what we read says human beings don't like change. If true, that implies that most people are satisfied living, working and thriving within the status quo. It doesn't occur to these individuals to test the current boundaries much – if at all. They like the current state. It works for them, at least to some level. They lack the confidence to believe that what *could be* can be better than what already exists. Even if they aren't particularly happy, they fear loss if/when the current state or conditions change. The status quo keeps most people within the bounds of what feels comfortable, even if they are curious about what sits outside that comfort zone. They accept the givens of the status quo. And this is good. We need these positive, talented status quo types to keep the world running well. They just aren't the folks to drive transformations. You need BOLD leaders for that.

> *"I start with the premise that the status quo is never sufficient."*
>
> — *President and CEO, Foundation*

This human aversion to change may also explain why BOLD leaders are so rare. The **believers** group have little patience for the status quo. They brim with confidence that they can find the next, better answer. Their curiosity drives them to pursue innovations, improvements, and wholesale changes. Status quo limitations, such as rules, walls, methods, and expectations, are meant to be tested, redefined, expanded, or completely eliminated and replaced with something suited to the next generation of growth and opportunity.

When interviewing our candidate BOLD leaders, the ones that stood out as true believers used phrases like, "I start with the premise that the status quo is never sufficient" and "I tend to look beyond the usual limits of conventional thought or action."

None of the BOLD leaders who scored high on confidence and curiosity in our survey see the status quo as a place to hang out.

If you have a major transformation or opportunity in front of you that requires something much different than what you have or know today, you need leadership capable of thinking and acting beyond your current organizational limits. They need to believe a better answer is achievable.

VISIONARY AND PLAYING THE LONG GAME

We can't start a conversation about **believing** without addressing the reluctance of many leaders to have the vision and long game conversation. They find it to be many things: too abstract, too sentimental, or personally unnecessary. If they don't need it, neither do others (or so they think). Or they mistakenly believe the vision to be self-evident ("Of course everyone understands it. Why would we need to discuss it?").

BOLD leaders believe in a vision. They carry it with them and share it in both their words and actions.

> *"The vision is so clear to me, I am living the vision in my mind as if it already exists."*
>
> — *Innovation Executive, Healthcare*

As Presidential candidate George H.W. Bush so painfully learned once he uttered, "Oh... the vision thing," vision matters – a lot. In 1987, *TIME Magazine* called out the then Vice President's response to a colleague's suggestion to search within himself (rather than ask others) to determine where he wanted to take the country. In a moment of exasperation (captured, quoted in *TIME*, and then repeated over and over again), Bush dismissed the advice, saying, "Oh... the vision thing." While he ultimately won the election, his lack of a clear direction for his presidency dogged him every day of his single term in office. He could never shake the criticism that he had no clear vision for where he wanted to take the country. What he stood for and **believed** in was unclear at the start. And it remained unclear throughout his term, inspiring criticism to this day.

BOLD leaders do not dismiss vision as fanciful or unnecessary. They know that if they want to make significant change and to have a meaningful impact, a vision and a course of action are essential. BOLD leaders see beyond the organization of today and imagine what could be. They set targets, then learn, test, and engage teams along the path to achieve them.

Not only do they carefully craft a vision, they share their belief in the direction consistently and regularly. It must be clear enough – not perfect, but compelling – so people can attach to it, so they feel excited about the prospects it implies, and so they are willing to engage in the difficult work to move toward it. Most often, these leaders know they are playing the long game. Between today and success, there will be plenty of static, doubts, and challenges. Noise will surface. They know they'll be tested, criticized, and sometimes attacked or ridiculed along the way.

"I'm not concerned with the noise because I'm playing the long game," said Jay Z. This is how a BOLD leader regards their vision. It is the belief in a clear and compelling vision that keeps them and their teams on track.

One of the BOLD leaders we interviewed described a stark difference between leading in companies he started and grew, and leading a large, long-standing corporate organization. In startup situations, especially founder-led organizations, he said, people sign up for you, the inventor leader. The vision and the person are one. In large organizations that have evolved through many chapters and turns of management, people need to know the vision. They need to *believe* in the future being proposed. They need to hear a clear direction. Only then will they feel willing to venture out, test current norms, and offer creative solutions. That's when believing turns into action and the long game for the organization comes to life.

CUSTOMER ORIENTATION

Visions are most powerful when they speak from the outside in. In other words, they consider the beneficiaries of your business – your customers. As Peter Drucker said so long ago, "The purpose of business is to create and keep a customer."

BOLD leaders *believe* in the power of starting with their customers. That outside orientation helps them enroll their employees and stakeholders into their vision and action plans.

Here's a quiz question for you: Are "customer orientation" and "customer experience" the same thing? Many people use them interchangeably. But should they?

We at Aveus would say no. The two are related, but distinctly different concepts. In our interviews, we discovered BOLD leaders understand them as two important, but separate ideas, and **believe** in both.

> *"You have to start with the customers and build an understanding of what they are trying to do. Then solve for that. And you have to have the flexibility to be able to see, design, and execute on these new requirements quickly."*
>
> — *CEO, Global Technology Company*

Customer experience (CX), as you will see in the "Do" section, is about actions and perceptions: how customers feel as they engage with you in the moment and over time. Customer experience shows, from a customer perspective, whether the decisions you make and the actions you take prove effective, drive distinction, improve results, and win hearts and minds.

By contrast, we consider customer orientation an aspect of culture. Customer orientation sets a firm foundation for all the decisions and actions made by an organization. When you hear BOLD leaders discussing being customer "oriented," "-driven," or "-centric," they are mostly speaking from a philosophical or value perspective about putting the customer at the heart of everything they do.

Many organizations have some version of customer orientation as one of their stated corporate values. It is an indicator to all employees that "carrying the customer around with you" and valuing this orientation in colleagues and others is important. Centricity is framed in the eye of the beholder. That's a good thing: Cultures built on valuing the customer or orienting around the customer lay the foundation for great customer experiences.

Because they are **believers** at heart, BOLD leaders use customer orientation as the foundation for every decision and action they take to drive strategy, growth, and performance, as well as improvements to the customer experience.

Customer orientation serves as a framework for all a BOLD leader's decisions and actions. Married with a customer experience discipline, this framework can help BOLD leaders understand how their decisions guide others and deliver the results they need.

GROWTH ORIENTATION

How much growth is enough? I've never been a proponent of growth for growth's sake, and lots of business consultants will tell you that "size is not a strategy." However, the ability to grow or scale is important. If you're passionate about transformative ideas, you need to grow fast enough to not get run over.

> *"I figure out my biggest impact, get other people involved and let it grow from there."*
>
> *— Co-founder and Entrepreneur*

In business, we most often discuss growth only in tangible – financial or operating – terms: revenue, market share, profitability, numbers of customers, employees, cubic feet or square miles of production capability, and more.

These are all legitimate ways to quantify and measure the growth of an organization. However, they miss the kind of growth that must come first, according to the BOLD leaders we have met. In addition to the "how much" question, we need to ask, "what kind" of growth orientation can drive transformation.

If you want to set the pace in your industry, growth must be part of the strategy. If you want to change the world with a concept that doesn't exist today, you have to both create and scale it. If your organization needs to transform, some level of growth is also required. In all cases, BOLD leaders start with *human growth* to achieve any of the other types. It might be their own development. Or that of a small team. Eventually it reaches the talent and capabilities across an entire organization. But growth always starts with people.

Human growth measured in skills and abilities leads to organizational capability and growth that can be realized and measured in all those tangible ways listed above (pace-setting, transformation, innovation). BOLD leaders **believe** in and develop their own abilities. More importantly, they select, develop, and push teams to grow so they continuously expand their capability, grow (literally and figuratively!) together, and drive exponentially bigger ideas.

BOLD leaders recognize that when people stretch their minds and expand their efforts, they gain confidence. They know approaching challenges with a sense of curiosity develops new solutions, expands capabilities, and creates growth.

A famous quote by Ronald Reagan neatly sums up the "behavior + purpose + results = growth orientation" we view as BOLD leadership: "There are no great limits to growth because there are no limits of human intelligence, imagination, and wonder."

INNOVATIVE AND ENTREPRENEURIAL IN WAYS THAT TRANSFORM

Casually throw out the word "BOLD," or use it in conversation, and a few current age standard business examples pop up: "Steve Jobs!" "Elon Musk!" "Howard Schultz!" People think immediately of innovators, and what I would call "extreme" or "iconic" entrepreneurs. These examples certainly match some BOLD definitions, but these aren't the BOLD leaders we refer to in this book. They are definitely innovative. All very entrepreneurial. And singular. They march to their own drum. These individuals are forces of nature.

When I hear, "We need more Steve Jobs!" (and surprisingly that idea comes up a lot), I laugh. There will only ever be one Steve Jobs. As with other great icons and larger-than-life figures (Albert Einstein, Stephen Hawking, Marie Curie, Nelson Mandela, to name a few) nobody else can fill those shoes.

"Innovation and agility are critical to our ability to navigate this shifting market, and sometimes a business our size feels like a wolverine in a cage."

— President and CEO, Healthcare Management

Trying to copy or clone any of these legends will not make someone BOLD. And I want to believe these icons wouldn't appreciate or value this copy-cat thinking. Learn from them, yes. But trying to be one of them, anyone other than yourself, won't make you BOLD. It won't make you innovative or entrepreneurial.

Nor will waiting or searching for the next "Steve Jobs" help an organization out of a transformation crisis. These icons don't step into existing organizations to drive change. They innovate, create and reshape markets from their own seat, in roles or companies of their own making.

What will help struggling companies change and adapt are the men and women who share with those iconic figures the characteristics of curiosity and confidence. Because embedded in those traits is the willingness to fail. Try again. Fail again. Learn each time. Albert Einstein is often quoted as saying, "A person who never made a mistake never tried anything new."

Innovation, by definition, requires new and creative thinking. It takes curiosity, especially when early attempts don't work or don't succeed at the level you need them to. And it takes confidence that you can – and will! – find your way to a better answer. The BOLD transformational leaders we meet know these innovative ideas must come from many corners of their organizations.

They are skilled at finding, encouraging, testing, and scaling ideas generated by the innovative spark they unleash in others, and not necessarily from their own brilliant ideas.

Most companies don't have the luxury of starting over or blowing up their current business to create a new one. They have customers. E mployees. Investors or shareholders. Legacy and obligations. The leaders that effectively drive these organizations to new places walk that fine line between not enough change and too much change. Their innovations must create momentum, open up creativity in others, and set a pace that the organization can absorb successfully.

"Entrepreneurial" is another term that gets thrown around a lot in organizations trying to shed the bureaucracy, lethargy, and weight of processes built up over time. The dictionary definition of entrepreneur is "a person who starts a business alone" or "someone who organizes, manages, and assumes the risks of a business or enterprise."

The definition emphasizes a person – like the iconic figures above. "Entrepreneurial" within an existing business setting makes for a slightly – but importantly – different concept.

Entrepreneurial leaders (sometimes referred to as "intrapreneurs") inside existing companies are as creative and skilled at navigating the culture and politics as they are at unleashing new ideas. They know they can only succeed with the help, endorsement, and actions of others. So they use their confidence and curiosity to build interest and support for new ideas. They use it to establish tolerance for the mistakes and failures that will naturally occur as new ideas get tested and refined. They use their entrepreneurial skills as much for creating an environment for success as for hatching the specific idea itself.

Believers in the potential of the organization – the leaders who think and act beyond existing organizational limits – are imaginative. They are willing to take risks to get rewarding results. These are the leaders who create new opportunities for their organizations.

INVESTMENT-ORIENTED AND WILLING TO PLACE SMART BETS ON STRATEGIC PRIORITIES

If you're involved in a business of any size, you probably face a budgeting process at least once a year. Often, especially if the company is not meeting its goals, this exercise turns into difficult choices about where to cut and where to spend, and how to make wise investment choices. In the worst-led cases, company executives wimp out on these decisions. They budget the status quo plus or minus. They fail to set clear direction. They let an unruly set of "priorities" fracture allocations. They refuse or fail to choose between talent, functions, capabilities, or asset investments based on some clear sense of what performance improvement requires. They don't, as Charlie Munger of Berkshire Hathaway said, "find a few intelligent things to do." Instead, they do stupid, cowardly things such as make across-the-board cuts. They adopt an "everyone has to take a haircut" mentality. That may sound harsh, but I've witnessed this failure to lead more times than I care to remember. The resulting fallout puts the organization in a weaker position to compete and succeed. All because the executive team was either unable or unwilling to make smart investments and stop non-productive activities.

> *"When you only have some information, you need to size up the risk and make a call. If we are wrong, nobody dies – we gather information and we move forward. You have to be confident in your ability to figure it out and nimble enough to make adjustments. You cannot wait until you have the right answer."*
>
> — *President and COO, Private Company*

At the other end of the spectrum, you may see companies that have money to invest, but they lack clarity about either their strategy or what actions and investments will most contribute to success. Rather than working to figure out the answers and make the tough choices, they fund a bunch of ideas a little bit. "Let a thousand poppies bloom," one of my former colleagues used to say. The only problem with that idea is none of these barely funded ideas develop enough to contribute or succeed at a meaningful level. The concepts that start to show promise starve for resources while other pet projects and/or non-contributing activities eat up the remainder of the available investment dollars.

BOLD leaders **believe** that making these hard investment choices is critical. They want to make these choices. They lead their teams through the process of evaluating, qualifying and advocating for the most important investments. They have enough confidence in their selections to stop activities no longer needed or contributing to the direction of the organization. Remember, these leaders are not attached to the status quo, so the idea of spending or investing resources for historical or nostalgic reasons will not pass muster with them.

Even – or especially – if funds are limited, BOLD leaders will do the work to understand the critical requirements needed to move the company strategically and effectively forward. Once clear, they will pour funding into the areas that need and deserve significant investments while making selective cuts in other areas. Painful at times, yes, but necessary.

This focus and tight investment orientation is perhaps most critical in situations where current performance and limited resources put a strain on the organization.

> "Get started quickly. Pick some early key change initiatives for wins. Don't wait for the complete plan to be developed."
>
> — CEO, Media Company

BOLD transformational leaders also manage their investment choices smartly. They will not throw money lavishly at projects. They have an investment strategy in mind but make initial small bets. They test, fail, learn, adjust, and place additional small, smart bets. In this way, they move their strategic developments forward while keeping solid control on the spending. This critical, eyes-wide-open style of investing helps the BOLD leader and team make smart and informed decisions when the direction is clear. At the same time, they keep an eye out for the best options for success to prove themselves in the marketplace.

BOLD leaders we have spoken with talk about the emotional and political challenges they face when taking on the status quo to change the investing focus and spending curve of an organization. It is easy to have conceptual discussions about investing wisely. But BOLD leaders know when these negotiations start, they represent only the first of many battles to come. Soon after, as early investments may and often do struggle, the pressures on them and on their team to perform will be intense. Another round of battling skeptics begins. Standing up to these naysayers requires true **belief** in the new direction, along with the courage to make tough decisions and the ability to follow through on the strategy.

BOLD leaders rely on their confidence and curiosity to guide them through their investment choices, through their learning process and actions, through negotiations, and on to advance the organization to the next set of decisions.

In summary, the *believer* abilities of a BOLD leader start with a deep curiosity that never lets them settle until they've found a better answer. Add to that curiosity a high level of confidence and you have a leader who can handle the challenges and criticisms of others who can't see or imagine what they can. Curiosity and confidence combine in the way *believers* craft a vision; structure small, disciplined tests; and learn and manage discoveries along the way.

Empathy is the grounding *believers* need to place themselves in the shoes of those affected by their actions during a transformation. BOLD leaders instinctively validate their ideas and critical information with these groups, including customers, employees, peers and bosses, and stakeholders of all stripes.

I occasionally catch eyes rolling when empathy comes up in conversations. Some people misunderstand it as too likely to put them in the position of just "doing what others want." But capitulation has nothing to do with empathy. And none of the BOLD leaders we have met even hinted at that idea. Empathy allows *believers* to take the uncertainty others feel in a situation, the "grey outside the window" as one BOLD interviewee described, and from it create meaningful tests and clarify inputs and decisions, so they can better chart the path ahead.

Finally, trust – both being trusted and sharing trust – is what allows *believers* to spread their optimism, their vision for future success. Having a solid trust platform allows BOLD leaders to develop others into *believers* willing to put their energy and skills into the work of making things happen.

Meet BOLD leader Brad Hewitt, CE O of Thrivent Financial.

"Bold leaders create stress." That conclusion came after a fast hour of "Brad-isms" as he dubbed them, and I have to say, this was one fun conversation.

"We're a slow growth company. This is a 50-year strategy, not 5-year strategy. I have to keep reminding my board and others that we are building for the long term."

Brad says he took on the CEO role to "do something, rather than be something."

"Stress is good. Comfort is what gets you in trouble!"

Read more of my conversation with Brad at http://aveusbold.com/blog/

OPEN

Given their *curiosity* and *empathy* orientation and their *trust-building* and *trustworthy* nature, BOLD leaders are naturally very **open** people. They know they can and will find answers, and they are *confident* in their ability to manage the dynamics of a transparent flow of information. They easily share and connect with those around them but show care when selecting those who ultimately become their trusted confidants. Being **open** does not mean being indecisive or passive. Quite the opposite: These leaders take in information to expand possibilities. Only then are they fully ready to carry the mantle of the decision responsibility.

In practice, these **open** individuals:

1. Start from a place of empathy
2. Are happy, positive people
3. Think "we," not "I"
4. Actively listen and seek input with confidence that they can isolate the most valuable information
5. Surround themselves with trusted colleagues
6. Communicate often with a wide set of constituents to grow support and engagement

Let's consider each of these perspectives individually, beginning with empathy, since empathy is the starting point for these *open* leaders.

START FROM A PLACE OF EMPATHY

Empathy and sympathy often get confused. Sometimes people use the words interchangeably. But they aren't the same. Understanding the difference is important if you want to appreciate how BOLD leaders start their change initiatives.

Sympathy is the harmony of feelings with another, often compassion. You might hear someone say, "I'm sympathetic to your situation or plight." But sympathy doesn't necessitate absorbing that harmony of feeling or using it to inform a decision or action. It is an expression of emotional connection. Nice, but not all that helpful to innovative change.

> *"If we design from the consumer's perspective and create products that consumers love – all the other stakeholders will eventually come on board."*
>
> *— CEO, Medical Technology*

Empathy is more nuanced and, therefore, harder to explain. It is the psychological identification with or vicarious experiencing of the feelings, thoughts, or attitudes of another. Ideally, through testing, observations, or other techniques, you experience what they experience and can translate what you learn into your decisions and actions. When you empathize with others, you understand at an intimate level what the challenge feels like to them and how it affects them. With this knowledge and appreciation – with empathy! – you start any change initiative from a more productive place.

Design thinking has become popular over the past few decades, led in large part by Ideo founder David M. Kelley. As Kelley explains, "The main tenet of design thinking is empathy for the people you're trying to design for. Leadership is exactly the same thing – building empathy for the people that you're entrusted to help." Design thinking is popular because, frankly, it works better for solving problems than some of the more traditional engineering and process approaches. Not that these traditional approaches are bad or obsolete. They can still be very useful. But it is easier to drive better design decisions and outcomes when you start with a customer-centered approach, with empathy, and with a process that constantly validates your efforts with the human experience.

BOLD leaders are born with the natural ability to empathize. They are *open* to the needs and ideas of others, and so they develop empathy instinctively. With time and the right experiences, they learn to hone this talent and apply it to all their work as they lead transformational change.

If you have identified BOLD leaders with natural empathy skills, develop them! Let them teach others and demonstrate their methods. If you have candidate leaders who need to learn and apply empathy, invest in their skill-building. You will see better results.

HAPPY, POSITIVE PEOPLE

A dozen or so interviews into our BOLD leader project, we were surprised to see an unexpected pattern emerge: These interviews were fun!

Why? Because we were interviewing **open**, positive, happy people. In retrospect, it was a bit of a "duh" moment when we made this discovery. Of course, these people would be happy and positive: They are wired to drive constructive change.

> *"Have fun. Make money. And change the world."*
>
> — *President, Innovation and Operations, Aircraft Manufacturer*

So why were we surprised? Why didn't we look for this perspective from the beginning? I think it comes down to two things:

- We started by talking to leaders we knew were capable of getting things done. But we hadn't yet locked in on the characteristics that make some stand out from the rest. "Positive orientation" wasn't a criterion for our interviews.

- We live in a world that excuses poor and boorish "leader"

behavior if the result is good enough. So we went into this effort thinking we might see a range of styles. We never thought specifically about positive, negative, happy or not.

However, once we started interviewing, it became immediately clear you can't have great outcomes if only the leader is rewarded – or if the outcome is mostly about the individual. We all know effective leaders who aren't at all pleasant. They get things done. But the news or the story is mostly about them. (And they often leave unintended negative consequences in their wake.) Although they get results, these weren't the leaders we wanted to understand. By the end of our research, it was clear that these kinds of leaders would fail our BOLD test on the most basic requirements.

You can't bring people with you if you aren't trustworthy, trusting, and empathetic. And, as we discovered, to be those things, it is virtually impossible to be anything but positive and happy. Fortunately, as Harvard trained, self-described "happiness researcher" Shawn Achor says, "Positivity is such a high predictor of success rates."

A leader whom we interviewed early on said, "I don't see any room in the Aveus rubric for negative, backward looking people. And you have to be intellectually honest, so not blind optimism either."

THINK "WE," NOT "I"

Trust is a bedrock characteristic for a leader who thinks in terms of *we*, not *I*. These leaders have a natural ability to build trust and to be trustworthy.

When you hear leaders speak of accomplishments, what pronouns do they use? "*I* did x." "*I* discovered y." "*I* am happy to announce..."

Or do they talk in "we" terms? "*We* had a spectacular year." "*We* came together and did the impossible." "*We* know it is within our reach..."

> "*Surround yourself with a talented team that is low on ego and high on achievement, and performance will soar.*"
>
> — President and CEO, Integrated Health System

The BOLD leaders we know attribute success to the people around them. They speak of their own accomplishments, but only or typically after prodding. Their own glory isn't the first thing on their minds. Instead, they focus on trust in and the wins of their people.

For many years at Aveus, we have used a trust model (see also "BOLD Defined") that assesses trust along three dimensions: capability, reliability, and motive. BOLD leaders find ways to build capability, reliability and positive motive in their teams. And they don't concern themselves much with who gets credit.

For many leaders and managers, if they question the capability of a person or a team, rather than deal directly with the deficiency, the temptation is often to think, "I need to do it myself" or "I need to find someone who can do this job right." It becomes about me.

If reliability is in question, the same things happen. Teams fall apart if some members are allowed to be unreliable. "I can't trust a team that can't deliver what they promise." Everyone gets hurt and it becomes again about me, the manager, to solve.

Motive is the hardest to really assess and is usually the quickest to be judged. If I am suspicious of your motive, as your manager, I must be ever watchful. It's about me.

BOLD leaders understand and resist this temptation to be the one to solve everything. They know they can't solve everything. And they are quick to deal with trust detractors. They can accomplish great things with others because they are **open**. They recruit, support, and develop individuals and teams who are capable, reliable and trustworthy. They are generous – and fussy – about who makes it into the "we" circle of accomplishment.

ACTIVELY LISTEN AND SEEK INPUT WITH CONFIDENCE, FILTERING IN THE MOST VALUABLE

Executives often find themselves in the "answer box." Because of their position, people around them and reporting to them expect them to have all the answers, certainly the "right" answers to any question posed. Unfortunately, nobody has all the right answers all the time. We have our opinions, our experience, and likely vast amounts of data and information at our disposal, but we certainly don't have all the answers.

And yet some leaders, perhaps full of good intention, think, speak and act as if they alone do have all the right answers. Often when they pose a question, they do so rhetorically, moving into answer mode before those around can respond or share a perspective. They cut people off, even as they invite input. As leadership guru Stephen Covey once famously noted, "Most people do not listen with the intent to understand; they listen with the intent to reply."

> *"[BOLD leaders] listen super hard. They listen neutrally. They listen for what is underneath."*
>
> *— North American President, Global Services Company*

Some leaders live with the operating assumption that their job as leader is to present all the critical answers. They surrender to the unrealistic expectation that others assume they are all-knowing.

These assumptions and expectations don't affect BOLD leaders, at least not those we have studied who drive creative and successful transformations.

In fact, the BOLD leaders we know understand they don't have all the answers. Nor can they be cajoled into behaving like they do. Lin Manuel Miranda, of *Hamilton* fame, spoke about the need to listen intently, listening to understand. He said, "I think a lot about trying to meet the moment as honestly as possible, because I don't pretend to have any answers. In fact, I have infinitely more questions than answers." When BOLD leaders ask a question, they are really asking to learn. They actively seek answers from others. They listen closely. They are **open** to alternative ideas and challenges to their own thinking.

BOLD leaders know better answers come when many minds and experiences inform a situation. Their strong confidence helps them in this pursuit of interesting and better answers. Their curiosity helps them actively listen. They develop a keen ability to sort through the information they gather, filtering out the unnecessary, distracting, pat, obviously self-serving, or uninformed ideas – while filtering in new information and ideas that can end up being more valuable.

Rather than falling into the "answer box" alone, they model **openness**. They give credit to others for advancing and improving ideas and actions. Their egos neither need nor want all the credit and adulation.

BOLD leaders take positions and make the critical decisions as they lead the organization forward with the collective support of extended and engaged teams. At Aveus, we call these scenarios "positive conspiracies." When BOLD leaders enter "telling and selling" mode as all executives do, especially in critical moments, they do so with confidence. Confidence in the direction they've set, confidence in the actions they propose, and confidence in the belief and support of their co-conspirators, who can help them enroll and inspire others.

SURROUND YOURSELF WITH TRUSTED COLLEAGUES WHO ARE SELECTIVELY CHOSEN

There's immense power behind the phrase, "I'd go into a foxhole with him/her." A foxhole is a place of shelter or offense on a battlefield where you hunker down with someone into whose hands you've effectively placed your life (and vice versa). The decisions you and your foxhole buddies make determine whether you live to fight another day. The military throws men and women together so they can learn through their training and on the field experience exactly what this obligation means.

> *"Responsible leaders, when they climb out of a difficult situation, are even more resilient, more capable, more competent than they were before the challenge."*
>
> — *Senior Policy Advisor on Leadership*

How often in your career have you felt about a colleague or set of colleagues, "I'd go into a foxhole with them"? A guess: that feeling, if you've ever thought about it and felt it, is rare.

Some businesses are literally in the business of life and death. Examples include healthcare, medical device, and critical instrumentation components that make it possible for planes, trains, and automobiles to move millions of people safely around the world each day. While most organizations don't work within life-or-death situations, they do contribute to – or detract from – the well-being of their customers, employees, communities, and other businesses.

Whether or not you realize it, you often place your livelihood, career, and personal reputation in someone else's hands. You do the same with the success or failure of the organization. Think about that for a moment. Sure, you may like and enjoy the company of many of your colleagues. But are you willing to rely on them making or breaking your work opportunities? Can they lead the organization through a challenging time successfully? Are you really willing to put your career, your compensation, your reputation – your future – fully in their hands?

BOLD leaders, focused on successful transformation and expanded opportunities for their organizations, decide very carefully whom they surround themselves with for exactly this reason. They know that in complex change situations, they will make business, organizational, career and opportunity decisions on behalf of customers, employees, shareholders, and other stakeholders. They are **open** to the challenge and responsible to those they serve. They need others around them who understand and can navigate the demands of serving these competing masters.

If you've ever experienced major organizational change without the right leader in place who can make the tough choices about team members and competencies, you know how frightening change can be. Everything falters without the right leader and the right team to weather those challenging times.

When you are that BOLD leader charged with driving the transformational change, each person you bring into the foxhole with you represents a critical decision – perhaps your most critical decisions. They are putting their trust and confidence in you. They are electing to follow you into the unknown, excited for what you can discover together.

You select the people who can inform your direction, support challenging ideas and questions, guide and inspire others, and remain steadfast battle after battle, phase after phase, strengthened by each new adventure. The people you choose make or break your ability to advance.

Choose well and the success of your organization will have no limits.

COMMUNICATE OFTEN, WITH A WIDE SET OF CONSTITUENTS TO GROW SUPPORT AND ENGAGEMENT

"Communicate" is a funny word. It is one we all know. In business, we toss it around without much thought. That is, unless your functional expertise is in communications. Then you deeply appreciate how easily communications gets taken for granted and how challenging it is to do well.

"Communicate" is a verb. According to dictionary.com, it specifically means: "Impart knowledge. To inform. To make known. To share thoughts, feelings, and information (easily!). To be connected." "Communication" is a noun. It is the act or process of having successfully communicated.

> *"Be clear, and people will want to follow. Connection and communication are key to making change happen."*
>
> — *Former CEO, Healthcare Entrepreneur*

There are a few other dictionary descriptions, but the above are enough to make a point. Communication is active, not passive. It implies a closed loop: What gets shared is understood or fully received.

And yet, in business settings you often hear leaders lament, "Well, I told them" or "How many times do I have to tell them?" They feel frustrated that whatever they shared was not received, understood, or accepted. In other words, these leaders did not truly fulfill their responsibility to communicate.

Whose fault is the miscommunication? That of the receivers? Maybe. They might not be listening. They might not like what they are hearing, and therefore they might reject it. They may simply not have been ready to absorb whatever was shared.

Or does the fault lie with the person who initiated the communication? More than likely, they don't actually communicate. They "tell."

"Telling" is also a verb. It is also active. But it is about proclamation. Announcing. Not waiting to confirm whether or not you've been understood. Many executives are great at pronouncements, but not so great at closing the loop of understanding.

There may be many reasons for this breakdown. Perhaps some of the information is too confidential to share. In an effort to be open, the leader generalizes. But along the way the real meaning gets lost or buried in "safe" language. Talk about a way to start rumors! In these cases, it is often better not to share anything. In other situations, a leader may not recognize they have full background while the receivers don't. The leaders may come to the conversation having discussed, studied, and weighed the pros and cons of whatever they are pronouncing over the course of several months. Meanwhile, their audiences – employees or customers or other stakeholders – are hearing the message for the first time. Without the necessary background, questions arise that the "teller" is unprepared to answer and frustrated to hear.

BOLD leaders are communicators in the truest sense of the word. Communication is one of their most important skills and tools. Remember that they are **open** by nature, which means they instinctively understand the need to both share and receive information. They provide information that is relevant and compelling to the people they need to influence. And they listen for information and questions, so they can evaluate whether they have been understood.

> *"There is power in stories. We all need to become better story tellers. Learn to create an image of outcomes people can start to believe in."*
> *— President, Health Plan*

When they know they've been understood clearly, they can move on to the next actions and communications. If confusion exists, they let the discussion inform the work ahead so they can bring along key constituents.

In rapidly changing situations, information management can often feel like a moving target. It is a balancing act to avoid getting ahead of yourself and communicating too much when the precise details will likely change. Yet you need to share enough so your teams and your broader employee base, or perhaps your customers and business partners, can understand and start processing the implications for themselves.

"Communications" sounds neat. In reality, it is messy. That mess is particularly pronounced in changing environments. Acceptance of occasional missteps forms part of the BOLD leader set of strengths. This realistic approach frees them from the guilt of feeling they failed to communicate. Instead, they process the input to better understand what should happen next. Communication gaps arise for many reasons. Perhaps you simply don't have all the answers yet. Or maybe decisions and actions haven't been fully understood by the broader audience. Or perhaps certain implications aren't able to be shared right away.

The only way BOLD leaders can communicate effectively through changing dynamics is by *opening* themselves up to hearing back from their constituents. Remember, these leaders are high on empathy and trust building, so they develop their communications skills in ways that let the receivers know they've been heard. With each communication, BOLD leaders take the next steps to clarify, share more, and provide more helpful examples. They also tap key influencers who can infuse the conversation with more ideas, energy and enthusiasm than one person can possibly deliver.

Dozens of change models exist. In one way or another, each points to communicating in a way that builds understanding, desire, and excitement to help with and participate in the changes underway. BOLD leaders know this rule of communication, and they work as hard at communicating as anything else they do.

In summary, the *open* nature of a BOLD leader pulls on all four core characteristics of curiosity, confidence, empathy, and trust. BOLD leaders have told us the risks are lower when they trust people, share, and open up to others rather than trying to hold and control all the variables.

Empathy and curiosity come together in a spirit of *openness* to the information and ideas that others possess. BOLD leaders know they need to expand and improve the decisions and actions that will make the transformation successful, and they can only do that by *opening* up to others.

We were struck by the willingness of BOLD leaders we didn't know well or at all to participate in our interview. I asked many of them why they answered the request. Their answers, pretty universally, added up to, "Why not!?" They appreciated that we were clear about the rules of engagement, and they felt confident in their ability to manage the discussion. Just like they manage their way through any situation. They said the idea sounded interesting. Many added that it sounded, and turned out to be, fun. (There goes that curiosity popping up again!)

Meet BOLD leader MayKao Hang, President and CEO of the Amherst Wilder Foundation.

"I start with the premise that the status quo is never sufficient." That is a classic BOLD leader comment. BOLD leaders, by definition, aren't satisfied with whatever exists today. There is always more opportunity for improvement and impact.

"Think of it as 'stealth' organizing" came up when MayKao was talking about her approach to uniting people, building capabilities and making needed organizational changes: community organizing inside your operation.

For years I've dubbed this idea: build a positive conspiracy.

You don't need everyone to start, but you do need a cadre of willing people with a shared vision and common approach to start influencing and help bring along others. MayKao calls this a "critical mass of early adopters."

Read more of my conversation with MayKao at http://aveusbold.com/blog/

LEARN

Learners quest for more and new information and skill-building they can apply to the transformation challenges they and their teams face. The *learner* orientation stems from a BOLD leader's *curiosity*, as well as the *empathy* they have for their customers, team members, and other stakeholders. As we have already observed, for a BOLD leader every experience is an opportunity to learn. New information or data is something to celebrate. Unanswered questions are exciting. Both good and disappointing results alike offer constructive and helpful insights into next steps. And failure signals an opportunity for further experience and learning.

Learners are driven by:

1. Their innate curiosity
2. Questions that help them connect the dots between what exists today and what is possible
3. Decisions and actions that drive momentum and lessons
4. Failures!
5. Data!
6. Possibilities, not problems!

Learning can often be academic or abstract – interesting, but not applicable. BOLD leaders seek lessons they can apply to the task at hand and build upon as they move forward.

INNATE CURIOSITY

Of the four essential BOLD leader characteristics that emerged from our work, none is more required than curiosity. And on our nature/nurture scale, we rated curiosity at about 90% nature. You must be born with it. Those lucky enough to have it can further develop and enhance it through experiences and education.However, our work showed that if a person isn't naturally curious, training and experience will never develop this characteristic in them sufficiently to reach BOLD status.

> *"I am always wanting to learn. Some people are very happy where they are. Not me."*
>
> — *President, Global Manufacturing*

Think of musical prodigies, who from an early age show extraordinary gifts of artistry, sometimes playing an instrument on first sight without instruction. These children grow into masters over years of study, and with practice. Other children can learn the music and can play the instrument, but they never achieve that elite ability. Trust me, after years of piano and violin lessons, I was proficient (well, good enough not to get kicked out of orchestra). But seriously, no one wants to hear me play either the piano or violin! Though I wished it, I would never be great no matter how much I practiced and studied.

Curiosity flows in a similar way. Leaders with this natural ability can seamlessly move from one environment to another, one challenge to another. They use their curiosity to kick-start their **learning,** and they never feel fully satisfied that they've learned enough. Their curiosity also allows them to be open to more than one "right" answer. While others may spend time wondering or pondering alternatives, the curious simply dive in and try it!

"No" or "We can't" or "That won't work" are words and phrases the curious routinely ignore. They move right into the mode of "What have we tried? What did we learn? Let's give this a try and see what happens." Because these leaders are not capricious and understand their actions have consequences for others (remember they are empathetic, too!), their curiosity causes them to study, prepare, and identify alternatives in case the trying leads to an ineffective outcome.

USE QUESTIONS TO CONNECT THE DOTS BETWEEN WHAT EXISTS TODAY AND WHAT IS POSSIBLE

A curious mind asks a lot of questions. We have probably all experienced that precocious two-year-old that has a never-ending supply of "Why?" questions stored up for any answer an adult may try to provide.

At two you're seeing a child with an unformed curiosity about everything. "Unformed," meaning it is more about the asker than the answer.

Combine that same level of intense curiosity with a healthy dose of empathy, experience, and maturity, and you get a BOLD leader asking, reframing, and asking again, a series of questions that can be used to connect the dots between ideas and solutions, between today and what is possible.

> "[BOLD leaders] are the ones demonstrating managerial courage, the ones in the room asking the profound question that others were afraid to ask. By their questions and actions, they change the dynamics of the conversation."
>
> — President, Financial Services

Many BOLD leaders in our interviews talked about searching for new inputs, or new ways to see and understand intractable problems. They pursue new inputs, view existing data through a different lens, and invite diverse perspectives into the mix so they can see something others might miss. In a quest to find new or better or more impactful answers, questions become an essential tool.

But, you may be thinking, how do BOLD leaders know which questions to ask? Well, the simple answer we have heard from many is that it doesn't really matter. Just start asking. Like that two-year-old, ask and ask again. Unlike the two-year old, listen. REALLY LISTEN to the responses.

Study the evidence that supports the answers and ask the next set of questions. And if you really don't know where to start, two of the best questions in your arsenal are the most obvious ones: "What?" and "Why?"

BOLD leaders are *learners*. One of the key ways they learn is by exploring through questions. They use the responses, the feedback, and any new information they gather to reshape and refine their thinking and to adjust their next set of questions. They use this approach to broaden possibilities when the answers seem too simplistic, too limiting, or stuck in the status quo. They also use questions to narrow in on the right set of facts or ideas that will help them and their team make transformative decisions.

Questions help shape and strengthen the original idea, guide implementation, validate what has been learned, highlight what needs adjusting, and inform what to try in the next round of experimentation or the next phase of implementation.

Learning happens through questions that help connect the dots.

DECISIONS AND ACTIONS THAT DRIVE MOMENTUM AND LESSONS

Early in our efforts to reach out and talk with successful executives and entrepreneurs we believed fit the BOLD profile, we had a notion they would behave and lead differently in times of positive and negative stress. What we mostly found was the opposite.

The stories they shared revealed that in good times and bad, they kept their focus on momentum and learning their way forward. The situation matters for sure. But on a from-to continuum, current state only anchors the "from" end and a new, desired position sets the "to" target at the other end. Momentum is what happens in the middle.

> *"To create confidence around change, don't punish failure but celebrate learnings from those teachable moments."*
>
> —*Innovation Executive*

Not to be cavalier, but when a company finds itself in a downward spiral (an example of a negative-stress situation), the decisions and actions required to change that trajectory are very different from the decisions and actions needed to harness and steer rapid growth and ascension (an example of a positive-stress situation).

Still, the decisions made and actions taken in both cases revolve around moving the organization in a desired direction. According to the BOLD leaders we interviewed, these actions include: halting decline, changing course, jump-starting growth in a sleepy organization, adding adjacent opportunities through innovation or acquisition, and steering and shaping accelerating growth.

BOLD leaders also ask questions and establish challenges to reset and clarify the work ahead. Two examples from our interviews:

- "Bring me solution options that do not require brick and mortar." (from the CEO of a real estate intensive organization)

- *"What* are we trying to do and *why* is this important? I wouldn't say I'm a great strategist, but what I am good at is asking the right questions and getting the right people – key participants and key sponsors – to be really clear about what we are about to do."

In these situations, as one CEO told us and several other executives affirmed, "BOLD leaders create stress."

BOLD leaders create stress with their questions as well as the decisions they make and actions they implement to move from status quo to a desired state. They use stress to create momentum. That is a good thing. Without some intentional unrest, very little helpful *learning* takes place, and positive momentum ceases.

BOLD leaders tap into the situation that already exists with their questions, so they can *learn* what decisions will motivate a change in behavior, and so they can focus and prioritize the actions that will have the most impact. BOLD leaders make decisions and actions that they know will generate discomfort, create urgency, and guide new behaviors. Their actions are tangible – in other words, they take on certain tasks and create outcomes that move the organization forward. Yet their behaviors are also symbolic: They demonstrate new expectations, model intended norms, and break through cultural walls they believe stand in the way of progress.

Not all an organization's decisions and actions are golden, perfectly defined or executed. Particularly in change situations, you can be sure that many fall short! Some are flaming failures. These are the exact situations in which you need the BOLD leader the most. BOLD leaders set the course, understand the risks, take interest in *learning* what works along the way, step up to make the tough calls, and weather adversity.

They do so by continually making informed decisions, acting in ways that capitalize on what they've *learned*, and driving momentum to power the organization through the needed change.

FAILURES!

We left the last essay about decisions and actions that drive momentum on a point about failures. We can't talk about BOLD or leadership or driving successful transformations without considering failures. They happen. If you sincerely believe you have never experienced failure, you are definitely not BOLD – or you've done a good job of hiding your skills! You might be great at your job, but you cannot drive meaningful change without failures – ideally failures you initiate through managed tests so you can *learn* from the outcomes.

> *"You have to focus and stick with it. We are persistent. Anything hard and worth it doesn't land the first time, or the second... you just keep going until you find the right path. We really don't get discouraged."*
>
> *— President and CEO, Integrated Health Network*

Miles Davis wasn't a genius musician because he followed the score someone else had written. He took music to new places, precisely because he didn't follow an existing path. Did he hit notes that were sometimes hard to hear? Yes. Did every improvisation work? No. Did he see them as failures? Absolutely not. He said, "Do not fear mistakes. There are none." In his view, a mistake was evidence of something tried. From it, new ideas were born.

Failures happen. What matters is understanding why they happened and what you choose to do with them.

You've likely heard innovators and geniuses (and those who study them) utter a version of the phrase, "fail fast and cheap." Still, in business, we often struggle with failure. School, at least Western education, teaches us there's always a right answer. If we work and study hard enough, we will find it. In reality, there are often multiple viable answers. Waiting for the "right" one is actually a more insidious form of failure. This notion of fast-cheap-and-often failure resonates with BOLD leaders because they also act as stewards of their organizations. That means as they *learn* and drive significant changes, they have to strike a balance: They can't bet the future of the organization in the process nor can they wait for the perfect answer to be revealed.

> "I see leaders freeze all the time because they don't have the answer. Often there is not a clear answer. We have to teach people to 'learn out loud.'"
>
> — President and COO, Private Company

Let's be clear: Failure born of sloppy work, poor planning, playing fast and loose with someone else's money, or risking other people's reputations or livelihoods for some ignored risks is not BOLD. It is reckless and selfish. Nor does it tend to drive the change you want (unless you're incredibly lucky). Sadly, if you read or listen to the business news on any given day, these kinds of failures do happen. A lot. But these failures are rarely the handiwork of a BOLD leader. More often, a BOLD leader is the one who winds up putting the pieces back together in the aftermath of this type of failure!

Failures that inform are BOLD. They are controlled, meaning limited in time, cost, or other risk dimensions (in other words: fast and cheap). They open up new or improved ideas and clarify decisions and actions for the next time around. They advance knowledge. As such, they are essential. They should be embraced. They are, in the spirit of Miles Davis, one more thing tried so new ideas can be born.

DATA!

We live in the age of big data. Staggeringly big data. The information that surrounds us and our businesses is vast, and growing rapidly. These examples will change and grow long before this is published – but to make a point:

- Hours of video uploaded to YouTube every minute: 300 – and growing!

- Monthly Facebook users: 2 billion – and growing!

- Tweets per second: 6,000 – and growing!

- Pages of structured and unstructured data in Watson: 300 million – and growing!

- Worldwide Google searches: 5 billion per day or 1.3 trillion per year – and growing!

- Ecommerce revenue: Estimated to reach $2 trillion in 2017 and $4 trillion by 2020

> *"If the data changes, make a new decision. Get smart people in a room – who aren't panicking – and confront the data – honestly. Then as the leader you make a call and move on."*
>
> — *President and CEO, Technology Company*

The list of examples goes on and on. And millions of somebodies around the world are analyzing every bit of underlying data. Guess what that creates? Right. More data!

What does this have to do with BOLD leaders? Well, a lot. Without a disciplined approach to data, more of it is not very helpful. We have seen it in many client and prospect organizations: In their quest to drive change, they collect volumes of data, often with little awareness of which data matters, why, and what to do with it. Collecting it, storing, it, securing it, and stirring around in it becomes an overwhelming task. The old phrase "boiling the ocean" comes to mind as people and machines collect and crunch more data without clear intended applications.

BOLD leaders know they are not experts in everything. They know when they need assistance with key functions, including intelligent data application. BOLD leaders find a valuable analyst with whom they can partner – someone who can look beyond the raw stats and mounds of unstructured data to find the useful nuggets and gems. Of course, this partner must share their purpose. The analyst must know how to uncover the right questions and clarify guideposts. It takes a curious brain and a dose of empathy to probe in ways that clear away millions and billions of units of data to find the handful of insights or themes relevant to those valuable questions.

These cogent, relevant outputs become the fodder for testing and theorizing – for *learning* – and to guide next actions. By testing and refining the questions and evidence-based hypotheses, BOLD leaders help their organizations step away from pursuing masses of data to *learn* the way forward based on focused insights. Using these insights, they can make better decisions more quickly and take precise actions against targeted outcomes.

Sir Arthur Conan Doyle (or rather his famous character Sherlock Holmes) had a lot to say about evidence and data. For example, in "A Scandal in Bohemia," Holmes opines, "It is a capital mistake to theorize before one has data." Holmes was also a master at selecting which data to study. BOLD leaders do the same for their organizations. If not great analysts themselves, they know enough to surround themselves with talented team members who can perform these functions for or with them.

POSSIBILITIES, NOT PROBLEMS!

As businesspeople, we undergo heavy conditioning to be problem solvers. We run at challenges. We "put our heads down" and we "muscle through" a crisis.

- We think in problems.
- We talk in problem statements.
- We work problems.
- We celebrate problems solved.

In many corporate cultures, the true heroes are those that – you guessed it – put out fires and solve immediate or regularly recurring problems. They get so busy fighting fires, they never have an opportunity to figure out how to avoid fires in the first place.

> "I love a roadblock. I am an optimist; I know I can figure a way around and I pull people in beside me who have the same orientation, who will challenge me and may have better ideas. And I like to have a 'steady Eddy' on the team, too, to keep us grounded."
>
> — Insurance Executive

With our heads-down determination and all our good intentions, we make things work. On the one hand, this is great. We need problem-solvers to keep the organization running and fulfilling its mission.

But with our heads down and short-term urgency always at the door, we sometimes miss the big picture. We miss what's coming. We miss opportunities to poke our heads up and look around. We fail to give ourselves time to learn new tricks, to experiment, and to invent.

BOLD leaders drive a lot of activity, so you might think of them in this same problem-solving vein. But that would be a mistake. BOLD leaders think in possibilities, not problems!

The BOLD leaders we interviewed think far beyond the immediate situation. They keep their eye on the horizon – or beyond. They orient everything they and their teams do toward new possibilities. They *learn* their way to new and inventive answers.

As they move forward, of course they run into many obstacles. But their orientation remains clear: They use all their natural-born and hard-won curiosity, confidence, empathy and trust to make forward progress every day.

- A wall is in the way? Tear it down.

- A roadblock pops up? Invent a way around it.

- Something you tried didn't work? *Learn* from it, then try a modification or something else. Whatever the outcome, capture the *learning*. And then try again and again.

- Or, find an alternative path!

On the journey to an exciting transformative outcome, setbacks occur. Surrender? Never. As Friedrich Nietzsche said more than 100 years ago, "That which does not kill us makes us stronger!"

BOLD leaders are willing to initiate and claim small wins, *learn* from what works and doesn't, and move forward through experimentation and critical evaluations. They frame choices as possibilities, not problems. That positive approach leads them to new and interesting options. They move, assess, and try again until they *learn* their way to the goal they were after.

Occasionally in our interview conversations, BOLD leaders would reflect with amusement and awe on the twists and turns they navigated with their teams along the way. Some even admitted they may have never started had they known the full scale of what they had set out to accomplish. But by thinking in possibilities, and putting one foot in front of the other, they *learned* their way to success.

In summary, the *learners* are a lot about curiosity – of course! But knowing something doesn't mean much in the world of transformation unless you can do something with it. That knowledge requires the confidence to look around the corner, take in information, and use empathy to shape the direction you will take.

Learning your way through a transformation requires testing ideas with discipline and sorting out the winning ideas from among many options. Virtually 100% of the time, learning through transformation means experiencing failures. And even small failures that correct with minor adjustments can be hard to process and move through any business setting. When a BOLD leader hits a big obstacle or a wall, it takes confidence and trust to keep going and find the path to the other side.

So, when we talk about the *learner* dimensions of the BOLD leader, remember: Think active, not passive – and think beyond the theoretical to applied learning.

Meet BOLD leader Sara Gavin, President of Weber Shandwick North America.

"I always walk in with the orientation, 'I'm going to learn.' I'm always being open – seeing, listening, experiencing the work in action. Great leaders make me do better work. They keep pushing our standards."

This comment prompted me to ask where Sara finds these leaders. "I'm very fortunate that I see many in my own organization and certainly among our clients. People that inspire me and others. Leaders are in lots of places around us. And, with the internet, I sometimes just try to open my mind and randomly jump into a TE D Talk, an MPR interview, some long-form articles, or social media. There are endless opportunities to learn if you're hungry enough."

Read more of my conversation with Sara at http://aveusbold.com/blog/

DO

The BOLD leader definition fully comes to life in doing. *Doers* tap the combination of *curiosity, confidence, empathy,* and *trust* to imagine the future, pursue creative ideas, enroll others, and generally just get things done! They show confidence in their approach to moving transformational changes forward. They enroll entire organizations in renewed success. You will notice their decisions and actions founded on some basic values. These leaders are happy to test and be tested. They will shape, learn, refine, inform, and pursue next steps until the vision is successfully completed.

Doers create transformative changes through:

1. Strategic direction
2. Action orientation
3. Customer experience
4. Course adjustment
5. Resourcefulness
6. Perseverance

Let's understand how these behaviors are reflected when *Doers* set to work getting things done.

STRATEGIC DIRECTION

At Aveus, we have a long-standing saying that strategy without action is just an idea. As "strategy" consultants, we meet plenty of competitor firms that stop at delivering the idea. And we meet prospective clients in love with their ideas and strategies, but they lack the tools and guidance to bring them to life. This market reality is one of the reasons we focus so much of our energy on execution in our practice – and why we look for BOLD leaders in our client relationships. BOLD leaders never stop at the idea and are all about making strategies real. They are *doers*.Strategy starts with setting the right direction. BOLD leaders know this is critical to the effort of arriving at worthy answers.

> *"The decisions we will make will decide the future of the company for years to come. Sure, you can fail. But I find this responsibility and the possibilities really exciting. You need energy and enthusiasm to move in a direction."*
>
> — *President, Global Manufacturing Company*

Direction-setting requires a proper framing of the starting point, as well as a clear picture of what success looks like. This up-front work provides the foundation for pursuing the dream, goal, or vision. Direction-setting also takes confidence in your ability to find the right answers – and to recognize them when they appear! Direction-setting requires curiosity to avoid settling for the most obvious or available ideas while pushing yourself and your organization to think bigger and more creatively about what is possible. Finally, the clarity that the BOLD leader creates encourages and motivates others to stay the course when the going gets difficult.

In the process of setting the strategy, empathy shapes and sharpens the questions that need answers and serves as a guide to the most important inputs. BOLD leaders continue to test lessons collected through implementation with empathy for their customers, colleagues, and other stakeholders. Trust is also required for enrolling others in strategic ideas and winning their willingness to assist. BOLD leaders *do* the work and sweat the details to create a strategic direction that not only looks good or sounds good, but IS good because it can be implemented to great success!

Strategy-in-action tests everyone's resolve. It takes the firm hand and mind of a BOLD leader to filter in helpful information and filter out distractions and diversions. It also requires a kind of doggedness to stay on the established path and, in many cases, certainly the biggest cases, to persevere through some dark days and long nights. Confidence in the strategy, in themselves, and in their teams allows the BOLD leader to do what it takes to reach success. BOLD leaders accomplish impactful changes where others might well abandon ship or settle for less.

"Strategy" gets thrown around a lot. *Doers* know the power of a well-formulated strategy extends beyond an idea. It comes from small moves made every day, and from the galvanizing energy for making big things happen.

ACTION ORIENTATION

I had the opportunity to meet Zig Ziglar (American author, salesman, and motivational speaker) one day, early in my career. He was speaking at a conference for the company I worked for, and I was his "host." It was my job to make sure he was ready to go on stage at the appropriate time and "wow" us. As I recall, he was very generous and gracious (unlike a couple other guest speakers that day) and really didn't need much help from me. He was ready. He had done this a few thousand times. He was a natural storyteller. And he had a central theme, summed up in one of his many quotes, "You don't have to be great to start, but you have to start to be great!"

> *"We never know what the final answer is, but we have to make decisions and move."*
>
> — *President and CEO, Financial Services Company*

His message was crystal clear: Too many people wait to be fully ready before they act. Consequently, they get little or nothing done. And they certainly don't accomplish great things.

There is always more information to gather, more questions to pursue, maybe a better idea around the corner. But if you want to get anything done, you have to act.

BOLD leaders take qualified action. They don't strike out thoughtlessly without any information or move without forethought, planning, or an objective. You've undoubtedly experienced the kind of leaders that leap at every idea and try to use their charm to keep the plates spinning. That behavior can work – and even seem fun for a moment. But it quickly disappoints as the plates begin to fall and break. This approach is not action orientation. It is attention deficiency!

Remember, BOLD leaders excel at surrounding themselves with smart, strong, able people who inform their action orientation. They also exercise discipline in the actions they take.

I fully believe what I hear many experts say: Adults learn best by *doing*. *Doing* requires a willingness to start, to pay attention, to gather facts, and to learn. That's what BOLD leaders who successfully drive transformational change *do*. They act, gather insights, evaluate, and act again. Along the way, they find the path to the outcome they need or want, and when really effective, to greatness.

CUSTOMER EXPERIENCE

When consulting, you need to deeply understand your client's starting point. At Aveus, one of the ways we begin to build this clarity is by asking what may seem like a straightforward question for business executives to answer:

Is your customer experience:

- Making you money?

- Costing you money?

- And, if you are uncertain, can you pinpoint what is creating that uncertainty?

My hunch is that Jeff Bezos (Amazon), Bob Iger (Disney) and Gary Kelly (Southwest Airlines) could and would answer "making money" to that question. And likely Eddie Lampert (Sears), Oscar Munoz (United Airlines), and Tim Sloan (Wells Fargo) could and should answer "costing money." In between the clear yeses and noes are millions of companies that probably can't answer that question definitively. Maybe they have a hunch or perhaps some empirical indicators (CSAT or NPS scores, for example). But, in our experience, most can't clearly articulate which aspects of their company's customer experience work to their financial benefit and satisfy customer needs.

> *"Companies need to keep their focus way out to the outer-edge of the customer experience... We need to pay attention to what customers are telling us is coming and needed."*
>
> — *Investor, Entrepreneur, Business Owner and Founder*

We have been asking that making/costing money question about customer experience since Aveus was formed in 1999. At first, we were surprised most companies don't know, with confidence, whether their customer experience works mostly for them or against them. Now we expect indecisive responses and are delighted to meet leaders who know the answer – good or bad. They know their starting point.

When we began interviewing BOLD leaders, we found it refreshing that these individuals consistently brought up the importance of well-crafted and distinctive customer experiences for any successful transformation. As *doers*, they know they will make and implement many decisions. As BOLD leaders, they know customer experience is a key to unlocking an organization's potential. They are very customer-wired people. They know the answer to our customer experience question. Some find themselves in the midst of addressing and repairing damaged customer relationships. Some are working to adjust and advance an "okay" (neither exceptional nor differentiated) experience today. Some are in the process of completely, radically redefining the experience to move exponentially ahead of where they and their competition operate today. All BOLD leaders know empathy – understanding intimately who they serve and what needs they solve – represents their guide to future financial success.

Customer experience has become "a thing." Tons of articles and books speak to the subject. Research is happening, and new measures define winning customer experiences. Yet far too many company leaders treat customer experience as optional, as something they can turn on or off when they need to, instead of using it as an operating lens that affects everything they do.

BOLD leaders do just the opposite. They believe and act on the understanding that great customer experiences are the key to future success. They know that pinpointing challenges and addressing negative experiences can dramatically shift the fortunes of the organization from floundering or failing to succeeding. They appreciate that any current experience is an evolving concept, impacted by every interaction and market change that touches their customers. Finally, they know their customers are the essential force that can inspire the organization to move and innovate.

"Who *better* than your customers to guide your thinking, strategies, and actions toward financial and market success?" a BOLD leader would ask.

COURSE ADJUSTMENT

Many of the BOLD leaders we talked with have described the ups and downs of the journeys they go on over, sometimes, very extended periods of time. These journeys quite literally take years in many cases. One BOLD leader said, "It's never a straight line from A to B." Another said, "There is no black and white." Yet another commented, "Looking back, it is amazing that we navigated our way through. In the middle, sometimes when it is more cloudy than clear, you're thinking, *What am I doing!?*"

"There is bureaucratic stuff in all organizations that gets in the way. Many people don't know how to effectively navigate it. They don't know how to get out of the hierarchy. My approach is: forget where you work and just start connecting dots. Think about and find answers that benefit the whole organization."

— President, Financial Services Company

None of these BOLD leaders thought about quitting. Rather, all of them talked about how they worked to figure out the next move. These are **doers**, after all.

If you recall any high school physics lessons, you might remember Newton's Law #3: "For every action, there is an equal and opposite reaction." That is part of what makes transformation work so complicated, requiring all the capabilities our BOLD leaders possess.

BOLD leaders gather facts, hypothesize, plan, lay out a sequence of logical steps, and start to implement. And almost immediately, the reactions begin to appear. If the intelligence in the planning process was sound, they likely anticipated some – but not all – of these reactions. They may have also anticipated certain kinds of resistance from several corners: from employees, from other leaders who feel (or actually are) threatened, and from external players who either don't like or don't understand the changes. Reactions happen. Newton's Law #3 guarantees it. They all provide fantastic inputs for the next moves if these leaders can stay open and avoid defensiveness; remain curious and not intimidated; and maintain the confidence to meet these reactions head-on.

Then the BOLD leader either advances to the next planned move, if it still makes sense, or adjusts based on new information. In this way, they take a step forward that is more powerful than it would have been without the reactions.

Reactions that surprise prove especially interesting. Weaker leaders, shocked by something they didn't anticipate, may retrench or call into question the entire direction. Resisters will show up with "new evidence" that the BOLD leader is causing problems or is the problem! Competitors, in turn, may do seemingly crazy things in response to knock a leader off base or at least throw a wrench into advancements. Examples we have seen include things like dropping price and selling at a loss or threatening customers with penalties or other negative switching consequences. The politics of reactions inside and outside the organization are real. Don't underestimate them!

BOLD leaders understand this reactivity – or they figure it out very quickly. They see each reaction as an opportunity to learn and advance. Responding and moving again may take recalibration of the carefully thought-out plan and sequence of activities. This is where BOLD leaders draw on their mix of capabilities to dissect the reactions, plot, and, if needed, redesign their next moves and go again. Each time, they get stronger.

One of our Aveus clients working to implement a customer experience-based strategic change asked for guidance from another of our clients a few steps ahead in a similar process. In the exchange between them, this topic came up. The latter observed that initial moves are based largely on (hopefully well-founded) hypotheses and concepts, not facts. As reactions play out and results come in, hypotheses are confirmed or altered, and concepts become more factual. The leader and the team get better and better at tightening their focus, and the success rate on next moves increases.

The idea is this: Instead of waiting until some magical ending point to measure results or focusing on the macro requirements of the strategy, start with smart steps that move you from well-formed ideas to well-researched and documented business cases with measurable results. Do so incrementally based on your next logical moves until you reach the momentum you need to drive the big wins.

RESOURCEFULNESS

When resourcefulness as a concept comes up in a business setting, it is very often associated with simply doing more with less, or modifying the way resources get used. "Resourcefulness" becomes code for "cost cutting." While it can certainly include cost cutting, resourcefulness is really so much more. In fact, cost cutting or doing more with less isn't even really the natural starting point to think about resourcefulness.

Dictionary.com defines resourcefulness as "the ability to deal skillfully and promptly with new situations, difficulties, etc."

> "It is easy to talk about being BOLD when you have options. Not so easy when there is no other viable option... you have to have a vision. You have to sell it, and to sell it, you have to believe it and keep reinforcing progress."
>
> — President and CEO, Technology Company

Resourcefulness emerges within the context of some challenge. The challenge creates a framework for new ideas. The greater the challenge or obstacle, the more interesting the ideas become. If you are one of our *doer* BOLD leaders, this is the time when you pull on all the empathy, trust and curiosity you can muster to find breakthroughs that you are confident will take you and your organization in a better direction.

Resourcefulness is a valuable lens through which you can view how you do anything – everything. How you allocate resources and decide whether you're getting the best benefits from them.

Any obstacle becomes the inspiration for unexplored answers. In some cases, that might mean using resources in a new way or for a changed purpose. It might mean combining resources to accomplish something completely different and significantly more valuable. Or it might mean dismantling some of them, taking them apart like LEGO® blocks and putting them back together in a new, more effective form to overcome the obstacle or meet the challenge.

Resourcefulness, when you think about it, is really a very important form of innovation.

Back in 2010, John Baldoni, an author and executive coach, wrote a great, simple piece for the *Harvard Business Review* titled, "The Importance of Resourcefulness." In it, he says, "You must first start with an open mind." We couldn't agree with him more. He also reminds us that resourcefulness isn't something to just pull out of the toolkit when times get tough. Its usefulness might actually be greatest in good times when you're challenging yourself and have opportunities to reach higher, try new ideas, and focus resources on clear and important goals.

Resourcefulness comes up in BOLD leader conversations because, almost universally, all of them are working toward something exciting and big. On the journey, they and their teams face new challenges routinely. They expect obstacles and surprises along the way. They know they will face these challenges many times over. Resourcefulness is how they push past them, solve them, and come out at a better place.

By being open, by refusing to accept historical assumptions about the right or best uses of resources, and by being willing to freely explore how better to *do* things internally and in the marketplace, BOLD leaders break through the next challenge – and the next, and the next.

PERSEVERANCE

I cleaned up their mess. I made my own mess. I cleaned up my own mess. I found partners and colleagues along the way to share the adventure. And for the past many years, we have been doing fine. When people ask me about my experience at Aveus, that's usually what I say. And it is the truth. It is also such a clean way to describe the early years, which were by any measure a stress-filled, chaotic, often painful, expensive, and soul-searching journey.

> *"It is easy to be innovative, aggressive, BOLD and risk taking as long as you have resources. When you're under huge constraints, or the bottom line is getting very flat, that is when you need to be even more BOLD, active, and engaged."*
>
> *– Senior Policy Advisor on Leadership*

I joined Aveus as its CEO when, in an earlier form and by a different name, it existed as a joint venture of a technology company and a design firm. The year was 1999, and we were all partying (nod to Prince) because the dot-com bubble surrounded us. Money flowed like crazy into equally crazy start-up internet projects. The predictions said that all old business rules would be out and we'd be living in a "new economy" with new rules.

The idea for the venture was to provide strategic consulting for the companies wanting to succeed in the new economy, which in turn would feed great projects to the design firm and the tech firm. I often tell people that although I think I'm smarter than the average bear, and I did what I thought was decent due diligence, I walked into a vortex. Inside, we were a mess. Outside, the market was just not ready for what we were designed to solve. And with the early 2000s came the dot-com crash. Things went downhill from there.

I write this in a piece about perseverance because on January 1, 2001, instead of closing up shop (a serious consideration at the time), I took over sole ownership of the firm from the original owners.

On the first workday of the new year, the staff presented to me a lovely Nomi plaque that reads:

"To create real change in this world, you have to have a vision, and you have to have enormous perseverance."

They kindly left off the rest of the quote by Marguerite W. Sallee:

"It's the same principle that applies in any entrepreneurial venture: You've got to be too stupid to quit."

I carry that last line with me to this day, as you can probably tell!

Each twist and turn of my "entrepreneurial" venture has taught me lessons that reshaped my thinking and my ability to withstand the next roller coaster ride. I would have always included among my competencies: persistence, focus, and commitment to getting a job done. And, on many scales, I was getting the job done. However, this was a new level of challenge.

The gift of a company like Aveus, however, is the opportunity to work with dozens of clients – now more than 150 organizations – in every industry and many corners of the world. We get to see and learn and grow every day as we work with clients, all trying to accomplish big things.

Our work has really sharpened my understanding of why things work – or don't – and how much is required of an individual if you really intend to set direction, focus the actions of a business, and actually follow through on your ideas.

This BOLD leader project has been a huge, somewhat unexpected, bonus to years of our own efforts. Through this process, we meet incredible, courageous, smart, accomplished – and rare – people who have this same streak of perseverance in them that we have grown over the years. Many of the leaders we interview take on much bigger, more complicated, and higher stakes challenges than we do.

There is no quitting. There is no taking the easy path over the better path. These are leaders who set out with confidence, declare a direction, enroll others, and learn their way to success. They are **doers** who start with one thing, then another, and another until they persevere to an event or transaction or handoff that fits with their vision of success.

I now know: They are too *smart* to quit.

In summary, **doers** get things done. That's the case for all effective leaders of substance. They have the ability either directly, or through others, to get things done.

What distinguishes BOLD **doers** from others is their natural curiosity, confidence, empathy and trust. With them since birth, these characteristics, developed over time and under challenging circumstances, making them stronger and more effective.

In **doing**, we complete the picture of the BOLD leader. The BOLD definition, again, is:

A BOLD leader is someone who thinks and acts beyond the existing organizational limits, is imaginative, and is willing to take risks to get rewarding results.

Doers use their imagination, their creativity, their ability to enroll others, their determination, and their high tolerance for taking on and managing risks to achieve transformative goals and rewarding results.

Meet BOLD leader Maureen Spivack. She has 30 plus years of investment banking experience with E & Y, Merrill Lynch, UBS, Morgan Keegan, and KPMG Corporate Finance and is now Senior Industry Partner for healthcare at New State Capital Partners.

As we've heard from many of the BOLD leaders through this interview series, the true test of that boldness and knowing thyself shows up when you hit a wall because of something unexpected. That's where the bulldog comes out in Maureen.

"I'm good on my feet. I'm tenacious, and I will find a way to get back on track and moving forward with an outcome that I can live with. It may not be the originally intended outcome, but it will be a positive outcome." She says to keep moving, pushing, and exploring. There are always options.

Read more about my conversation with Maureen at http://aveusbold.com/blog/

BOLD: A C-SUITE CONVERSATION

Hello, Mr. or Ms. CEO, C-suite executive – and Ms. or Mr. "on the path to the C-suite" executive. So glad you've arrived at this point!

It is hard to hold a two-way communication effectively in text, but let me set up the conversation I hope you will have with yourself and with others in your organization.

> *"The most important thing I can do is develop people. Find people with the BOLD traits for success."*
>
> — *Former Global Hedge Fund Manager, Now Nonprofit CEO*

If you're currently in a C-suite role or rapidly heading that way, you are likely a highly effective organizational leader and manager with strong attributes of your own that have fueled your success. One of them is most certainly the ability to lead and manage a complex and growing organization. That may or may not mean you are BOLD by the definition provided earlier.

That is fine. For the purposes of this conversation, let's assume you are ***highly effective but not BOLD.***

In your position, you know people can make or break your success. As many of our BOLD interviewees noted, finding great talent and matching it to marketplace and organizational needs is one of the most important (if not the single most important) jobs of any executive leader. You need the best talent you can find to join you in accomplishing your critical goals.

Taking the leap that you agree with this point of view, consider next:

What are the biggest strategic challenges your organization will face in the next year? In five years? Beyond?

And then:

How confident are you that you have the right people in place to tackle these big strategic challenges? Do you have people who can think beyond existing organizational limits, who are imaginative and capable of finding the best answers for you, and who have the right risk profile to drive rewarding results – without burning down the house in the process?

You might even want to have a candid conversation with your team about:

How does unsatisfactory work contribute to market opportunities lost? Organizational stresses? And what are the hard financial cost implications of critical work that is not getting done to your satisfaction today?

When you don't have the right leaders matched to your biggest transformative needs, lost performance can show up in many forms. Here are just a few examples:

- Disconnects from your customer base: They leave, reduce their involvement with your organization, or get lured away by competitors or emerging alternatives.

- Losing competitive battles for new business

- Slow time to market on innovation efforts or disappointing results from highly anticipated product launches

- Surprises that catch you off guard in the marketplace – changes you didn't see coming that require your response

- Stalling in the starting blocks on what you've decided are the real drivers of your future success

- Talent drains as some of your best, most capable people get frustrated and either leave or get recruited away

- Hard dollar cost implications that force you into short-term budget and investment choices, which work against the long-term strategies you want and need to put in place

When you discuss these challenges openly, critically, and with evidence (not just opinion), you learn something about whether your organization has effectively matched BOLD leaders to your biggest transformational needs.

Whether you are satisfied with your conclusions or are now deeply frustrated by the answers, an obvious next question arises:

KNOWING THE CLEAR CONNECTION BETWEEN BOLD LEADERSHIP AND FUTURE SUCCESS, WHY DON'T ORGANIZATIONS ALWAYS SELECT AND SUPPORT BOLD LEADERS IN ALL SIGNIFICANT CHANGE SITUATIONS?

I wish we could give you one, but there is no singular answer to this question. How many times have you seen change agents hired, only to be fired when the changes they were brought on to make get too uncomfortable? Maybe you've done this. Maybe it has happened to you.

You have likely seen in action some of the following scenarios that demonstrate how and why companies fail to put the right BOLD leadership in place for the transformation they need to accomplish and/or fail to support them:

- Politics: This one is an unfortunately common scenario. Too often top executives bow to, allow, or without much thought, default to the existing hierarchy, turf, or silos to control the implementation. Sometimes even when a potentially great BOLD leader gets identified within an organization's ranks, management holds them back by keeping them stuck in their existing role. In other cases, BOLD leaders are instructed to keep their current role and layer on the transformational work. When this happens, the current work and current boss overshadow any transformational work. The initiative suffers or fails. In the end, frustrated, the potentially great BOLD leader leaves.

- Overestimating current talent: Politics isn't always the culprit. Sometimes organizations simply overestimate the abilities of the team, failing to appreciate the specific skills and capabilities required. Or leadership underestimates the work required to accomplish the transformation objectives. After all, they think, how hard can it be? The answer is: very hard. If you sense a mismatch of talent and skills to the difficulty of the undertaking, put the challenge in terms executives understand. Ask the simple question: "Is this really the team *you* (we) plan to entrust with *your* (our) future and the future success of *your* (our) business?" If the immediate gut response to that question is "No!" reality can set in and the hunt for the right talent can begin.

- No BOLD leaders in sight: Sometimes company executives don't spot a BOLD leader in their midst, so they settle for a lesser option. This culture of settling builds up over time. It contributes to driving out creativity and locking in the operational status quo. Similarly, as companies mature, a level of risk avoidance can naturally settle in, particularly if performance is "good enough." This settled, satisfied orientation can be the biggest obstacle to new ideas, and it can literally stop transformations from taking place. Why rock the boat? Why change what is working? These organizations don't attract or keep BOLD leader talent, so when confronted with the need, the right resources aren't available to be tapped for the assignment. The organization settles for current-level performance (and potential decline) when they settle on a team that can't see beyond the existing limits of the organization, and isn't capable, motivated, or incented to attempt BOLD acts.

- Selected but not supported: Let's return to our hired-and-expelled change agent. Very often organizations do understand the need for BOLD talent, then pursue and put it in place. But they completely drop the ball when it comes to supporting this person.

You've probably heard the phrase, "buying the answer." Some organizations are notorious for "buying" talent and creating a revolving door. Everyone suffers in this scenario. The swirl definitely creates change, but from what we have seen, it generally isn't the positive kind. Sometimes organizations buy the "flashy, showy" definition of "bold," which by now you know is far from BOLD. Just as often, however, these organizations do find wonderful talent but don't think about or appreciate what it will take to effectively support them. It is a little like spending the money to buy a high-performance sports car, then failing to fill it with high-octane fuel or follow recommended maintenance routines. Soon, the engine begins to knock, and other problems show up because this beautiful acquisition doesn't receive the proper care. The car becomes a burden and is blamed for low performance, when in fact its caretakers created the problems.

Organizations that fail to select or support BOLD leaders don't necessarily do so intentionally. Sabotage from peers or cultural rejection happens, but the culprit can simply be organizational ineptness.

Additionally, **BOLD leaders** who can successfully navigate an organization's culture, embedded systems, and politics, then successfully communicate a vision that extends beyond the organization's ability to see today, **are rare**. And that's probably the biggest reason organizations don't immediately and always put them into these critical positions.

Now think back to your answers to the question posed above: Does your organization always select and support BOLD leaders in all significant change situations? Have you experienced any, some, or all of the scenarios above? If yes, consider how effective you are as a company at leading and managing transformational change – and what you can do to improve that effectiveness.

Don't forget to evaluate your own readiness for the change challenge ahead while you're assessing the readiness of others. We see people fall into this trap too often. We have met many highly effective executives who are not BOLD, but who make sure to surround themselves with the right talent – and succeed. The executives who come up short despite this foresight often make one of two mistakes. **Because they are** *currently* **highly effective executives:**

1. *They assume their skills will carry them through a transformative change.* These leaders can't see or can't admit they don't have the profile and "born with" characteristics of the BOLD leaders we describe.
2. *They believe they are BOLD leaders (How else could they have accomplished so much?!).* They fail to critically consider whether the skills that work well for them in the current setting are the ones the organization requires for transformation. This unchecked belief causes mistakes.

One example that plays out in the scenarios above: Your organization is doing well today. You pick high potential talent who are succeeding under current conditions and move them to a transformational task they are wholly unsuited to perform. They suffer. Your current operations suffer. The transformative initiative suffers. You suffer.

Admittedly, it is an intimidating thought to confront yourself and your executive team with an open conversation about the BOLD skills you and your organization do or don't have. Executives rise and succeed with many important skill sets, but for some it can be painful to think they might be missing some of the BOLD requirements. It is also an essential conversation to have. We encourage you to set aside the inner voices that might be saying things like:

- "I have to be the BOLD leader."

- "I can't accept others wearing the BOLD hat."

- "Anyone can learn to be a BOLD leader."

- "I want everyone to be a BOLD leader."

None of these thoughts are helpful. They only minimize the effectiveness of you and any of your BOLD leaders.

Why should you shush these voices? It may seem odd, but be selfish for a minute here: If you can avoid buying into the false notions above, you can better serve your organization and yourself by focusing on, finding, recruiting, developing, and supporting the BOLD talent you need.

We want to be clear that we fully believe many kinds of strong, positive leaders exist. They are great stewards of their organizations. They deliver results. They possess a variety of creative and operational leadership and management skills. Skills that are required every day for success. To use a couple old adages, they "make the trains run on time" and "keep the lights on." They bring in customers and make them happy. They recruit and build talent. They provide a steady hand and a critical eye to the organization. They manage broad functions and large teams very well. Some work well with current operations. Some have the ability to ensure operational excellence, quality, and short-term performance. Some are the "steady Eddies," as one of our BOLD leaders called them, that do a great job of ensuring balance and effective risk management.

When you accept that not all highly effective leaders are BOLD, you put yourself and your organization in a stronger position.

Many successful CEOs and other executives we have met and interviewed are NOT BOLD leaders, by our definition of their core behaviors and characteristics. We have heard several CEOs say, "I don't have an empathy bone in my body!" or a version of, "I got to where I am by managing down risks and sticking to a playbook."

Your role is not to try to become something you are not. That doesn't serve you or anyone else, and you've been successful getting to the station you are at.

Instead, your roles are to:

- Identify and assign BOLD leaders when you face critical transformational challenges,

- Give them clear assignments and expectations,

- Provide resources and some rope to dive in and execute, and

- Support them with cover to do the change and transformation work you need them to do.

> *"He cleared the path and that has made a tremendous difference."*
>
> — *President and Innovator, Insurance Company*

One of the BOLD leaders we interviewed described her CEO as her most incredible ally: "He cleared the path and made a tremendous difference." He didn't drive the transformation himself, but he set up the challenge, picked the right talent, and brokered negotiations between the emerging business and the current state. He acted as her safety net with peers who felt threatened by her work and provided the comfort and strength the whole organization needed to bridge from the current to the new. This BOLD leader admitted she could not have been the BOLD leader she was and driven the results she did without her CEO. And during a conversation with the CEO, it was clear he knew the organization would not have moved as far as it did, as effectively as it did, without this BOLD leader.

Guiding and mentoring BOLD leaders when you're not one of them can be a tricky thing. The first challenge is learning to communicate and negotiate with each other. It requires deep trust to acknowledge that although the BOLD leader does things you would never have thought to do (or would have done differently), they belong in their role because of their special abilities – talents you've acknowledged are different from yours. Having different orientations can be very helpful. Remember, the BOLD leader is a learner and very open. They will soak up your point of view and incorporate it into their decisions and actions – even if they go a different direction. The perspective you share is invaluable to them.

BY THIS POINT YOU MAY BE THINKING: I'VE READ THIS AND GET THE NEED TO MATCH BOLD LEADERS TO TRANSFORMATIVE PRIORITIES IN MY COMPANY. HOW DO I DO THAT EFFECTIVELY?

If you find yourself thinking your organization faces specific challenges that require this kind of leadership, you are likely also asking yourself:

- How do I identify BOLD leaders?

- Once I do, how do I develop their potential?

- How can I best support them in the efforts we need to accomplish as an organization?

FINDING AND ASSIGNING BOLD

We know from our own experiences in identifying BOLD leaders and driving transformational changes, time is usually at a premium. With this in mind, we captured the needed decisions and actions in several main steps:

<u>Create an initial BOLD leader talent pool</u>

Hopefully, through the descriptions in this book, you can close your eyes and quickly scan the talent around you, identifying highly likely BOLD candidates. Early readers of the book said they could simply look at the definitions of BOLD and ask, "Is this person..."

- A Believer – A true believer who demonstrates interesting ideas about our future? Yes/No

- Open – An open listener who values the input of others? Someone who puts the organization needs above their own? Yes/No

- A Learner – Constantly in a learning mode, challenging themselves and driving their own development? Yes/No

- A Doer – Focused on doing: driving results and learning from failures, managing risk, and advancing the organization through their actions? Yes/No

With all the candidates that get a clear YES from you, create your initial talent pool. If you get mixed results or feel unsure but more positive than negative, include those candidates and move on to assessing them.

- It is important to know if the candidate(s) have the required characteristics of curiosity, confidence, empathy, and trust. That requires some simple testing. Our quick self-assessment tool effectively sorts likely candidates into "definitely BOLD," "definitely not BOLD," and "uncertain." This tool takes only minutes for each candidate to complete. You will find it at AveusBOLD.com.

- With the assessment data in hand, confirm your likely BOLD leader pool.

Before moving on, *a special note if you are HIRING for BOLD*: You may not have the internal candidates you need, so perhaps you're looking outside for the right person. Add the self-assessment to your screening process. An interview alone – and other testing – will not necessarily give you the information you need to know whether this person has the requisite curiosity, confidence, empathy and trust to be BOLD. A quick assessment will help inform your hiring decision.

<u>Validate your BOLD leaders through peer assessment and field testing:</u>

Colleagues who work closely with a candidate BOLD leader can easily confirm their potential if you ask them the right questions. A companion assessment that takes just minutes to complete and can be given to a candidate's peers, subordinates or immediate supervisor is also available, learn more about it at AveusBOLD.com. You can even start with the simple BOLD Yes/No questions above. If the candidate is an obvious BOLD leader, that may be all you need.

With the self and peer assessments complete, you will quickly validate that you're looking at a BOLD leader and see how ready they are to deploy to transformation challenges. You will find some with the right "born with" profile who are early enough in their careers that they need targeted development. Others you will recognize as ready for something bigger as evidenced by their work history, current portfolio, and the assessments.

You never really know if your recruited candidate is a BOLD leader until you work together. So, starting them on an initial project and incorporating the peer assessments can help validate your hunch.

Field testing offers another effective way to observe a BOLD candidate in a controlled environment. During the field test, set up a scenario or hypothesis with controlled conditions. The BOLD candidate must use trial and error to develop effective change options so you can assess their ability to push boundaries, use their imagination, manage risks, engage with others, and get to the test result in creative ways.

<u>Challenge your BOLD talent through targeted assignments as a logical next step</u>

The time has come to match your BOLD leader to one of your transformational challenges. Depending on their experience, you can scale assignments over time.

- If you're in a real bind and the challenge is large, do your earlier screening against very senior candidates.

- BOLD leaders with prior experience in change situations should be able to swim in the deep end of the pool – as long as they have support (as outlined earlier in the chapter) from you and others.

- To do their best work (and for you and your organization to reap the best benefits), free your BOLD leader of any current-state management responsibilities so they can fully focus on designing and executing the transformation.

- If you qualify a highly experienced BOLD leader, move them into action with some clear direction. If they are truly experienced and BOLD, they won't need many guard rails.

- For a high potential, but untested BOLD leader, identify a learning and development venue for them to put their talents to use.

  - Define stretch assignments where their curiosity, empathy and confidence can shine.

  - Set expectations to find creative, breakthrough solutions to big questions or challenges.

  - Require that they demonstrate their ability to select and motivate a team while building trust with peers and others during this engagement.

SUPPORTING BOLD

Mentoring is a must. The BOLD leaders we have met and interviewed all mention special role models or mentors in their lives. Some had a formal structure, while others developed informally.

We believe the best candidate for a mentor is a formal, non-boss mentor who understands what is at stake in the transformation, and who has broad respect within the organization. Mentors are especially important in these situations because you are asking the BOLD leader to take on an entrenched organization and introduce ideas that will create stress. They need a strong, sophisticated guide and ally. As we discussed earlier, BOLD leaders are rare and can find themselves in lonely situations, particularly in the early days as the transformation work begins – and especially if the BOLD leader is new to the organization. Having a touchstone in someone with more experience, someone they know has their back, is important. These relationships will become deeply trusting over time. The right match will advance the BOLD leader's skills, preparing them to take on bigger and more critical challenges.

For anyone working with a BOLD leader, as we noted earlier, the first challenge is learning to communicate and negotiate with each other. You can build deep trust and a relationship with a BOLD leader by acknowledging your different talents. Explore how your strengths complement each other. They will, by their nature, be open with you and to your ideas. You can be the same with them. Share your point of view and stay open to theirs. Work to understand their challenges. Help them navigate the organization and advocate for them if/when others act out against them. Learn from them and share your knowledge with them.

Here are a few things to consider that will help you both think about the leadership you provide, and where your work and that of the BOLD leader may collide:

- Test your own attachment to the status quo. Where do

you take things for granted? Where do you see areas that deserve further critical thought and evaluation?

- If, like most of us, you received conditioning through your education to believe there is just "one right answer," challenge that thinking. Participate in the exploration process so you can appreciate how the transformation team is working through options to reveal the best answers.

- Draft your own vision of "the long game" for your organization. Use it to inform your interactions, your listening, and your influence in your own organization. Pay attention to where your strategic assumptions match your peer BOLD leader's assumptions, and where they do not.

- Offer to work with the BOLD leader on important communications. Help them practice. Practice your supportive endorsements. Give straight and clear feedback.

- While you're doing your job, keep an ear to the ground. Pay attention to conversations and rumors about the transformation. Don't fan the flames! Share important feedback – with suggestions.

- Observe (or better yet – interview) someone you know to be a BOLD leader. Figure out how to incorporate what fits for you as you develop your own style.

- Sensitize yourself to what it is like to walk in a BOLD leader's shoes. Take on a project that feels uncomfortable. Stretch yourself. If a professional opportunity doesn't exist, volunteer for an organization that supports a passion of yours.

In summary, you know from your own experience that organizations, especially those with some long histories, will resist the very things you're asking them to do to change. The BOLD leader can handle that reality and respect the resistance (because they are empathetic). But they only can succeed with your support and endorsement. Much like the CEO described earlier, you can help them by acting as a buffer, a champion, a realist, and a facilitator when the challenges from others in your organization show up. And you know they will.

Meet BOLD leader Damien Harmon, VP of Operations at Bridgestone Retail Operations.

Damien shared that when you are humble, you are naturally able to make your purpose and message much higher than yourself. It's not about being right; it's about having extreme focus on customer outcomes and knowing you alone don't have all the answers on how to get there.

"People can say 'I'm in' to an organizational vision or strategy – but they oftentimes don't change their behavior, mostly because they don't know how. As a leader, I believe my responsibility is to help people change one step at a time; there is only so much that a person can digest at once. When a company is going through large change, it's critical to slow down and make sure you bring people along."

Read more about our conversation with Damien at http://aveusbold.com/blog/

BOLD LEADERSHIP UNLOCKED

Finally, let's talk about you, **yes, you, BOLD leader in the C-suite or on your way there!** You score high in the characteristics of curiosity, confidence, empathy, and trust. Through your behaviors, others see you as:

A Believer: You see beyond today – you have a vision of greater possibilities and you are customer-, growth-, and investment-oriented. You're innovative, and status quo limits frustrate you.

Open: Empathy comes naturally to you. You are a great listener and keep the confidences of others. You are a "we" person, preferring to solve challenges with others and sharing the credit for work well done. You attend to stakeholders and communicate often. You are good at and fussy about building your team. Others would describe you as happy and positive, and that's how you see yourself!

A Learner: You can't help it – you are curious, you ask a lot of questions, and you work to connect the data and the perspectives you gather from many sources. You get right to work and absorb lessons from failures as well as successes. You don't see a day when you'd ever want to stop exploring, creating, and learning.

A Doer: You get things done no matter how thorny, untried, or difficult – and you love it. You care about customer experiences and how your transformative work will impact others. You have a strategy, and you constantly take actions to refine it, move it forward, and collect results. You are resourceful. You persevere, finding creative ways around roadblocks, walls, and other impediments – they only make you stronger.

Your skills within each of these BOLD dimensions will develop naturally through all the "doing" you will undertake. But you can also take charge of your development in a more disciplined way. Here are a few examples of how to further refine your talents:

Develop your own "long view:" Do the work to think ahead of your organization and for your organization. You can share your long view or use it as your private touchstone. Use this vision or "North Star" to inform your interactions, your listening, and where you choose to influence activities – or not. Make sure you understand (and test) your own assumptions and hypotheses. Pay close attention to where your strategic assumptions match – or diverge from – the assumptions of others. If they do align, decide whether you might be stuck in a status quo assumption. If they don't match, consider what you see that others miss. On the other hand, what do they see that you don't? What evidence can you gather to clarify the importance of the assumption and validate your direction?

<u>Evaluate your time and resource use:</u> Many folks avoid this eye-opening effort for fear of the answers, but take a moment to evaluate where you as a leader and your team are spending your time, resources, and budget. If you had to start completely over – you had no team, no meetings on your calendar, no dollars currently allocated – what would you do? Here are a few more questions to add to that exercise:

- Give yourself 10 open positions – undefined. Fill them with your dream team. What kind of team and mix of skills would you assemble?

- 100% of your time is free. What activities are worthy of a time allocation? Choose wisely! What would a typical day, week, month look like?

- You have a $100 budget to spend (or $100 thousand or $100 million). How will you allocate those dollars based on your priorities?

  - Name two things you would defund or reduce spending on and why.

- You have $100 or $500,000 or $10,000,000 in investment capital to spend. You can invest in up to 3 initiatives. What would they be?

<u>Feed your curiosity:</u> Your desire to learn is almost infinite. So, exercise your desire to learn and try new things. When the daily grind gets a hold of you, it is easy to put your own development interests aside for "when I have time." Find reasons to test and stretch your imagination. Do simple and silly things to push your creativity:

- Read a book!

- Listen to random Ted Talks.

- Interview leaders in other businesses and sort out the relevant lessons for your business and situation.

- Create your own list of activities to do – one new thing every month.

- Volunteer outside of work for something you're passionate about – get out of your comfort zone.

I know a couple BOLD leaders who literally schedule learning time because it is such a priority to them. Swap out one administrative task or something that can be delegated for some learning time!

Practice communicating: You have natural gifts many wish they had, so master them. Start with two-way communications. Practice presenting and responding, listening, and building one-to-one, one-to-a-few, and one-to-many communication skills. From the day you step into your BOLD in a leadership role, you will be communicating in many different ways. As you develop teams and lead others through changes they may not fully understand, your ability to inform, inspire, appreciate and move others will make you stronger and more effective. A few simple ideas:

- Role-play important communications with a trusted colleague or team. Present something to them and then test their understanding of what you shared.

  - Did you get questions you might have anticipated?

  - Was your colleague or team able to clearly convey the key messages you wanted them to receive?

- Were they able to understand and engage with the information you shared, and respond with interesting and helpful ideas?

- Take a class. There is nothing like putting yourself in front of a speech or communications group to sharpen your skills!

- If you're leading an important transformation right now, develop a discipline of testing communications before they are widely shared:

  - Gather feedback once information is shared.

  - Tap key influencers to give you regular feedback and suggestions. Are you sharing the right information in the right tone? If not, adjust before you strike

<u>Find a mentor:</u> If you have a mentor, excellent! You are off to a good start. If you don't yet have a natural or assigned mentor, find one or ask someone to help you identify and recruit one.

<u>Observe others:</u> A quick personal aside: One of my earliest corporate jobs had me serve a group of 50 or so banks as a regional marketing staff person. What a gift to a curious 20-something. I got to see all kinds of leader and manager behaviors. Some I wanted to emulate and practiced incorporating into my own development. Others I never wanted to model or repeat! To this day, I pay attention to others and how they are or are not effective leaders. And I regularly check how my own behaviors affect others.

Simply paying attention pays dividends. You will collect a clear portfolio of ideas and methods used by the best leaders you encounter to inspire, guide, model, direct, and take actions that get results. You also learn and sharpen your own expectations of yourself by observing and checking your approaches to leading against those whose practices you never want to follow.

Experiment: A lot of information exists these days about placing small bets, failing fast, failing cheap, and experimenting your way to answers. We covered many of these topics earlier in the "BOLD Defined" chapter of the book. They are worth a quick reminder here.

- Practice the art of small moves every day.

- Learn how to place small bets and control risks.

- When you make decisions to pivot or persevere, make sure everyone who needs to know understands your choices.

- Collect your lessons learned. Collect your wins. Move again, and invite others to join you.

You are oriented to *do*: act and learn. Get started and own your destiny as you master your BOLD. So finally, simply, get out there!

Meet BOLD leader Dr. Penny Wheeler, President and CEO of Allina Health.

Dr. Penny Wheeler skipped directly from her obstetrics/gynecology medical practice to chief clinical officer and then to president and CEO of Allina Health. She leads a very large, complicated, dynamic healthcare organization. "I'm of no illusions that I know everything or have all the answers" was her remark when reflecting on the leaps she has taken into new areas and ever-widening scopes of responsibility.

During our conversation, one story about a nurses strike in 2016 that drew national attention kept resurfacing. Dr. Wheeler also saw this conflict as a test of "short-term pain for long-term benefit." She has that BOLD leader ability to see beyond the organizational limits of today and imagine possibilities long past this chapter. She demonstrated the will to take risks and confidence to accomplish what she knew needed to happen.

Read more about our conversation with Dr. Wheeler at http://aveusbold.com/blog/

ONE CLOSING THOUGHT

We have spent years leading transformative change efforts, as well as researching, interviewing, working directly with clients to assist with their imperatives, and reading the "masters" in change, leadership, and management. All this experience has brought us to one inescapable conclusion:

When an organization succeeds where others fail, it does so as the result of one very clear factor:

A BOLD leader makes it happen.

We have concluded that all other variables are important to solve, but they fail when they lack a certain kind of leadership – BOLD leadership – from the beginning of the transformative assignment to the end result.

Consider this:

- Methods and tools: There are literally thousands of tools and processes available to you. Take your pick of all the methodologies for change, organizational development, process and project management, and design that have mushroomed over the years. We work with many of them, based on client preferences. Find the ones that will work best for your organization.

- Gurus: Choose whichever expert(s) you most relate to and study them. Follow them. Try their methods. Some prefer 5 steps, or 7, or 8... But they all are talking about similar approaches to driving change, and their advice is useful.

Parenthetically, search "change management" or "leadership" on Amazon: They will serve up 100 pages of book options.

- Consultants: Select from the biggest names to boutiques. Collectively, they have been paid billions by organizations hoping they can deliver a leg up on more effective transformations. As consultants ourselves, of course we know consultants can help, but they cannot own the change. Leadership must come from inside the organization.

Despite evolving methodologies, better tools, smarter consultants, and more market pressure to adapt, survive, and thrive – transformative initiatives still fail. In a 2000 *Harvard Business Review* article, co-authors Nitin Nohria and Michael Beer write, "The brutal fact is that about 70% of all change initiatives fail." (Many others about that time were using that same number.) A November 2015 UNC Executive Development blog cites David Leonard and Claude Coltea of Gallup, asserting that "70 percent of all change initiatives fail." If you do your own search, you will find many experts opining on this topic year after year, and they all point to similar failure rates.

Let that sink in a minute. 15 years of new theories, new methods, new process recommendations, new tools, new experts, billions of dollars and uncounted hours spent, and still, here we sit at ± 70% fail rates.

When these initiatives fail, what happens?

- Organizations get hurt. They often turn inward and backward. Sometimes they must absorb a great setback, and over time, some just disappear.

- People get hurt. People get fired. Jobs are lost. The ones who hurt the most are those directly impacted, including:

  - Your customers

  - Your employees

  - You

- Shareholders and other stakeholders are also hurt and move to find other, better options.

Research conducted by prestigious academics and consulting organizations identify many reasons change initiatives fail. They offer some helpful tools, methods, and practices to improve the likelihood of success.

We see these researched scenarios play out repeatedly in our consulting practice and have boiled them down to a list of 10 (we like the nice round number), confirmed them, and written about them many times. If you want to see all 10, check out the series of blog posts by my Aveus partner Duane White at http://aveusbold.com/blog/.

If you are simply satisfied w ith i mproving t he o dds of success, great. These tools can help.

However, until you do one important thing, failure (to some lesser or greater degree) is way more likely than success.

That one thing?

Place a BOLD leader at the helm of your initiative and support them.

Take this critical step particularly if your organization's future depends on an absolutely successful transformative change.

BOLD ONLINE

As we summarized in the Foreword, a book can only do so much. This one is intended to spur interest in starting a BOLD conversation. One we would love to continue to explore and develop together with you online.

We know this work and this book are just the beginning of discovering, developing, and applying BOLD ideas. You will find companion resources to this book at AveusBOLD.com.

RESOURCES FOR INDIVIDUALS

- More BOLD insights, blog posts, white papers and other resources

- Interviews with BOLD leaders

- The **BOLD Self-Assessment** referenced in this book

- Opportunities to participate in open discussions and post questions

- A **BOLD** community – for those who take the self-assessment and score as a BOLD leader

RESOURCES FOR ORGANIZATIONS

- Background on the **methodology** used to refine our BOLD definition and its underlying characteristics

- **Recommendations** for how to use the BOLD Self-Assessment in a more formalized development program to build out your organization's BOLD capabilities

- Materials with tips for initiating a BOLD leadership program: Find, support, nurture, and benefit from BOLD leadership

- Related transformation white papers and resources

- Opportunities to participate in open discussions and post questions

ACKNOWLEDGMENTS

Our Aveus team would like to thank all the people who helped us find our way on this subject:

- All our clients over the past 20 years from whom we have learned so much and who opened the door to this BOLD exploration. We are so thankful for the opportunity to work with you.

- The individual leaders we have met through this work, who were among our earliest contacts in this initiative. You gave us your precious time, your great ideas, and your referrals to expand our network of conversations.

- Every leader who participated in a BOLD interview, many of whom appeared in posts at our blog and many who preferred to remain anonymous.

- Every leader who participated in our assessment testing.

I would personally like to thank the "Aveusian" team: staff – present and past, advisory board, and our network of friends and associates who all contributed to this work. Thank you to Deb McMahon, Sammi Guseyn-Zade, Pam Sveinson, and Molly Danielson for your individual contributions to the content, editing, and design process. An extra nod to Deb McMahon, who leads the development of AveusBOLD.com and all the related BOLD marketing efforts. A special thank you to my Aveus partner Duane White, whose guidance was essential to the shaping of our BOLD work and who always amazes me with his ability to distill the important from the insignificant. And a specific thank you to Ali Shirvani-Mahdavi for his kindness, sharing his absolute brilliance, and the work he did to help guide Duane and me through the maze of literature, research, and testing to get to our final BOLD conclusions and tools.

And thank you Daniel Mahai. Again. Past. Present. Forever.

ABOUT THE AUTHOR: CHRIS LAVICTOIRE MAHAI

Chris is the President of Aveus, a global strategy and operational change firm. Over the span of her corporate executive and consulting career, Chris has led, developed, and implemented successful strategic and transformative changes in companies around the world. While at Aveus, Chris has worked with more than 100 organizations from large global enterprises to family-owned businesses and startups, non-profits, a nd other service organizations. She has served on the boards of several businesses and non-profit o rganizations a nd i s an active investor in women-owned and -led businesses.

Chris has been called a "practical brainiac" and a "change catalyst," both descriptions she happily wears. Her clients hug her as often as they give her a handshake. That should tell you all you need to know about her style and orientation as a client advocate.

OTHER PUBLISHED WORKS BY CHRIS LAVICTOIRE MAHAI

ROAR: Strengthening business performance through speed, predictability, flexibility, and leverage

THEM: The Handy Experience Manual (with Linda Ireland)

CPSIA information can be obtained
at www.ICGtesting.com
Printed in the USA
LVHW080046131021
700272LV00004B/11/J